Praise for "The Occurrence"

"Heartbreaking, yet still a must read. The realities you'll never find in the news. It can happen to you! And it's worse than you think, for everyone involved. Well written account and no pulled punches." - John A.

"Will seem shockingly frank to those fortunate enough to have never walked this hellish road. Stay the course, for this is raw and real. Nuggets of hope, wit that will cause you to laugh unexpectedly, no judgment. Those who have lived this will be grateful for the courage to say what we've thought, but without the guts to admit it. A vulnerable, painful process of acceptance." – Jennifer E.

"Thank you for sharing your story, for being so honest and open, for writing with clarity, and also with humor. Your voice is very resonant and natural, and I appreciated that throughout. Thank you for your beautiful generosity of spirit. The world needs more of just that! Your book has had a meaningful impact on me, and my guess is that it will for many." – Jill K.

"A must read. Very well written. Don't think it can't happen to you or someone you know or love. My heart goes out to both families." – Kenneth K.

"This book knocked me out. When I saw what it was about, I decided to wait for the right time to read it because I knew it would upset me. So powerful and beautifully written, I devoured it over two days. I hope others will read this important cautionary tale, which would make a powerful movie. I am so sorry you had to write it, but it is filled with so much wisdom, it must have been very healing as well." – James L.

"A factual narrative, harrowing story, a vehicle for so many discussions. A summation of love, of vulnerability, of motherhood, of riding the rapids of Life and coming out bloody, bruised, and triumphant all at the same time. It might be that it takes an earthquake of this magnitude to shake us so hard that we crack, and the light shines out of us." – Paul S.

"I've never read a book that talks about this... something we should all be aware of. A deep dive into a terrible and not well known situation." – Viola

"The combination of personal memoir, humor, and graphic detail, add up to very compelling reading about a very serious topic. Then there's the actual ramifications of it all. Whoa. Gotta say that last chapter is sheer genius." – Ira W.

"Compassionate, inviting, and gracious. Reverent, but irreverent. Comprehensive, yet accessible. The witty yet heartfelt observations and commentary will endear this book to many who find themselves in the same shoes. Well done." – Chris. Y.

~One~

"Until a day is over, there's always a chance you'll remember it for something else."

Rebecca Pearson (Mandy Moore) in "This is Us,"
Season 6, Episode 3, Teleplay by Dan Fogelman,
Casey Johnson, and David Windsor

So it seems that this is the book I was meant to write. And it all started on the worst day of my life. (So far. %-)

I've always wanted to write, but never had the discipline. I can't sustain a gym membership either, and there are similarities. When I come back from the gym, I always feel virtuous, more healthy both physically and emotionally, and I feel the same way after a session of writing. And yet, when it is next time to go to the gym or to sit down and write, I feel the same inner resistance. I want to have done it, but I don't want to do it.

I'm told that I write wonderful letters, and a friend of mine tells me that she has saved all of my correspondence. But no one writes letters anymore. First we were reduced to email and then Twitter, now Snapchat. I expect "The Collected Snapchats of Pope Francis" to be published in 2039.

I used to write a humorous newsletter at the off-Broadway theater where

I worked, purely for the amusement of my co-workers. Our Musical Theater Program Director, Ira Weitzman, tells me that he saved every number of these staff meeting minutes. But I recently reread one of them, and I couldn't remember half of the references to people or to incidents that had happened so long ago. I suppose – I hope – that they were funny at the time, but they have no shelf life. You really did have to be there.

The only remark that still made me laugh, more than 30 years on, was not mine. I simply transcribed something our Literary Manager, Eric Overmyer, said at one of our staff meetings.

Eric was charged with reading and evaluating both solicited and unsolicited manuscripts from hopeful playwrights, with an eye toward possible production in one of our two performance spaces. And although this was the mission of our theater, both Eric and his responsibilities remained mysterious to the rest of us. We bustled about on the second floor of the crumbling old building on 42nd Street between 8th and 9th Avenues in Manhattan, a former burlesque house back in the days when New York was more dangerous and interesting and less sanitized, back when Times Square was teeming with cars and trucks and hookers and pimps and arcades and triple-X porn movies instead of over-priced half-price theater tickets and fat tourists sweating and collapsed into wrought-iron patio furniture.

Those of us who worked on the second floor were in marketing, business, fundraising, box office, casting, production -- occupations we all pretty much understood, at least vaguely. On the first floor was our main theater space and lobby, which were self-explanatory. The sight of lights and sets and costumes, the smell of sawdust and make-up and dusty velvet upholstery and then, on performance nights the rising buzz in the lobby as guests greeted friends, the intoxicating aroma of mingled perfumes, and then the mad rush and flutter of closing chatter in the audience as the house lights dimmed. This was the mission, the goal, the dream, the reason we were all here.

But Eric lived in a strange netherworld, a cramped little office down a flight of dark steps at the back of the building, off the business office. At the bottom of the steps was a long, dark hallway lined floor to ceiling on both sides with brown cardboard boxes containing all of the archives of Playwrights Horizons: manuscripts, playbills, posters, photographs, correspondence, the yellowing parchment record of decades of artistry and creativity. A perilous life-threatening hazard inexplicably never flagged by the fire marshals.

At the end of this hallway was a small, cramped room set like a crow's nest over the building's front door, redeemed by the light from a wide floor to ceiling arched window that faced out onto 42nd Street. Here Eric and his intern sat, knees to knees, surrounded by towers of play scripts, and they read plays all day, occasionally remarking to one another on some brilliant or dreadful bit of writing they had come across, or sitting up straight for a moment to stretch, crack their necks from side to side, and passively regard the carnival of 42nd Street passing by.

Eric's job was to go back to before the beginning, before the necessity for fundraising and marketing and casting. He held in his hands every day the tear-stained and coffee-ringed products of hours and days and weeks and months and sometimes years of solitary, soul-grinding labor and hope on the part of would-be playwrights from all across the country and around the world. Every once in a while he would emerge from his lair to head for the bathroom or to engage in some other mysterious errand above ground, and his posture reflected both his habitual environment and his working life. He was pale, blond, shaggy-haired, and bespectacled, somewhat hunched over at the neck and shoulders, his posture permanently altered by a career spent looking down at the words that had somehow found their way into his lap.

"People often ask me what I do," Eric said with an exhausted sigh at one of our weekly staff meetings. "Well. Today, for example, I'm reading a play entitled 'Electra-cution, or: You're Under Orestes.'" He paused, sighed again, and gazed balefully around the circle at the rest of us. "And that's what I do."

This struck me as hilarious at the time, and it still does, both the play's painfully punny title and Eric's resigned reaction to it. But, seriously, why has this play not been produced? I would totally go. "You're Under Orestes." That just kills me.

Mostly because I worked at a theater and was steeped in it, I wrote a play called "Knights of Doubt." I took the title from a poem, a hymn, by an obscure Danish poet (is there any other kind?) named Bernhard Severin Ingemann that begins as follows:

Through the night of doubt and sorrow
onward goes the pilgrim band,
singing songs of expectation,
marching to the promised land.

I was trying to channel Chekhov in "The Three Sisters" and Lanford Wilson in "Fifth of July," so my play conjured up an apt description I once read about New Yorker short stories. To paraphrase: "Nothing much really happens... but you feel sort of sad about it anyway."

Alas, "Knights of Doubt" wasn't good enough to be worthy of production, and not bad enough to be interesting. I received a pity reading at Playwrights Horizons, thanks to the generosity of my former boss, the Artistic Director André Bishop, and I cast it with my friends, wonderful actors all. It passed unremarked into obscurity, and rightly so. I'm not a dramatist. "Drama" doesn't just imply drama; it states it right out loud. It's called "Drama." And for someone like me, who is conflict-averse, drama is a tough haul. So my play consisted of a lot of smart people sitting around talking. Smartly. Which might be amusing, but will never be riveting, or life-changing, like the best theater.

I love to read, more than just about anything in the world. To read is to enter the mind of another, to live another life. There are probably a lot of people, like me, who may think they want to write, because they love to read. It's hard to make a living just reading, so what's the next best alternative? Writing.

I actually did read for a living at one brief point in my life. I read books and scripts for MGM, was what they called a "D-girl" in the movie business, for "Development Girl." These are people – mostly women, at least traditionally – who read through a slush pile of books or screenplays looking for something bankable, although no property has ever been produced from a work read by a D-Girl. Never. Not one thing. The "D" should stand for "Dead End." It's the perfect pointless job.

And it's a miserable job. Yes, you get to read, but you cannot choose what you read, and then you must write up a summary and recommendation afterwards. As I recall, I was paid $50.00 for every property read which, if you do the math on a typical script or book, plus the writing of the summary and recommendation for further action (i.e., none), comes out to probably $5.00 an hour, max, without benefits.

And any time you're not reading, you're not making money. So it became impossible for me, during this period of my life, to enjoy a brunch or drink with friends because during times that should have been pleasant, making memories in my youth, I would be thinking, "I could be reading some dreadful science fiction story this moment about the planet Meepzor, thereby paying my rent and for this brunch and this drink." I was miserable.

So I suppose I've always wanted to write, in a desultory sort of way, or just "to be a writer." But I don't know that I have the disposition, the stamina, the attention span, (or the talent) for it.

Still, I'm going to write this, because maybe I can help someone.

Maybe I can even help you, or someone you love. I hope so.

It started around 6:00 a.m. on the morning of February 9, 2018 when my husband and I received probably the second worst phone call a parent can receive. Or maybe the third worst. Or maybe fourth or fifth. I don't know. There are a lot of terrible phone calls out there, as it turns out, and I've become much more sensitive to them after what happened to us. We spend our lives dreading and anticipating those phone calls so that when one comes, we're almost relieved, or at least vindicated. Ah, here it is, at last, as I always knew it would be.

The day before had been ordinary and uneventful, forgettable, as all the best days are. The only notable news: the Dow plunged over 1,000 points to close below 24,000 for the first time since the previous November, Bermuda rolled back gay marriage legalization to domestic partnership, and curling kicked off the Winter Olympics in Sochi.

But then everything changed in less than a second.

If my co-workers and all but my closest friends and family were to find out what I'm going through right now, have been going through now for years, they would be shocked that I can continue working and living and breathing and laughing every day. What happened was horrible, and continues to be horrible, and will always be horrible, but I've learned that people are carrying around a lot of burdens you would never guess about. I know I am.

I've also discovered that a traumatic event changes not only the present and the future, it changes the past as well. A dark curtain has fallen over my family's life, and life's entire meaning has been altered, as has the meaning of the lives of everyone who came before me: my parents, my grandparents, and ancestors unknown.

It takes only one error in judgment, one moment, less time than it takes to draw a breath. I can't go back in time to change the past, but I hope that I can prevent one person from making the same tragic mistake. To prevent the end of a life. To prevent the death of a life.

Because there is more than one kind of death. The people we were before – myself, my husband, my daughter – those people are all gone, as surely as if our ashes had been scattered into the sea. I look now at pictures of us – posing together for a 5th grade school picture, sitting on the grass up at Brinkie's Brae in the Orkney Islands of Scotland, on the beach in the Dominican Republic – and they might as well be sepia-toned, so remote are those images from the life we live now, and what the future holds for us. Those people are lost to us forever. I still remember them, but only just, because memory fades.

We can never return to the time before that phone call. All we can do, with whatever time is left to us, is try to move on from here, to find purpose and meaning in what remains.

"... in a real dark night of the soul, it is always three o'clock in the morning...."

F. Scott Fitzgerald, "The Crack Up"

When it happened, I thought that it was the worst thing that had ever happened to anyone. But that idea barely stood up to scrutiny for even a moment. Because then, just five days later, three adults and 14 children were slaughtered at the Margery Stoneman Douglas High School in Parkland, Florida. Since then there have been hurricanes and flooding. Twenty people were killed in a wedding limousine crash in upstate New York, including four sisters and two pedestrians. Eleven people were killed in a synagogue in Pittsburgh. The opioid crisis kills over a hundred Americans every single day. Nine children died of adenovirus at a Haskell, New Jersey nursing facility. There's the war in Yemen. North Korea. St. Jude Children's Hospital, drownings, bicycle accidents, falls from ladders. The bathroom is the most dangerous room in the house.

Turns out there's a lot of misery in the world. That's why, if you tossed your troubles onto the table with everyone else's, dreadful as they are, you'd probably end up clawing yours back, embracing them.

In my own life, I've seen and heard of a lot of suffering.

I worked briefly as personal assistant to the actress Dina Merrill. It would be hard to find a person who might inspire more envy than Dina. She was beautiful, gracious, and impossibly wealthy. Her parents were Marjorie Merriweather Post (Post cereals) and Edward Francis Hutton (E.F. Hutton; when he talked, people listened). She was married to the heir to the Colgate-Palmolive empire, and then to movie star Cliff Robertson. At one point, her net worth was estimated to be $5 billion.

She also buried two of her four children: David, who died in a boating accident at 24, and Heather, who died of cancer at 38.

Would you take Dina's fortune, along with her troubles, or would you keep your own? Keep your debts and keep your children.

I recently learned that an old college friend lost her young adult son to a sudden, mysterious virus. Another dear college friend shot herself in the head in the woods behind a motel in Virginia.

I worked at Playwrights Horizons with a woman called Stefanie Verkauf, who was one of the funniest people I've ever known. She loved Bruce Springsteen and Jackson Browne. When tabloid reports of domestic abuse allegations came out regarding Browne and his then girlfriend, the actress Daryl Hannah, I asked Stefanie what she thought of him now. She sighed wistfully and said, "Oh, if only he cared enough about me to beat me up."

Domestic abuse is a serious problem, but still. That is some serious funny.

Stefanie died of a brain tumor at 43, leaving behind a husband, and three children under the age of 10.

I worked with a 3rd grader who suddenly started stumbling and weaving through the school hallways like a drunk. He had a brain-stem tumor, and was dead within six months.

So, as it turns out, I had led a rather charmed life up to that moment in 2018.

I came home from work on February 8 and told my husband about a youtube video I had watched at lunchtime featuring Dr. Jordan Peterson, he of the "12 Rules for Life." Dr. Peterson was shown polling one of his psychology lecture classes, asking them to raise their hands if they had never in their lives experienced a two-week period of sustained and serious pain, suffering, and depression. Only one lone person in the back raised her hand. Dr. Peterson seemed momentarily taken aback. His eyebrows shot up. "Oh! Good for you!" he said after a moment. And then, more ruefully, shaking his head, "It's coming."

And about twelve hours later, it came for us.

"It is fate, destiny, nemesis. Perhaps the dawning of knowledge, the coming of sin. Or more prosaically, the catastrophe that awaits everyone from a single false move, wrong turn, fatal encounter. Every life has such a moment. What distinguishes us is whether – and how – we ever come back."

Charles Krauthammer

When I say that a traumatic event not only changes the present and the future, but also changes the past, I mean that a trauma becomes the beginning of a "new normal," but it also becomes the final event, the destination, the meaning of everything that came before, as though it were inevitable. This turns out to be where we were heading all along. All of my memories, especially the happy ones, are now colored by this event, as though my entire life was just marking time to this moment. I can never look back without thinking of this, or look forward, or even live in the present. This single event inhabits me as I inhabit it, and always will.

In her magnificent book "The Proud Tower," about the late 19th and early 20th century years in Europe, the years leading up to 1914, the brilliant historian Barbara Tuchman describes the First World War as "...[lying] like a band of scorched earth dividing that time from ours.... [creating] a physical as well as psychological gulf between two epochs."

Individuals and families can have their own bands of scorched earth.

I like to get up early, at least two hours before I leave for work. My husband Philip and daughter Andrea need to eat as soon as their feet touch the floor, but I must ease into it. Coffee. Coffee is proof that God loves us and wants us to be happy. I pet one of our two lap cats, Betty and Wilma, watch a little television news, work on my Duolingo Spanish app.

I read somewhere a long time ago that something absurd like 75% of Americans eat at least one meal a day in their cars, which explains why, when someone offers you a ride, they have to apologize while they clear out what looks like the contents of a McDonald's dumpster from the passenger side, throwing everything into the back, on top of another dumpster's worth of debris, creating sedimentary layers of wrappers, bags, plastic cutlery, and napkins to be explored and puzzled over by archaeologists centuries from now.

Not me. I like to take my time and eat at home.

So I was sitting in the Queen Anne chair in the living room with Wilma in my lap when Philip came down the stairs looking pensively at his phone. "Cole just called," he said. Cole was Andrea's housemate, a nice kid, some kind of tech wizard entrepreneur. Very Aspergersy. "Apparently, our daughter was arrested this morning at 3 a.m. for a DUI."

I couldn't even get upset, which is a sign of growth for me, a chronic worrier. In a way, it was inevitable. She lives in Austin, Texas, where everybody is young, everybody loves music, and everybody is drinking. The columnist Kevin D. Williamson has described Austin as a place "where the average drinker drinks more than average." Andrea had been 21 for almost 10 months, so was relatively new to legal drinking. Did she drink before she was 21? Yes, like most young people, I fear. But then she would call us, as we had urged her to.

"Mom? Remember when you said that if I ever needed a ride home I could just call you and you would...?"

"Yes," I interrupted her. "Where are you?" And so we went and got her. No questions asked, no recriminations, just advice to not do it again. It happened only once that I know of when she was still in high school.

But were there times when she didn't call? Almost certainly.

Our old friend Ben was also our family lawyer, based in Dallas. He had drawn up our wills, living trust, end of life advanced directives. And since he was only about three hours north of her, he had told Andrea, "If you ever need anything, if you get picked up for a DUI..." So I guess even Ben was expecting it, even if we weren't. The DUI is the common cold of Austin, Texas.

We hadn't seen Andrea since Thanksgiving, which we spent with her in Austin. She was supposed to come home for Christmas, but her pug Giacomo, the love of her life, suffered a mysterious anaphylactic reaction to something, we know not what, around the middle of December, and she didn't want to leave him in care. We couldn't stay in the second bedroom of the house because Cole lived there now, and Andrea had been working for four months at the front desk of the Westin Austin Downtown, so she would be busy during the holidays anyway.

Andrea and I had spent a couple of weeks in August 2017 walking into the top hotels in downtown Austin, trying to find her a job. Andrea looks like my mother-in-law, who was quite beautiful, and she is smart, funny, and articulate. Rather than applying for jobs the way young people do nowadays, by uploading a resume and simply hitting "Send," I suggested that she walk in, resume in hand, and ask to see the manager. And it worked. Andrea is the person you want to see at the front desk when you finally arrive at your hotel on your thirty-seventh business trip of the year, or when you show up for your best friend's destination bachelor party.

"Is she okay?" I asked Philip.

"Yes, apparently, but Cole says it sounds as though someone got hurt."

At 3 a.m. on a Friday morning in Austin?

"She must have rear-ended someone," I said. We all know about the hazards of drinking before driving and texting while driving, which some say is even worse, but one of my student's parents was a police officer, and he told me that in his experience most accidents are caused in just that moment when the driver looks down at the radio, to adjust the dial or the volume level. Hence the design in many late model cars putting the radio controls on the steering wheel.

I fired up the Ring video doorbell footage and looked to 3 a.m. The battery on the front door had died, but by the front eaves camera I could see Andrea arrive home. She made too wide a turn into the driveway, hit and knocked over a corner of the neighbor's fence, backed up and righted herself, and pulled straight into the driveway. So there was a fence we would have to pay for.

On the east camera I could see the top of her silver Jeep Wrangler pull up to the front door. The image was grainy, but from above, the grill, hood, and fenders of the car appeared to be intact. I heard her get out of the car, shut the door, and climb the steps to the front door of the house. She did not walk around to the front of the car to check for any damage.

"The front of the car looks fine, at least from this angle," I said. "It can't have been much of an accident," I told Philip.

I looked ahead a few minutes on the Ring and saw the police arrive at the house. So where had the accident happened? One officer was looking at the far fender, the right front, and looking under the front of the car. I could hear Andrea in the background saying to one of the officers, "My car is all fucked up."

"No," I said to myself, "it sounds as though you're all fucked up, my dear." In a way, perhaps it would be a wake-up call for her, I thought. The Dixie Chicks sing about sending your kids out there into the wide open spaces, "room to make the big mistakes." Maybe this would be a valuable lesson going forward. I hoped that no one was seriously injured.

I showed up at school early, as usual. I was a speech-language pathologist at an elementary school in Tenafly, New Jersey, an upper middle class enclave just across the Hudson River from Manhattan, a quick hop onto the George Washington Bridge.

Most people, when they think of speech-language therapy at all, think only of speech articulation, stuttering, voice. But most of our clients and students these days are those with significant language delays and disorders, auditory processing disorders, children and young adults on the autism spectrum, older clients who are post-stroke, post-traumatic brain injury, or having swallowing difficulties. The range of issues we address is wide and deep, so it can be frustrating when people think that all I do is turn a "wabbit" into a "rabbit" or a "bowl of thoop" into a "bowl of soup."

So I arrived at school an hour early, as usual, and didn't even think about what might be going on down in Austin. Philip would be in touch with Ben, and Ben would straighten things out. I set up my room for my kids, got out my therapy materials, checked e-mail, and went to an early Child Study meeting with a set of parents, teachers, our assistant principal.

When I got back to my room, I pressed the wake-up button on my phone and the screen lit up with a text from Philip saying simply, "Call me."

I think I knew then, and everything seemed to slow down. I didn't feel panic or weak in the knees, but suddenly lethargic, like a suspension of time and space. I thought it might feel nice to lie down on the floor and just curl up and go to sleep. My legs and arms heavy, I walked across the room to the wall phone, because I have a hard time hearing properly on cell phones, and I prefer to use them only for texting, or for emergencies. I dialed Philip's number, and the voice that answered sounded like a deeper, older version of him, like someone who had only just reluctantly emerged from a coma.

"It's me," I said.

"Honey." he said hoarsely. And then I heard him swallow hard and clear his throat so that he could speak again.

"She killed somebody."

TRANSCRIPT OF
OFFICER'S INTERVIEW WITH ANDREA SCOTT
STATE OF TEXAS VS. ANDREA SCOTT
IN TRAVIS COUNTY, TEXAS

Original Statement given by Andrea Scott
upon first contact with APD Officers

The following proceedings were transcribed from Officers' first contact with Andrea Scott and the subsequent "on scene" interview and field sobriety tests involving Officer H and Andrea Scott (Defendant) at 3:15 a.m. on February 9, 2018.

UNKNOWN OFFICER (Time: 3:20:53 AM): (Andrea opens the front door to her house.) Hi, how you doing? Uh, whose vehicle is the Jeep?

AS: That's mine

UNKNOWN OFFICER: That's yours?

AS: Yeah, what's up?

UNKNOWN OFFICER: What happened to it?

AS: What do you mean?

UNKNOWN OFFICER: Do you wanna take a step out and see what happened to your Jeep? Who was driving that tonight?

AS: Yeah, that was mine (sic).

UNKNOWN OFFICER: Were you driving?

AS: I was.

UNKNOWN OFFICER: You just get home?

AS: I don't know, like 30 or 40 minutes ago.

UNKNOWN OFFICER: 30 or 40 minutes ago? Where were you coming from?

AS: I was coming from downtown.

UNKNOWN OFFICER: Yeah? Were you drinking tonight?

AS: I was.

UNKNOWN OFFICER: You were?

AS: Yeah.

UNKNOWN OFFICER: Do you, uh, have a driver's license with you right now?

AS: Not with me off the top of my hand (sic).

UNKNOWN OFFICER: Will you go ahead and turn around for me. Go ahead and turn around. Right now you're being detained, okay?

AS: Are you sure you don't want my driver's license?

UNKNOWN OFFICER: You can just give us your name and date of birth.

AS: Can you... can you lock my house though?

UNKNOWN OFFICER: We can. Do you got keys inside we can get to? So we can lock it for you.

AS: I mean, yeah, somewhere inside, but it's in that purse, but, like, my dog is going to come at the door.

UNKNOWN OFFICER: Okay, what kinda dog?

AS: He's a pug.

UNKNOWN OFFICER: Okay.

AS: Please be careful, I might have locked him in my room.

UNKNOWN OFFICER: Is there anybody else in the house?

AS: Yeah, my roommate.

UNKNOWN OFFICER: Your roommate is in the house?

AS: In the room to the left, if you go down the hall to the left.

UNKNOWN OFFICER: Okay. And where is your purse at? Are these your keys?

AS: What? What... what's he asking? I don't have anything.

2nd UNKNOWN OFFICER: Nothing at all?

AS: Nothing at all. I promise. I wouldn't lie. Please... Please close the door before he goes wandering.

2nd UNKNOWN OFFICER: Go ahead and sit down please, go ahead and sit down.

AS: I just want the dog to be safe. That's all I care about.

2nd UNKNOWN OFFICER: Okay.

AS: I just want the dog to be safe. (Inaudible dialogue about the dog.)

2nd UNKNOWN OFFICER: Yeah I know, I hear ya. I mean your roommate is here, right? Hey, hey sit down. Please stay right there, stay right there.

AS: I... I am not going to hurt anybody (inaudible dialogue)

2nd UNKNOWN OFFICER: What's your last name?

AS: (Spells last name.)

2nd UNKNOWN OFFICER: (Repeats spelling.)

AS: (Verifies spelling.)

2nd UNKNOWN OFFICER: Your first name?

AS: Andrea.

2nd UNKNOWN OFFICER: Andrea. What's your birthday, Andrea?

AS: (Gives date of birth.)

2nd UNKNOWN OFFICER: (Repeats date of birth.) Is it in here, your ID?

AS: My ID, no it's, do you know where my phone is?

2nd UNKNOWN OFFICER: Is it in here?

AS: Yeah, probably. If it's not in there....

2nd UNKNOWN OFFICER: This one?

AS: Yeah, yeah.

2nd UNKNOWN OFFICER: Your dog is just fine. He's in the bedroom.

AS: (Inaudible dialogue.)

2nd UNKNOWN OFFICER: No, no, he's just in the bedroom.

3rd UNKNOWN OFFICER: I want to wake her up, to make sure we got the right person here.

AS: No, no, he's a him. His name is Cole Campbell. He's in the other room.

3rd UNKNOWN OFFICER: Is he going to bite me? (Talking to AS about her dog.)

AS: He's not going to bite you. He's a pug in the other room.

UNKNOWN OFFICER (Time 3:27:44 am): Reads Miranda Rights to Andrea.

AS: Responds she understands to each of the questions (begins crying leading to inaudible dialogue).

UNKNOWN OFFICER: (Speaking to Roommate Cole Campbell.)

AS: Are you, were you talking to Cole?

UNKNOWN OFFICER: I was.

AS: Do you have water?

2nd UNKNOWN OFFICER: Have water? I do not.

AS: Cole didn't do anything. Cole did nothing. (Begins speaking inaudibly to another officer.)

UNKNOWN OFFICER (Time: 3:33:29 AM): Andrea, do you know what's going on?

AS: I have no idea.

UNKNOWN OFFICER: Is that because you don't remember, or you're kinda putting it together now? Or has someone told you?

AS: Yeah, a little bit of both.

UNKNOWN OFFICER: Okay. So is there anything you're not telling us at this point?

AS: No.

UNKNOWN OFFICER: No? Okay, where were you coming from?

AS: (Indicates she does not know.)

UNKNOWN OFFICER: You don't know? Earlier you were telling us you were coming from downtown? Were you working tonight?

AS: (Responds inaudibly.)

UNKNOWN OFFICER: Did you hang out with friends afterwards? You don't want to talk to us? You need some shoes?

2nd UNKNOWN OFFICER: If she wants some socks and shoes, I can find her some.

AS: It's on the left, I mean right (indicating location of her room).

NO FURTHER AUDIBLE COMMUNICATION WITH AS UNTIL OFFICER H BEGINS INTERVIEWING HER.

OFFICER H (Time: 4:25:24 AM): Hey, how you doing ma'am?

AS: I'm okay.

OFFICER H: My name is Officer H, with APD, what's your name?

AS: (Gives her name.)

OFFICER H: What's your DOB?

AS: (Gives her date of birth.)

OFFICER H: What's a good address for you?

AS: (Gives her address.)

OFFICER H: What's a good phone number for you?

AS: (Gives her phone number.)

OFFICER H: All right, so let me ask you this. Do you know why we, ten, fifteen of us are here? Do you know why we're out here?

AS: More or less, it seems like there was an accident.

OFFICER H: All right, so can you tell me what happened?

AS: I can't.

OFFICER H: Why not?

AS: Because I don't know.

OFFICER H: You don't know?

AS: No.

OFFICER H: Okay, um, let me backtrack just a little bit, okay? Let's start with this. So do you know what day it is?

AS: It's February 8, 2018.

OFFICER H: All right. Let me ask you this. Without looking at a watch or time piece, what time do you think it is right now.

AS: Probably some time after 2:00 AM.

OFFICER H (Time: 4:27:20 AM): All right, so I'm actually going to correct you on one thing, just the date. The date is actually February the 9th, the morning of, and the time is 4:23 AM according to my watch, okay?

AS: Okay.

OFFICER H: All right, so I just wanted, that way we can establish a base here, okay?

AS: Yeah.

OFFICER H: All right. So let me ask you this. What's the last thing you remember?

AS: I remember being in bed with my dog and, I don't know, I couldn't tell you what time it was, but it was after I got off work, which is 11:30.

OFFICER H: 11:30 PM or AM?

AS: PM.

OFFICER H: So you got off work at 11:30 PM?

AS: Yeah, February 8th.

OFFICER H: Okay.

AS: And I was asleep, and that's the last thing I remember.

OFFICER H: When do you usually get to work?

AS: 3:00 PM.

OFFICER H: So you worked from 3:00 until 11:30 AM? Excuse me, I mean 11:30 PM.

AS: Yeah, 3:00 PM to 11:30 PM.

OFFICER H: All right, so eight and a half hours you were at work. Where do you work at?

AS: (Gives name of workplace.)

OFFICER H: Is that the hotel?

AS: Yeah.

OFFICER H: Okay, all right.

AS: I'm a Front Desk Agent.

OFFICER H: All right, front desk?

AS: Yeah.

OFFICER H: Okay, so from 11:30 PM to now, you don't remember anything?

AS: No.

OFFICER H: You don't remember getting a knock at the door?

AS: I do remember someone knocking at the door and I went to answer it, and at that point I went outside my house because my dog is kinda forward and likes to answer the door with me. So I went outside my house and there were police officers there and at that point I was answering questions.

OFFICER H: What kinda questions did they ask you?

AS: Where I was and at what time, basically.

OFFICER H: And what was your answer?

AS: It was what I remembered at the time. So I think, it started around 2... 2:00 AM, something like that, and I answered where I was at 2:00 AM. I feel like at that point I would have been driving.

OFFICER H: Okay, so at 2:00 AM you feel like you would have been driving?

AS: Mhmm.

OFFICER H: Why would you have felt like you would've been driving?

AS: Because I was leaving the area around which I was driving to go home.

OFFICER H: Okay, so where were you at during that time period?

AS: I was downtown.

OFFICER H: Where at downtown?

AS: Umm, Latitude, something like that. Then I went to another gay bar nearby Latitude. I think it's on Colorado.

OFFICER H: Colorado? Okay.

AS: Something like that.

OFFICER H: Let me ask you, so we've already established that you went to work at 3:00 PM and got off at 11:30 PM, right? Is that correct?

AS: Mhmm.

OFFICER H: All right, so let me ask you this. When you left work at 11:30 PM, where did you go as soon as you left work?

AS: As soon as I left work, I went to my colleague's house.

OFFICER H: If you don't mind me asking, where is that located?

AS: Somewhere in south Austin. She was looking for her passport.

OFFICER H: Okay, so you went to south Austin to a colleague's house. About what time did you get to her house?

AS (Time: 4:30:59 AM): 11:45?

OFFICER H: All right, 11:45, about 15 minutes after you got off work?

AS: Yeah.

OFFICER H: All right, so from 11:45 after you got to your colleague's house, what happened?

AS: Uh, we went to from there, and then there was someplace called the High Ball? High End? Something "high."

OFFICER: Is that located downtown as well? Or...

AS: Yeah. It's a gay bar, I know that much.

OFFICER H: All right, so...

AS: Then we went there.

OFFICER H: Is that the one that you said was on Colorado, or is that a different one?

AS: It's, yeah, I feel like it's off of Colorado, so I think it's a little bit to the... to the west.

OFFICER H: All right, so 11:45 y'all came downtown, went to the bar Latitude. Is that correct?

AS: Mhmm.

OFFICER H: And after Latitude, you went to, don't know the name of it, but another bar?

AS: Mhmm.

OFFICER H: All right, let me ask you this: from 11:45 to the time you went to the second bar, what time do you estimate it would have been at that time?

AS: From the time I went to the second bar to the time I went to the other bar? It wouldn't have been very long; it would have been like five minutes. And I feel like that one, the name of it starts with "high," it was like "High Ball."

OFFICER H: Let me ask you this, I'll make it simple, what time did you leave that bar on Colorado?

AS: Probably around like 1:30.

OFFICER H: 1:30? Mmk.

AS: Yeah, I mean I'm estimating but, yeah.

OFFICER H: Okay, so you left at 1:30. After leaving at 1:30, what happened?

AS: I went to my car which was nearby my friend's car and then I went to go get cigarettes. Then we came back to the area where our cars were. Then we had a cigarette and then after that point it's a little more amorphous.

OFFICER H: Okay, I just want to make sure I understand correctly. So, you say you left the bar and went to your vehicle. Do you remember where your vehicle was parked at?

AS: It was parked in the Brazos lot next to Westin.

OFFICER H (Time: 4:33:16): Brazos lot, is that 5th and Brazos? Do you know what the cross street there is?

AS: 5th and San Jacinto, I feel like. I mean it's 5th and Brazos or 5th and San Jacinto. Somewhere in there.

OFFICER H: Okay.

AS: Yeah, it's the Brazos lot.

OFFICER H: Okay, so you was parked there. Did y'all walk to your vehicle at that time?

AS: Yeah, my car is always in that lot.

OFFICER H: Okay, so you walked there. It sounds like the way you're telling me, I just want to make sure, did you actually drive your vehicle to get cigarettes, or did you...

AS: No, we... we parked my car and then we went over to Scruffy's, which is a convenience store on 6th, and then we got cigarettes and then we left.

OFFICER H: All right, so you basically walked to Scruffy's and then walked back to your vehicle and then you left?

AS: Yeah.

OFFICER H: All right, and about what time do you think that was?

AS: Probably somewhere around 1:45-ish.

OFFICER H: 1:45?

AS: Yeah.

OFFICER H: So after leaving, like literally driving, after the garage, what happened?

AS: By the garage, you mean, like, lot?

OFFICER H: Yes, ma'am, it's a garage or is it a flat area?

AS: I mean it's a garage... I mean it's just a lot where you leave.

OFFICER H: Okay, so it's just a lot. Sorry about that.

AS: You don't have to apologize for anything.

OFFICER H: Okay, so you left the lot and then what happened?

AS: I mean, I just remember going home at that point because I usually park in that lot, I have parking privileges in that lot, and I have a little decal on my car that says I can park over there because I work at Westin. So I parked there, and then I drove home. That's pretty much the... the gist of it.

OFFICER H: All right, so you left the lot, what route do you normally take home?

AS: I go... okay, I go north from... from the Brazos lot, so that means going up Brazos towards 6th or 7th. I think it's 7th, because I take a right. And then I take a left, and I'm not sure if that's onto Red River or the road that leads to Red River, because I know that I take that left. And then I wind up going towards Red River towards home.

OFFICER H (Time: 4:35:32): Mmk, okay, so normally... I just want to verify for a minute. Okay, so you left the lot, you went north on Brazos, made a right on 7th Street, um, not sure if you took Red River or you took another street, but basically went north. Okay, I'm trying to track with you.

AS: Yeah.

OFFICER H: So I'm trying to think about Red River... so you're making a left... okay.

AS: Left on Red River near the hospital, near the hospital where it begins.

OFFICER H: Okay, okay, I'm tracking with you. So you are right, Red River does run into the new Dell Seton at UT. So if you're talking about there, then...

AS: Yeah, yeah.

OFFICER H: Is that where you ended up at?

AS: I mean, I don't know. I went past the hospital because I know there's kinda more than one hospital, but I don't know if they're affiliated with each other. So, it's like I went left from Red River and then going right after that point, but the same street, so I think it's MLK at that point, so it sorta transitions into the same street, so I went left and I know there's a hospital kinda on my left and my right, but mostly on my left, so I kept going on Red River, and I don't know if there's a hospital on 32nd and Red River because I've been there before. So I don't know if they're the same.

OFFICER H: But you know that you made a left onto MLK?

AS: Exactly.

OFFICER H: Okay.

AS: At that point, I was on Red River.

OFFICER H: So, at what point, so, so you remember getting to MLK or making a couple lefts, at what point do you remember getting to your house?

AS: I mean, I don't know how to answer that, like shortly before I arrived at my house, I remember getting to my house.

OFFICER H (Time: 4:39:00): Do you remember any significant events from the time you left downtown, 'til the time you got to your house?

AS: I remember there being a bump.

OFFICER H: You remember there being a bump? Do you remember where the bump took place?

AS: Somewhere between 32nd and here, 32nd and 37th.

OFFICER H: So when you felt that bump, what did you think it was?

AS: I didn't really think anything of it. I just thought something had happened but, I mean, my car has sorta been messed up for a while. I don't know if anyone else smelled it, but my car has been giving off a gasoline fuel smell overall for a few days. At this point, it's been a few weeks, but I work most days so I don't really have a lot of time to take it over to the shop, which I knew that I should've done between the time I first noticed the fuel gasoline smell and now... ummmm.

OFFICER H: So you felt a bump, but you didn't think to stop and look what that bump was?

AS: No.

OFFICER H (Time: 4:40:14): Did you think at all that you hit anything?

AS: I mean, I thought that maybe I hit an animal, but like a raccoon or a possum or something. I didn't think like anything beyond that. I thought it was just road kill, you know.

OFFICER H: Okay, so how did that, where you may have possibly hit it, how did it affect your vehicle?

AS: How did it hit my vehicle?

OFFICER H: How did it affect your vehicle?

AS: It didn't.

OFFICER H: So nothing was wrong with your vehicle?

AS: No.

OFFICER H: Okay. So it didn't stop and smoke or anything?

AS: No.

OFFICER H: So it drove like normal?

AS: Yeah. No, I mean like my Jeep, it's like a 4-wheel car, so it just sorta goes, you know, so it doesn't.... it doesn't...

OFFICER H: It didn't steer or anything different?

AS: No. It doesn't... it doesn't act differently depending on what happened to it in the last couple of minutes. I mean, it's a 4-wheel drive, so it doesn't.

OFFICER H (Time: 4:41:20): All right, sounds good. So let me ask you this. I understand not stopping in the middle of the street after you hear a bump, um, when you got back to your residence, did you look at your vehicle?

AS: Not really.

OFFICER H: So even after feeling a bump, not wanting to stop on the dangerous streets and highways, I understand that, but when you got here you didn't even look at it to see what had taken place?

AS: Not so much. No. I mean like 'cause this isn't unusual for my car, where like either there's dry roads, I don't know, but like it's either that or something happens to it where it just like goes over a bump or something happens where it has a reaction to it, and I don't really go out of my way to figure out what it is.

OFFICER H: Do you normally hit bumps going home?

AS: Sometimes. Sorta around 32nd.

OFFICER H: What do you mean... specifically?

AS: I think it's somewhere around where I go right before 32nd Street and the street right after that. I don't know if it's like 33rd. I don't think that's a thing in the neighborhood. But like there's a bump that happens between 32nd and my house, so I thought it was that. Ummm, but I'm not sure, you know, I know that there are some bumps that happened between 32nd and my house, and it's usually like one significant one somewhere between 32nd and my house. But I haven't really thought much about it. And I mean, I know, I know that there's something wrong with my car because it does give off a fuel smell, which can't be a good sign, but I haven't taken it to the shop or gone out of my way to figure out what it is because it's been working fine. I take it to work and park in the Brazos lot and I go to work from there and everything's been working okay.

OFFICER H: Okay. Let me ask you this: so from what I understand, from what you've told me so far is that from the time you went downtown, sounds like you went to two bars, correct?

AS: Latitude and, uh, High something or another.

OFFICER H: Latitude, thank you. So, while you were at Latitude, how many alcoholic beverages did you have?

AS: Two.

OFFICER H: Okay, two. What exactly did you drink?

AS: I would've had I mean whatever shots, Nicole was having, but after that one...

OFFICER H: Okay, you know what that was?

AS: Off the top of my head, no, like they just gave me whatever was there and I mean it smelled awful, I know there was Coca Cola in it. Probably tequila and whiskey and orange juice, but I, like...

OFFICER H: Okay, but what I'm trying to figure out, was it, like, two shots or, like, two sets of shots or was it, like, two mixed drinks?

AS (Time: 4:44:59) : Mmm, it was one drink, so I don't know how many shots they put in it, but it was somewhere between one and two.

OFFICER H: Okay, so I'm still a little bit unclear, so I just want to make sure I got it right. So you said... 'cause it sounds like you went from two to one, so I want to make sure I'm clear.

AS: Somewhere between one and two for the first drink.

OFFICER H: Okay, and then you had a separate drink.

AS: I did.

OFFICER H: Okay, okay. So that first drink could've been a combination between one and two. So how big would you say that drink was?

AS: It was either, in terms of, like, drinks? In size of drinks, that was somewhere between one and two, probably more towards two.

OFFICER H: Okay, how big would you say?

AS: Umm, do you mean, like, ounces wise?

OFFICER H: If you want to use ounces, yes, ma'am.

AS: Probably something like 16, but not, like, all of alcohol.

OFFICER H: Okay, I see what you're saying. So it was a bigger drink, that's why you were saying it could've been one or two.

AS: Yeah.

OFFICER H: Okay, that makes sense to me, okay. That's what I was trying to clarify, sorry.

AS: Yeah, of course.

OFFICER H: Okay, so the second drink, how big was that one?

AS: The second drink? It was like this (motioning with her hands).

OFFICER H: In terms of ounces, how big would that be?

AS: In terms of alcohol?

OFFICER H: Just in general.

AS: In general, this would be about 15 to 20 ounces.

OFFICER H: All right, so that's the second drink?

AS: Yes, but, like, alcohol wise it would be more like four to six.

OFFICER H: Okay, exactly what was that one?

AS: Tequila and vodka, I would... I imagine.

OFFICER H: Okay, so you're not exactly sure what was in it?

AS: No.

OFFICER H: Okay. Do you remember what they, like, the name of what they served to you. It's been a while since I've been to a bar, but most of the time I can ask for a Grey Goose and cranberry drink. So there's my chaser, you know what I'm saying, so did they give you a name or anything?

AS: I think it was a Long Island Iced Tea.

OFFICER H: It was a Long Island Iced Tea. Was that the second drink or the first drink?

AS: That was the second.

OFFICER H: All right, second drink coulda...

AS: There were multiple liqueurs in it, but overall.

OFFICER H: Overall, a Long Island Iced Tea. What about the name of the first one?

AS: Umm, that one was just a shot. Whatever they were serving.

OFFICER H: All right, so you're not exactly certain what that one was?

AS: No.

OFFICER H: All right, perfect. All right, so that was at Latitude, so those were your two drinks. When you went to... what did you call it again? The High...

AS: I want to say another, like, Long Island Iced Tea.

OFFICER H: Okay, and what else did you have there?

AS: Nothing else.

OFFICER H: Nothing else?

AS: No.

OFFICER H: All right so, just at those two bars you only had three drinks?

AS: Yes.

OFFICER H: Three different drinks?

AS: Yeah.

OFFICER H: All right, so where else did you go besides those two bars?

AS (Time: 4:48:10): There was another bar after that, one that was a little bit to the east of that one and then north. Which I can't remember the name of that one either. But I know that I had another Long Island Iced Tea or something to that effect there. But overall it was only four in the night, and I left shortly after that last drink.

OFFICER H: All right, sounds good. So, let me ask you this question. Have you taken any type of medication.

AS: No. I mean yes, I have taken Wellbutrin... I think it's XR.

OFFICER H: When do you take that?

AS: I take that every morning.

OFFICER H: Okay, so it's a morning dosage?

AS: Mhmm.

OFFICER H: Gotcha, okay. What else, what other medications do you take?

AS: I take Vyvanse, which is around the afternoon, umm, that's 50 mg. a day.

OFFICER H: Okay, and is that a daily dose for you? And what else do you take?

AS: Nothing.

OFFICER H: All right, so, Wellbutrin in the morning and Vyvanse about mid-afternoon?

AS: Yeah.

OFFICER H: Okay. Ummm, any type of illegal drugs?

AS: No.

OFFICER H: All right, so let me ask you this. When you arrived at your residence, what did you do once you got inside?

AS: I got inside, changed my clothes, and I got in bed with my dog.

OFFICER H: All right, I just want to be as specific as possible. Did you take a shower?

AS: No.

OFFICER H: Did you brush your teeth?

AS: (Shakes head no.)

OFFICER H: Did you eat any type of food?

AS: No.

OFFICER H: Did you drink any alcoholic beverages?

AS: No.

OFFICER H: Umm, did you do anything of note once you got in the house besides changing your clothes and getting in bed with your dog?

AS: No.

OFFICER H: All right, so I just want to clarify one more time. So while you was at the residence, you literally walked inside, put your clothes on, got in bed, and then you were awakened by officers at your door?

AS: Mhmm.

OFFICER H: Is that safe to say?

AS: Yes.

OFFICER H: Is that everything that happened as soon as you got to the house?

AS: Yeah.

OFFICER H: Not even mouthwash?

AS: Not even mouthwash.

OFFICER H: All right, I just gotta ask.

AS: No, I understand that. You have to ask.

OFFICER H: All right, let me ask you this. In the last six months, have you been involved in any major collisions?

AS: No.

OFFICER H: Suffered from any major head trauma?

AS: No.

OFFICER H (Time: 4:51:01): Can you see out of both of your eyes? Do you wear glasses or contacts?

AS: I do. Glasses, not contacts.

OFFICER H: All right, now let me ask you this. For the glasses... do you leave 'em... is it more, like, just for reading, or is it something you wear every day?

AS: I prefer to wear them every day, it's not really for reading at all. 'Cause it's for astigmatism, so it's, like, far away. I prefer to wear them every day, and I tend to. Apart from my days off, which don't count as much to me in my mind as my regular work days. But, umm, yeah, I wear glasses.

OFFICER H: I think I asked you earlier, I may have not, when was the last time you ate some food?

AS: Ate some food? Somewhere around 11.

OFFICER H: 11 a.m. or p.m.?

AS: p.m.

OFFICER H: Okay, p.m. What exactly did you eat, if you don't mind my asking?

AS: Popcorn.

OFFICER H (Time: 4:52:01): Okay, that's when you had the popcorn? 11 p.m.?

AS: Before that, it was around 8 or 9, and it was, like, half of a pesto wrap.

OFFICER H: Okay, all right. So it's safe to say meal wise that you probably haven't eaten since around 8 or 9 o'clock?

AS: Yeah, something around that.

OFFICER H: All right, um, have you ever been diagnosed with diabetes?

AS: Not diabetes.

OFFICER H: All right, sounds like you got something else in there. What have you been diagnosed with?

AS: I have an eating disorder.

OFFICER H: What did you say? An eating disorder?

AS: Yeah, it's been around since, like... I mean, I was diagnosed with it when I was 18 or 19, but that's been around since I was 13 or 14.

OFFICER H: Do you take any type of medication for that or anything?

AS: I mean, apart from the Wellbutrin and Vyvanse, nothing.

OFFICER H: Okay, fair enough. Do you have anything physically wrong with your legs, knees, ankles, lower back, or hips?

AS: No.

OFFICER H: Okay. Um, Imma ask you this question here, okay? So on a scale of 0 to 10, 0 is sober, not consuming any alcohol beverages, 10 is the most intoxicated you've ever been in your life. Where would you put yourself at right now?

AS: Right now?

OFFICER H: Yes, ma'am.

AS: Probably a 3.5.

OFFICER H: A 3.5?

AS: Mhmm.

OFFICER H: All right, Imma ask a huge favor of you, okay? Imma ask you to stand there, right where my light is. Imma ask you to turn and face me. Can you turn and face me? You're perfect, just fine. I'm going to have you pull your hands out of your pockets for me and just put 'em down to your side, okay? Do you understand these instructions?

AS: I do.

OFFICER H: All right.

(Time: 4:53:57) Inaudible dialogue with another officer, Officer H walks out of view of camera.

OFFICER H: All right, so once again, feet together, arms down by your side and just stay in that position for me until I give further instruction. Do you understand these instructions?

AS: (Nods yes.)

OFFICER H: Huge favor, can I have you take your hood off for me?

AS: Okay.

OFFICER H: Thank you. Can you see the light right there on the top of my pin? And what color is that light?

AS: Yes, bluish, but not exactly, kind of like a light... light color.

OFFICER H: Okay, what I'm going to do is move it back and forth. I'm going to ask you to keep your head still just like you have it, once again, keep your head still. Do you understand those instructions?

AS: Okay, I do.

OFFICER H (Time: 4:55:00): Okay.

Officer H begins HGN Field Test. The Horizontal Gaze Nystagmus test is part of the sobriety field test. It involves asking the subject to follow a light with gaze only. *Alcohol consumption exacerbates nystagmus, which is the involuntary jerking of the eye, where a smooth eye gaze would be expected. An example of natural nystagmus would be gazing out a window at a passing train. The eye jerks back and forth, trying to follow the movement of the train, while returning to the original gaze position.*

OFFICER H: And we'll go up and down, okay? (Time 4:56:58) End of HGN Test.

OFFICER H: Thank you, ma'am. All right, do me a favor and just relax for a second. (Officer H walks off screen to talk to another officer about watching AS during other tests due to observed swaying.) All right, Andrea, do me a favor. Imma have you stand right here, and I want you to turn and face this way. So I'm going to put my light right there.

AS: Mhmm.

OFFICER H: Turn and face me. There you go, perfect. Put your feet together for me and just relax. Once again, Imma have you take your hands out of your pockets for me, okay?

AS: Where do you want them?

OFFICER H: Oh, you... just relax, just relax, all right. So what Imma ask you to do right now is to imagine a straight line running from your person to however long you imagine that straight line to be. The width of that line is going to be the width of your foot. Do you understand that?

AS: Okay, yep.

OFFICER H: All right, so on this imaginary straight line right now,

Imma ask you to take your left foot and put it in the middle of it for me. Take your right foot and place it directly in front of your left foot, making sure your heels and toes are touching. Put your arms down to your side, and stay in that position until I give you further instructions, okay?

AS: Mhmm.

OFFICER H: Do not move from that position until I tell you to do so. Do you understand those instructions?

AS: Yeah, mhmm.

OFFICER H: All right, when I tell you to do so, I want you to take nine heel-to-toe steps down, turn in a manner that I'm going to show you, then take nine heel-to-toe steps back down the line, okay?

AS: Mhmm.

OFFICER H: While you're doing so, keep your arms down to your side. You're going to look down at your feet and you're going to count each step out loud. Okay?

AS: Mhmm.

OFFICER H: It's going to look like this (Officer H demonstrates The Walk and Turn Test). One, two, three, all the way to nine, okay?

AS: Mhmm.

OFFICER H: When you get to that ninth step, keeping this lead foot forward, you're going to take a series of small steps just like this, then turn

around and take nine heel-to-toe steps back down the line. One, two, three...
all the way to nine, okay? Once again, arms will stay down to your side, you
will look down at your feet, and you will count each step out loud, okay?

AS: Mhmm.

OFFICER H: And once you start, do not stop. Do you understand those
instructions?

AS: I do.

OFFICER H: All right, ma'am, when you are ready, you may begin.

AS: (Begins Walk and Turn Test at 4:59:28.)

OFFICER H: All right. Another huge favor, can I ask you to turn around
and face me, please?

AS: Mhmm.

OFFICER H: Imma have you stand right here where my light is, there you
go. All right. Imma ask you to put your feet together for me, take your hands
out of your pockets and keep 'em down by your side for me, please. Imma
ask you to stay in this position until I give you further instructions. Do you
understand those instructions?

AS: I do.

OFFICER H: All right, when I tell you to do so, whichever foot you're
comfortable with, I want you to raise it approximately six inches up off the
ground. Make sure both your legs stay straight Make sure whichever foot you

choose stays parallel to the ground. Your arms are going to stay down by your side. You're going to look at your raised foot, and you're going to count out loud, one thousand one, one thousand two, one thousand three, and you're going to keep going until I tell you to stop, okay? So once again, whichever foot you choose to raise, keep it about six inches up off the ground. Make sure your foot stays parallel to the ground. Arms will stay down to the side...

AS: As you're standing now?

OFFICER H: Yep, as I'm standing now, yes, ma'am. Don't do it yet, please. Put your leg down, please. Once again, make sure both your legs stay straight. Whichever foot you decide to raise stays six inches off the ground and foot stays parallel to the ground. Arms stay down by the side, look down at this raised leg, and count out loud just like I did.

AS: Okay.

OFFICER H: Do you understand those instructions?

AS: I do.

OFFICER H: All right.

AS: When... when do I stop counting?

OFFICER H: When I tell you to stop counting, yes, ma'am, and you just keep going until I tell you to stop, okay? Do you understand these instructions?

AS: I do.

OFFICER H: All right, when you raise your leg, we will begin.

AS: Okay. (Begins the One Leg Stand Test at 5:01:59.) One thousand one, one thousand two, one thousand three, one thousand four, one thousand five, one thousand six, one thousand seven, one thousand eight, one thousand nine, one thousand ten, one thousand eleven, one thousand twelve, one thousand thirteen, one thousand fourteen, one thousand fifteen, one thousand sixteen, one thousand seventeen. (Loses balance and puts both feet on ground.) Do you want me to start again?

OFFICER H: Yes, ma'am.

AS: One thousand sixteen, one thousand seventeen, one thousand eighteen, one thousand nineteen...

OFFICER H: You can stop there.

[Note: The One Leg Stand Test generally requires 30 seconds of balancing to completion.]

OFFICER H: All right, last thing Imma ask you to do for me, stand right here for me, feet together for me, arm down by your side. Stay in that position until I give you further instructions.

AS: Mhmm.

OFFICER H: All right, so once again, arms down by your side, feet together, stay in that position until I give you further instructions. Do you understand those instructions?

AS: Mhmm.

OFFICER H: All right, when I tell you to do so, I want you to lean your head back and close your eyes, okay?

AS: Mhmm.

OFFICER H: When you lean your head back and close your eyes, in your head I want you to estimate 30 seconds, okay?

AS: Okay.

OFFICER H: Once you've estimated those 30 seconds you'll lean your head back forward, open your eyes, and tell me to stop, okay?

AS: Okay, all right.

OFFICER H: One thing I do want to mention is that I only want you to estimate 30 seconds in your head. I don't care how you do it, but don't count out loud, okay?

AS: Okay.

OFFICER H: All right. Do me a favor, and put your hands down by your side, and just stay in that position, okay?

AS: Sure.

OFFICER H: Do you understand those instructions?

AS: I do.

OFFICER H: All right, ma'am, when you lean your head back and close your eyes, we will begin.

AS: (Begins Rhomberg Balance Test at 5:03:05.)

AS: (Time: 5:04:31 tilts her head forward and opens her eyes. Elapsed time: 1 minute and 26 seconds.)

OFFICER H: Stopping there?

AS: Mhmm.

OFFICER H: All right, so how many seconds did you estimate?

AS: Thirty.

OFFICER H: You estimated 30. How did you get to 30?

AS: I counted to 30.

OFFICER H: Okay, all right. (Walks out of view of camera.)

AS: (Inaudibly talking with another officer.)

OFFICER H: All right, so this right here is called a P.B.T., okay (Preliminary Breath Test). It's something that we as police are supposed to carry to allow the citizens to show they're below a .08. It does not affect your license or your ability to drive; it's not admissible in court, okay?

AS: Mhmm.

OFFICER H: Do you understand everything I just told you?

AS: I do.

OFFICER H: I want you to take it. Have you ever blown into a balloon for a party before?

AS: I have.

OFFICER H: Okay, same concept, okay? Take a deep breath for me, okay?

AS: Mhmm.

OFFICER H: And blow... (AS blows into Portable Breath Tester at 5:06:00.) Keep going, keep going, keep going, keep going, keep going, keep going... and stop. (Time: 5:06:03.) All right, ma'am, do me a favor. Take your hands out of your pockets for me, put your hands behind your back. You are being arrested for driving while intoxicated, okay? (Places AS in handcuffs at 5:06:20.)

AS: As long as my door is locked.

OFFICER H: Door to what?

AS: My door to my house.

OFFICER H: Okay, all right. We can check on that for you.

AS: Yeah, Cole should probably still be inside.

OFFICER H: Is he pretty friendly, your dog?

AS: No, my roommate.

OFFICER H: Oh, oh, oh, that's your roommate. I'm sorry, I thought you was talkin' about your dog.

AS: I was not, no.

OFFICER H: All right, I'm sorry.

AS (Time: 5:06:54): You don't have to be sorry. I'm the one who should be sorry. Where are we going?

OFFICER H: All right, we're going to go over to my car here. So... Imma use the back of my hand real quick just to check your pockets, okay?

AS: Yeah. Yeah, I mean, I feel a little ridiculous 'cause I'm kinda in a onesie.

OFFICER H: Nah, you're good. Do you have anything underneath?

AS: No.

OFFICER H: Okay.

AS: Am I going in the backseat?

OFFICER H: Yes, ma'am. And actually, real fast, Imma actually turn the light on so you can see where you're sitting.

AS: I appreciate it.

OFFICER H: All right, yes, ma'am. Have a seat for me. Watch your head. I am going to reach across you just one time to put the seat belt on you, okay?

AS: Mhmm.

OFFICER H: Hey, Andrea, sorry to wake you up one more time. I need to read you a form. Actually, can you see in this light, do you want me to use my flash light? It's a little bit more light.

AS: I mean, like, what part of it are you reading?

OFFICER H: Imma read the whole thing to you.

AS: Okay.

OFFICER H: All right, so can you see it in the light here? Or do you want the flash light?

AS: Either one, it's fine.

OFFICER H: Okay, all right. Imma use the light here. Just let me know if you can't see it okay? Can you see it?

AS: Mhmm, I can.

OFFICER H: All right, first it's called a statutory warning, okay? (Officer H. proceeds to read statutory warning to AS.) I am now requesting a specimen of your blood, and what is your answer, ma'am?

AS: (Nods her head yes.)

OFFICER H: All right.

UNKNOWN OFFICER: What's your birthday, ma'am?

AS: (Gives her date of birth)

UNKNOWN OFFICER: You said you're 5'2"?

AS: I'm 5'4".

UNKNOWN OFFICER (Time 5:14:41): How much do you weigh?

AS: I don't know off the top of my head, but somewhere between 135 and 140. I would imagine.

UNKNOWN OFFICER: Okay. Blue eyes?

AS: Yeah.

UNKNOWN OFFICER: What's your natural hair color, ma'am?

AS: Blondish natural, blonde, brown something.

UNKNOWN OFFICER: Okay.

(Transport from scene to Austin Downtown Lockup begins at 5:16:24 a.m., arriving at Austin Downtown Lockup at 5:33:04 a.m.)

OFFICER H: Hey, Andrea?

AS: Mhmm

OFFICER H: I'm gonna ask you to wake up for me, okay? Imma have you... we gonna get you out here, okay? Let me know if you need help getting up. You need help? You got it.

AS: I think I got it.

OFFICER H: Okay, come on out. Okay? All right.

**END OF VIDEO: 5:34:48 a.m. **

I should say right up front that if you are the sensitive sort, who balks at some dark humor, this book might not be right for you.

Let me stipulate right now that Mr. Boyd's death was a serious occurrence that has stayed with me every moment of every day since it happened, and will be with me for the rest of my life, will probably be the very last thing I think of as I go off myself to whatever he has found before me.

People – good people – who have unintentionally taken a life torture themselves with this knowledge forever. There is no worse punishment you can inflict upon them than that which they inflict upon themselves every day.

So I could wear a hair shirt and rend my garments, chew up my heart, and throw myself on the mercy of the reader, but how tiresome a book would that be? I want to take you to all the places I have found in my soul through this experience. There will be sadness, guilt, grief, terror, sickness, anger, and some humor, because without some humor, even some dark humor, we – I – cannot go on. I want to write a book that will help to prevent this from happening to you, or perhaps to someone you love. But I also want to write a book that will give you hope if this does happen to you.

And, yes, this happened to me. It happened to Mr. Boyd and his friends and loved ones, and to my daughter and to my husband and to our family and to our friends and to our dogs and to our cats. If I were ever to rate an obituary, Mr. Boyd's death and my relationship to it would be in the very first sentence. If you were to ask me, "What is the most important thing I should know about you?" it would be this. It informs my every waking thought, my every waking deed. It belongs to me.

And because it belongs to me, I give myself permission to write about it any way I see fit. When and if you come to write about the worst thing that ever happened to you, you will have my full support in writing about it in your own voice. As the memoirist Jerry Stahl observed, "If you had to live it, you get to write it." Amen, brother.

Come along with me and enter a cautionary tale for everyone. But be warned that you might read some things that will make you uncomfortable, upset, angry, that might "trigger" you. If you're the queasy type, turn back now; no one will judge you.

But if you have courage and you want the truth, get on board.

Let's go.

~Two~

"The man who has a conscience suffers whilst acknowledging his sin. That is his punishment."

Fyodor Dostoyevsky, "Crime and Punishment"

We all have thoughts that will make us ashamed.

I remember holding on to the phone receiver and saying, "Oh my God, oh my God, oh my God, oh my God, oh my God" countless times, but I was still aware that just on the other side of the door, my colleague Casey was working with some of the children we shared. "What will they think?" I wondered in the back of my mind. But I still couldn't stop gasping, "Oh my God, oh my God, oh my God, oh my God, oh my God."

There are moments besides death when your whole life flashes before you. I knew immediately that my daughter's life, my husband's life, and my life would never be the same again. That band of scorched earth...

Philip must have told me more, but I don't remember him saying much else. I knew that she had been arrested at home, so he must have told me that. There was one victim, a man. A victim. A man. A dead man.

I hung up the phone and began to make my way down the hall toward our principal's office. I saw colleagues along the way, and I think I tried to flash a wan smile, because social conventions die hard.

Our assistant principal, Julie Cosgrove, was filling in for our principal, who was on paternity leave after his wife had given birth to twins. I stood in Julie's doorway and asked if I could speak with her privately. I'm sure I looked a fright. As soon as the door closed, I broke down. I told Julie that I had to leave for Austin with Philip right away, and that I didn't know how long I might have to be gone.

I had the odd sensation that I was standing outside my body watching myself telling Jodie what had happened, and sobbing, judging my own crying as though it were somehow performative and not real. I remember having the odd thought that this event was "extra," sort of an "add-on." I thought vaguely that we must all be reconciled to the inevitable calamities of life: growing old, getting sick, and then dying. The trick, it seemed to me, was to avoid all those "bonus" events we never count on, such as this one. But it appeared that we had not been able to avoid an unexpected catastrophe after all. So it would be the unspeakable enormity of this, and then the requisite growing old, getting sick, and then dying. We would be spared nothing in exchange for this.

I remember driving very carefully the two miles from school to home. And I remember having only the most shameful thought over and over again as I carefully came to a full stop at each Stop sign, checking all my mirrors every few seconds, clutching the steering wheel until my hands cramped.

I remember thinking, "Please, God. Please make it be someone I don't have to care about." Maybe it was just some poor homeless person by the side of the road. There are a lot of them in Austin. Maybe he was lying in the gutter, covered with newspapers, or he stumbled into the street from out of nowhere, from between parked cars.

It's a sad fact that some people's lives are worth more than others. We all know it, but no one wants to say it out loud. All lives have the same value, we say, all lives are sacred. But we know we're lying. So then, why do we say it? Maybe we're superstitious.

Maybe it will keep us and our loved ones safe if we mouth the right platitudes.

But please, God, don't let it be a surgeon on his way home from the late shift at St. David's. A surgeon with a wife, and with three young children in private school, who saved eight lives today, with loving parents who slaved to put him through medical school, with two brothers and two sisters who will spend next Thanksgiving staring at an empty chair, and whose fatherless children will spend their lives despising us, googling us, stalking us, standing outside our house late at night, staring at the lighted windows, bitterly looking for any signs of peace or joy, the peace and joy of which they have been robbed.

"Please, God. Please make it be someone I don't have to care about."

These are the thoughts I think. And I'm ashamed. But I think them anyway.

When I got home, I found Philip making the flight arrangements. We packed in a daze, shuffling past each other from the closet to the dresser to the suitcases on the bed. My mouth tasted like ashes, and it was hard to swallow.

I don't remember much about the ride to the airport or the flight, but I remember that Philip and I held hands, which is something we never do. But I needed that sense of firm connection, of being tethered to something, because everything that held any meaning for me in life had been shattered into a million tiny pieces.

We're not hand-holders. But in the coach plane seats, we held hands, and I stared down at the hideous patterned carpet designed to conceal soda stains.

I don't remember a lot of details about those first few days. We went to the Austin house to walk and feed the dog, and saw Cole, Andrea's housemate. The house is a little two bedroom/one bath ranch near the University of Texas stadium. When we were looking at colleges for Andrea, UT Austin was on the short list because Andrea wanted to major in screenwriting and UT boasts a world-class film school. She ultimately decided to go to southern California, but Philip and I had fallen in love with the city and thought it might be a good place to retire one day.

Austin bills itself as "The Live Music Capital of the World" and, thanks to the university, it's a young, lively city, with something always going on, from museums and local artists to vintage and indie movie theaters, and now a thriving stand-up comedy scene, thanks to Joe Rogan. It's a "NORC," a "Naturally Occurring Retirement Community" for oldsters like us who don't want to live in traditional retirement communities, those designed primarily for 100% unemployment, shuffleboard, pickleball, and rampant syphilis transmission.

Our lawyer and friend Ben came down from Dallas and met us at a local hotel on I-35. I remember that Philip and Ben were both able to eat, but I wasn't. Men can always eat.

Ben is one of Philip's oldest friends, born and raised in Dallas. He and Philip met in the late 70s as actors in drama school at LAMDA, the London Academy of Music and Dramatic Art. Ben had reinvented himself many times over, as an actor, a director, a writer, eventually going to law school and opening up his own practice in order to fund and sustain his theater habit. He and his actress wife Althea worked often in the vibrant Dallas/Fort Worth theater scene.

Ben is tall and broad, shoulders back, with a slight paunch that precedes him into a room by a half second. He has a rocking gait, like a giant toddler. He's smart and well-read, but is also a deeply silly man, with a highly developed set of Three Stooges, Laurel & Hardy, and Abbot & Costello impressions. Althea is his always-elegant counterpart in colorful caftan. When our two couples get together, we usually all laugh until we cry and pee in our pants. But not this time.

I remember those first few days as a patchwork of bits and pieces of information and impressions, and the sources of much of the early information we received are vague and disjointed in my memory, like a bad online meeting connection where the picture freezes at times and some audio cuts out intermittently.

We learned through Ben that the victim's name was Thomas Boyd, 46 years old, that he lived alone, had no parents living, no wife, no children. He was said to be on permanent disability for some sort of brain injury. He reportedly had a half-brother who lived out of state and some friend in Massachusetts, I believe I recall, one or the other of whom reportedly said that "he was the nicest guy you'd ever wanna meet, and would never want to see a young girl's life ruined over something like this." He was said by someone – I'm not sure who – the friend, the brother, the police, the prosecutor, the insurance investigator, a doctor – to suffer from a crippling social anxiety disorder that moved him to do his grocery shopping at 3:00 a.m., when he would encounter as few people as possible on his errand. Later we learned about other reasons for his nocturnal wanderings, but these were the first snatches of information we could gather.

There were ironies attached to this early description. Andrea herself suffers from anxiety and frequent bouts of depression, and could easily have been one of the few people Mr. Boyd would encounter at H.E.B. in the middle of the night. I have worked with children and adults who suffer from similar disabilities, which interfere with their ability to communicate with others effectively. In another life, Mr. Boyd and Andrea might have been friends. He might have been one of my clients. We might have been professional acquaintances, nodding neighbors, might have been able to help one another navigate the perilous social terrain. Unfortunately, instead, our lives intersected under brutally tragic circumstances.

We learned that Mr. Boyd had been riding a small, early model Yamaha motor scooter and that when the impact occurred a young woman in a nearby apartment building was awakened by the noise and went outside to investigate before calling 911 when she came upon Mr. Boyd's body in the street. When the police and medical services arrived, it was first thought that he had been a pedestrian, because no trace of a vehicle was immediately apparent. However, the scooter had evidently become lodged under the chassis of the Jeep and the police soon noticed a thin trail of glass and metal parts leading away from the incident site, north and then east, taking them straight to our driveway, like a trail of bread crumbs.

Because the incident happened in the middle of the night, in order to take photographs the police had sprayed the street with green fluorescent paint, cryptically marking where they had found various parts of Mr. Boyd's motor scooter. From the River Road intersection they had also painted a bright green dotted line with dashes spaced about five feet apart straight from Red River and turning into our driveway. Areas of the driveway gravel were also circled in green to indicate places where evidence had been found.

It was a vivid "Scarlet Letter" map to our door, and at least one old ghoul made his way up the next morning and just stood across the street from the house, staring at it, clearly basking in the misery of others. I went outside, sat on our bench, and stared him down from the front porch until he became embarrassed enough to turn and head back down the street. I went out into the middle of the street and stood there, watching his slow progress toward Red River, where he turned and looked back at me from the length of a city block.

We both stood there for about a minute, sizing each other up like Gary Cooper and Ian MacDonald at the end of "High Noon." He blinked first, turned, and headed down the street.

I hope he felt some measure of shame. He can't possibly have gotten that old without having regrets, mistakes, actions in his past he would reverse, if he could, if he had it to do over. He couldn't possibly have gotten that old without having someone he loved make a terrible, tragic mistake. He can't possibly have gotten that old without having experienced some tremendous pain, loss, agony. Why would he bestir himself to follow that ghastly line to our door, like a succubus, to stand there and – what? – feel superior, invincible? Safe?

Ben kept checking in with Central Booking, and at first there was one charge: Intoxication Manslaughter. But when he and Philip and I got back from another dinner I couldn't eat, another charge had been added: Accident Involving Injury. This is the equivalent of "Failure to Stop and Render Aid," or FSRA, leaving the scene. Ben said to the clerk on the phone, "I won't hold you to this, of course, but in your experience what would be the total bail amount for charges like these?" The clerk paused for a moment, and then said that she would estimate bail on these charges to be set at about $50,000.00.

But Andrea's bail was ultimately set at $175,000.00. $100,000.00 for the manslaughter and $75,000.00 for the FSRA.

Travis County Sheriff
ANDREA SCOTT

Booked: 2/9/2018 06:20

Arresting Agency: AUSTIN POLICE DEPT

ACCIDENT INVOLVING INJURY
Bond: $75,000.00

INTOXICATION MANSLAUGHTER W/VEHICLE
Bond: $100,000.00

1st Court Appearance Docket
2/26/18 @ 9 a.m. in court room

Bail Bonds – Austin

SECURITY AGREEMENT

For value received, I, PHILIP SCOTT, acting as Co-Signor for ANDREA SCOTT, Defendant, do hereby agree and acknowledge by my signature, that LIBERTAD BAIL BONDS may possess the property described below to secure LIBERTAD BAIL BONDS against any and all losses, debts, and obligations of the undersigned.

The following property is transferred to LIBERTAD BAIL BONDS as COLLATERAL/SECURITY, to wit: Value $175,000.00 Lien on Real Estate Property.

The undersigned further agree with LIBERTAD BAIL BONDS hereinafter referred to as COMPANY, as follows: That, upon failure to perform the agreement terms and conditions of the bond, COMPANY is authorized and empowered to sell the securities then held in pledge hereunder, and receive the proceeds of such sale. We assume no responsibility for damage related to hurricane, tornado, or any other act of God.

These items are being held to ensure that the defendant will appear in court and will be returned ONLY after the COMPANY is completely discharged of any liability for all bonds posted with no loss to COMPANY.

EXECUTED ON THIS, THE 11th day of February, 2018.

LIBERTAD BAIL BONDS   Williamson County   Travis County

Date: 02/11/2018
INDEMNITOR INFORMATION RE: ANDREA SCOTT
Name: PHILIP SCOTT

Contract to Indemnify

For and in consideration of LIBERTAD BAIL BONDS, hereinafter referred to as Bonding Company, securing the release from jail of ANDREA SCOTT, hereinafter referred to as Bonded Person, I, PHILIP SCOTT, hereinafter referred to as Indemnitor, agree to pay the sum of $175,000.00 in Georgetown, Williamson County, TX, within thirty (30) days of a bond forfeiture of Bonded Person.

A bond forfeiture occurs when it appears to the judge of the court where Bonded Person's case is docketed that Bonded Person did not appear in court and the judge so designates the same on the court's docket.

I have fully read this contract and agree to its terms and conditions.

EXECUTED ON THIS, THE 11th day of February, 2018.

"Little solace comes to those who grieve when thoughts keep drifting as walls keep shifting and this great blue world of ours seems a house of leaves moments before the wind."

Mark Z. Danielewski

When Andrea first arrived at the police station, she was fingerprinted and the mugshot that would pop up in any Google search for the rest of her life was taken and released to the press, along with her name and significant portions of her initial interview with the police. At that point an officer, a woman at the booking desk, looked up at her and said, "You know someone died tonight, right?" And Andrea put her head down on the table and sobbed.

She was on suicide watch while in jail, with someone coming by to check on her every 20 minutes or so. Her cell had a cot, a sink, and a toilet. There was supposed to be a cup for drinking, but there wasn't one, so she scooped water out of the sink by the handful and drank, wiping the drips off her chin with her sleeve.

Breakfast, lunch, and dinner were all the same, dropped through the bars in a paper sack. Four slices of white bread, two slices of processed cheese, eight slices of faux bologna, an apple, and a bag of pretzels. No condiments. No cup. Cot, sink, toilet. Drinking water from sink. Breakfast, lunch, and dinner.

Everyone was very kind to her in jail. By the third day, as her father and I were getting bail together, one of the staffers told Andrea, with an eager joy usually reserved for infinitely better news, that she might soon be eligible for a tray, as she had been there long enough. But the tray turned out to be worse than the bag: some unidentifiable glop and a side of applesauce.

My friend Kathy once told me that she and some college friends had identified the four basic food groups in the Yale cafeteria: meat, plants, glop, and dessert. And it works. Anything you can think of is either one or a combination of these four elements. Chicken = meat. Broccoli = plant. Creamed chipped beef = meat and glop. Ice cream = dessert and glop. Applesauce = plant and glop. Most food, it would appear, either is or is accompanied by some form of glop.

Turns out the menu at the Austin lockup is pretty much the same as the menu in the Yale cafeteria.

On the fourth day, we were slated to pick her up, and we were able to speak on the phone briefly beforehand. "Mom," she said sheepishly, "when I was arrested, I was wearing a onesie." A onesie is an adult sleeping garment that looks as though it should be worn by a three-year old child: flannel, fleece, or faux versions thereof, fuzzy and colorful from the neck to the toes, zipped up the front. She would have nothing else to wear out of the building, so I told her that I would bring her some clothes to change into.

After she processed out, she had to sit in the lobby of the jail waiting for us in all her flannel finery. A middle-aged cop, hardened by Austin nightlife, walked out one of the doors into the lobby, took one look at her and deadpanned, "Whatd'ya get in a pillow fight?"

"I believe in Christianity as I believe that the sun has risen: not only because I see it, but because by it I see everything else."

C.S. Lewis

Five months before the incident, there appeared in The New Yorker magazine an article about people who have accidentally killed or seriously injured another. The article is by Alice Gregory and it's entitled "The Sorrow and Shame of the Accidental Killer." The piece details the story of Maryann Gray, who accidentally struck and killed a little boy with her car when she was 22 years old. Gregory notes that there are self-help books out there for everyone: "...alcoholics and opiate abusers; for widows, rape victims, gambling addicts, and anorexics; for the parents of children with disabilities; for sufferers of acne and shopping compulsions; for cancer survivors, asexuals, and people who just aren't that happy and don't know why. But there are no self-help books for anyone who has unintentionally killed another person."

Maryann Gray founded a website called Accidental Impacts, now The Hyacinth Fellowship, which basically has no competition online and receives over one hundred novel hits per day. I logged onto the site in anticipation of writing this chapter, and just since my daughter's incident, as of this writing, I find gut-wrenching personal stories from a man who killed a pedestrian with his bicycle; someone who ran over a three-year old child; a woman who hit a man standing next to his car and severed the man's leg; a man who struck and killed a 16-year old cyclist; a woman who – when she was eight years old – accidentally scalded her infant brother, leaving him scarred over 90% of his body; a woman who fell asleep at the wheel with her 24-year old daughter in the car; another man who ran over a six-year old boy; a woman who – 38 years ago – allowed her drunk boyfriend to drive, resulting in his death and the death of another young man driving an oncoming car; a woman who feels guilty for not intervening to prevent the suicide of her niece; even a man who accidentally left his dog in a hot car and a woman who commiserated with him because she had accidentally left her cat to die in a hot suitcase.

Maryann Gray traces the origin of her website to an accident that happened in 2003 near where she lived at the time, in Santa Monica, when an 86-year-old man mistook his accelerator for his brake, plowing into a crowd of people, killing 10 and injuring dozens. While others leapt on the incident, slavering, calling the man a "murderer," Gray felt sympathy for him, being familiar with the deep moral injury that lay ahead for him (he was ultimately convicted of manslaughter at age 89). She emailed her reaction to NPR, which asked her to read a version on the air, which she did, in July 2003. Gray expected negative blowback, but the response was overwhelmingly positive, and many people who had been living with the guilt of having caused a death reached out to her with gratitude. So she started Accidental Impacts.

The group has recently changed its name to The Hyacinth Fellowship, because the word "accident" has become problematic. There are many people seeking support because they were truly blameless. They may have been driving soberly and responsibly, like Maryann, when a little boy named Bryan, in childhood exuberance, dashed out into the middle of the street, and she was unable to swerve or brake in time.

But there are others for whom "accident" may be misleading, because some accidents don't just happen; they are caused. Andrea's incident fell into that category, stemming as it did through a series of events resulting from poor judgment, cognitive impairment, and just plain dumb bad luck.

The namesake Hyacinth comes from the Greek myth about the god Apollo and his friend and lover, Hyacinth. One day they were playing catch in a field when Apollo's discus went astray, hitting Hyacinth in the head, mortally wounding him. With all his godly power, Apollo was powerless to save his friend's life. As Hyacinth lay dying in Apollo's grieving arms, drops of his blood (or perhaps Apollo's tears) fell to the earth, and from these sprang the glorious flower we know today as the Hyacinth.

And so Maryann Gray devoted her life to providing hope and comfort to damaged, broken souls who all belong in a club to which no one would seek membership.

On the site, you can find articles, books, podcasts, and personal stories designed to help people navigate through the dreadful aftermath of having caused the grievous injury or death of another person. It is currently estimated that in this country alone 30,000 people every year cause unintentional death or serious injury to another. That's more than 82 people a day, or at least one every 20 minutes.

My daughter had been drinking at the time of her incident, and I'm sure you will find very few (I haven't found any) testimonials on the website from people who killed someone while driving drunk or "impaired" or "buzzed," or who are willing to admit that they did. The shame is simply too great, and many have been advised correctly by their attorneys that they should be silent about culpability until their cases have been adjudicated. These people have graduated to a higher level of blame and shame and guilt. It's one thing if you look down to adjust the radio, or even to text, or turn around to yell at unruly children in the backseat, if you nod off near the end of a long journey, or simply lose sight of someone in the blind spot created by that bar that connects the driver's window to the windshield as you're making that left turn. Those are genuine accidents, momentary distractions, forgivable, if you will.

But I wonder. I would never excuse it. I'm guilty of it myself. But driving after consuming alcohol seems to be unique among the vast array of bad judgments that can result in an accident because it stems from the exercise of bad judgment that occurs, by definition, when judgment is impaired.

Presumably, the decision to change that radio channel, to send that text, to turn around in the driver's seat to swat at those annoying little brats, to bend over to pick the dropped phone off the car floor – those were conscious, reasoned decisions made in an instant in the sober light of day. What about those of us who get behind the wheel when we know we're too tired to drive? Those of us who find ourselves nodding off, so we turn the radio up, sing a song, roll down the windows for a blast of cold air, only to find ourselves once again, head jerking up, eyes flying open, bumping along on the median? (This happened to me in 1973 on my way home, sober, from a college party.) What of those who drive angry, as Bill Murray exhorts the herald of spring on his lap to refrain from doing in the immortal "Groundhog Day?" So why does the drunk driver come in for special condemnation?

I'll tell you why. Because all of those other people are "innocent." Our vision of the texter, the phone dropper, the radio tuner, the sleeper, the distracted, and the angry: those visions are of good people who simply made a momentary mistake. What do you see when you picture someone texting? It's yourself. You just want to let your husband know you're on your way. You see the commuter on his way home listening to the traffic and weather glancing down for a second to push the button for 1010 WINS.

Or how many times have you run a stop sign or red light because you were simply distracted, lost in your own thoughts, not paying attention, thinking of something else? The outcome could have been horrific, but you were spared. There was no one else around. Thank God. You're still a good person.

But what do you envision when you hear the phrase "drunk driver?" I'll tell you. You see a guy who looks like he just got up on the wrong side of the floor. You see a paunchy, dissipated lush with ratty hair all akimbo, sunken eyes, broken capillaries on a florid nose, bad teeth, three days worth of silvering stubble, and a wasted, vacant expression. He's standing in front of a wallboard that marks his height at 5'9". You see Frank Gallagher from "Shameless."

But is that who the drunk driver is? Or is he me? Is he you? Is he someone you love? Is he the guy driving home from a business lunch or the suburban white wine mom on her way to pick up her kids from soccer practice?

Or is he the family man who just took his wife and two children out to dinner, where he had two Manhattans and a beer over an hour and a half or two hours? Because let me tell you, my friend, that man is probably legally drunk. There are thousands of those people on the road right now, and most of them will get home okay. But for an unlucky few, this will be the last day of their lives or the last day of the lives they have known. After tonight, nothing will ever be the same.

I recently met for coffee a friend from the Hyacinth Fellowship, the first time we've met outside of Zoom. He was 19 years old at the time of his accident, and unimpaired. It was broad, bright daylight. Too bright, in fact, because he was blinded by the glare of the low-hanging sun, grazed the median, was catapulted into oncoming traffic, and struck a couple on a motorcycle. The driver survived with injuries. His passenger girlfriend was declared dead at the scene.

Damien didn't drink at the time, but developed a drinking problem a few years later, partly due to the guilt and moral injury of having caused the death of another human being, or at least of having been the instrument of that death. He told me over coffee that when he started drinking, he would stop in at bars on the way home from work and find himself surrounded by many others who had done the same thing, of course. One drink, two drinks, three drinks, four. "How had they all gotten here?" he wondered at the time, and how were they getting home? It made no sense. None of them should be driving home.

And then it occurred to him, the logical answer. Just like him, they all were, in fact, driving home. It was simply accepted, it was natural. Tough day at work. You stop at a bar after work, you have "a few drinks to take the edge off," and then you "go home," by which we mean "drive home." It happened all the time, every day, everywhere. He looked around the bar again. "How are these places even legal?" he wondered.

That's a good question, isn't it? Maybe they're legal because we absolve ourselves by posting electronic billboards on the 4th of July saying, "If it's red, white, and booze, don't do it. Don't drink and drive." And by adding the tag line "please drink responsibly" to liquor ads.

Here's the bar. Here's the warning sign. Here's the drink. Here's the disclaimer. Do it. But don't do it. Nudge-nudge, wink-wink.

The "Real Housewives" get smashed every episode. It's fun, it's funny. It's "reality." When one of them stops drinking, the others all get suspicious, defensive, aggressive. Why are you not drinking? But who wants to watch a bunch of sober, middle-aged, spoiled, Botoxed, talentless women sit around a seminar table discussing Foucault and Derrida? Nobody. Sometimes we see them pick themselves up off the floor, stagger out to the driveway, and we might then catch a glimpse of a hired driver as the ladies crawl into the backseat of a black town car or a Sprinter van. But that level of perspicacity is only obliquely and occasionally suggested. If you blink, you could miss it. That's not what we came for. We came for the skinny-dipping in the pool and the falling in the bushes, the tantrums and childish fights that break out when inhibitions are low. That's television. That's fun. That's entertainment.

At the school where I worked at the time of the incident, several parents sponsor an annual benefit at a lovely local restaurant. The money raised is used to fund special events, as well as pricey equipment such as state-of-the-art electronics. There is food, music, a live as well as silent auction, and an open bar. Parents and other attendees are encouraged to drink liberally so that they might bid recklessly and thus fill the coffers of the school for the following academic year. SmartBoards don't come cheap (they aren't even smart).

And if you go to that venue the next morning at, say, 5:00 or 5:30 a.m., what will you find? Will you find a parking lot full of cars because everyone emerged from the event the night before and said, "You know, honey, I had a few drinks in there, and I feel fine to drive. But let's just play it safe and take an Uber home. I can pick up the car tomorrow morning."

No. You will find an empty parking lot. I know because I went to that parking lot the next morning, and that's what I found. Because everyone emerged from that venue the night before and thought to themselves what we all think, "Sure, I had a few drinks in there, but I feel fine to drive." And drive they did. And most of them – all of them, I hope – will get home okay. And everyone else will get home okay, too. But not because they're better people than my daughter is, or because they're better drivers, or even because they're better drunk drivers. No. They will get home okay if they are lucky.

Well, my daughter was not lucky that night, and Mr. Boyd was very unlucky. And the fabric of our lives was torn in half.

I have some advice for you, my friends. Try not to be so smug.

Ask not for whom the bell tolls. And, yes, send for an Uber.

Here is the link to the Hyacinth Fellowship:
https://hyacinthfellowship.org/

Here is the link to Alice Gregory's article about Maryann Gray and her mission:
https://www.newyorker.com/magazine/2017/09/18/the-sorrow-and-the-shame-of-the-accidental-killer

And here is Maryann Jacobi Gray's TED Talk:
https://www.youtube.com/watch?v=Xb-JneauRzs

"Where did I go wrong?
I lost a friend
Somewhere along in the bitterness
And I would have stayed up with you all night
Had I known how to save a life."

Isaac Slade and Joe King of The Fray

It's all my fault, really. All of it. Or at least, it's my responsibility. I wasn't one of those parents who want to be her child's friend, but I wanted to be pragmatic, practical, realistic. I knew Andrea would want to rebel, to stretch her wings before she was ready to fly, and I wanted her to be able to do that in a "safe" environment.

I was one of those parents.

By the time she was 20, that meant allowing her to drink in our presence, and when we knew she wouldn't be driving, because we would be the ones doing the driving.

Let me say right here that I do not condone underage drinking, but I will also note that in Canada, as well as most of Europe, the drinking age is 18 (in Italy it's 16). The theory is that young people are going to drink anyway, so they might as well learn how to do it early, safely, and responsibly. It's a reasonable theory.

Drunk driving is a problem in Europe, which boasts the highest level of alcohol consumption in the world, but the rate of drunk driving deaths is lower than it is in the United States. This may be partially explained by the fact that driving distances are shorter in Europe, and European countries have a much more widespread and sophisticated mass transit system. Many Europeans of drinking and driving age do not own cars.

So when should we have realized that we might have a problem?

Well, that day might have been July 22, 2016.

In July 2016, we all scored tickets to see Louis C.K. at Forest Hills Stadium, very exciting. We were big fans and remain so to this day (he can masturbate in front of me any time he wants to, so shut up).

Philip and I had seats in the stands, while Andrea and her friend José were attending a wine tasting at the stadium before taking their seats. Andrea was 20 at the time, but the wine purveyors evidently weren't carding, and Philip was driving, so we felt comfortable. Philip drove us out to Queens and we parted from the kids at the stadium gate, to meet up after the show.

Security and confidentiality were taken seriously. There were signs on all the seats stating that anyone caught using their cell phones during the performance – to speak, record, photograph, video, text, tweet, blog, snapchat, check their hair, you name it – would be escorted from the venue immediately. No refund, no discussion.

I spent some time in my 20s hanging around with young comics at the clubs, and they're not as much fun as you might think. First of all, most true comedy is a reflection of pain and anger, and these were some seriously dysfunctional people. They convert this turmoil into a reflection of life to which we can all relate, and which we can convert to laughter at our shared human condition. The product of comedy is sublime and life-affirming, cathartic, but the process, the sausage-making, can be dark and ugly.

"The Tonight Show with Johnny Carson" was broadcast from 1962 to 1992, and it was where many comedians made their biggest splash. Steve Martin, Robin Williams, Ellen DeGeneres, Andy Kaufman, George Carlin, David Brenner, Roseanne Barr, Jay Leno, Jerry Seinfeld, Eddie Murphy, Jim Carrey. It was the dream to do material on the Carson show, but every comic knew that once that appearance had been made, the material itself – sometimes worked and honed to perfection over weeks, months, and years – would have to be retired. Everyone had seen it now on Carson, so you couldn't do it in the clubs anymore. It was time to go back to the drawing board.

So Louis was in no mood to have the material he was workshopping in venues around the country, ultimately destined for a NetFlix special, captured by cell phone pirates.

I was excited about seeing C.K., but almost more excited to be in this cathedral of tennis. The stadium seats only about 14,000 and, like most places – and people – is revealed to be much smaller in person than in the imagination. Billie Jean King, Arthur Ashe, Chris Evert, Jimmy Connors, John McEnroe, Rod Laver, Margaret Court. They all played and won here, and I could feel the energy of tennis history vibrating in the cool evening air.

The show was very funny, of course, but I don't remember any of the jokes, not after the way the night turned out. I was busy imagining Andrea's evening, and searching for her and José in the stands. At one point, I saw her passing below us on the field, following a security guard through a curtain I imagined led backstage. I wondered if she was going to be able to meet Louis himself, what they would say to one another. I pictured him recognizing her intelligence and wit, offering her on the spot a job on the writing staff of his next series. We do live vicariously through our children, and often dream dreams for them they would never imagine for themselves.

When the show came down, we made our way along with the throngs leaving the stadium and stopped just outside so that we could text Andrea our location. The wait was long, with no response to our texts. I remember becoming irritated with her. Surely she would realize that we had to arrange a rendezvous before heading back to the car together. Why wouldn't she respond? Five minutes became ten.

Then Philip's phone rang and he spoke briefly before grabbing my hand and beginning to push through the crowd. It was slow going, we moved at a desultory pace, borne along by happy, lazy, summer evening shufflers in no hurry for the night to end.

I don't remember at what point Philip told me that he had been talking to José and that he and Andrea were in the medical tent. He said he could hear her in the background, crying or shouting, he couldn't tell which. When we emerged from the throngs, we found a policeman and asked for the location of the medical tent, but he didn't know where it was.

We headed clockwise around the stadium, through the dark narrow sidewalks and lush arboreal jungle of Forest Hills. Ironically, if we had turned left just outside the stadium gate, we would have stumbled on the medical tent almost immediately and saved ourselves a half hour of cold parental panic running frantically around an unfamiliar borough. The stadium sits in a residential area, so the streetlights are few and far between, and we had no idea where we were or where Andrea was.

I alternated running and walking, running in panic, then walking when my breath ran out. My mouth was dry and I couldn't swallow. I was sweating in the heavy, humid air of July in New York, and my baby was in a medical tent I couldn't find. We stopped several people on the street for information, but no one was able to help us. It was a classic nightmare.

Philip's phone rang again, and it was a nurse telling him that they would have to put Andrea in an ambulance within the next few minutes, if we failed to arrive. The nurse wasn't sure which city hospital she would be taken to, that would depend on dispatch.

We finally rounded another dark corner and spotted the ambulance at the end of the block. We had woven our way all the way around the stadium and deep into Forest Hills, like a corn maze in Hell. I hate corn mazes. Confusion, frustration, being lost, feeling tricked, corn. What's fun about that?

I broke into a run toward the ambulance, and I remember thinking, "Well, so much for UT Austin. She's not going there now. I'll never let her out of my sight again." The nurse called out to me, "It's all right, Mom, you don't have to run. It's okay." So I staggered the last few yards to the ambulance, with Philip right behind me.

Andrea was already inside, strapped into a gurney. She was conscious, but her face betrayed her general disorientation, and she was flailing about. Philip stopped outside the ambulance to talk with José, who was standing outside.

I held Andrea's hand and tried to calm and steady her, while adrenaline coursed through me and I struggled to manage my own breathing and heart rate. How to describe her affect at this moment? She was hyperactive but disorganized, her head rolling and turning and lolling, her eyes unfocused. Her legs were strapped into the gurney, but her arms were free, and she was writhing in place. I don't remember anything she said, but nothing she said was making sense. She smiled at times, then laughed, then cried. She kept apologizing to me saying, "I'm sorry, I'm sorry, I'm sorry," and I kept assuring her that there was nothing for her to feel sorry about, that we loved her, that we were there for her, and that she would be all right. She let me hold her hand, which was something she would never do if she were in her right mind.

Philip said later that he wished he had video-recorded her on his phone so that he could show her later, because her behavior would be so difficult to describe. He told me that he was afraid she had suffered some sort of permanent brain damage.

This was not drunkenness. I've seen drunk. I've been drunk.

And this was not that.

Outside the ambulance, José had described to Philip the events of the evening. He and Andrea had gone to the wine tasting, and she had some wine, but there was no food. Their tickets were supposed to include the tasting as well as seats for the show, but the affair was very disorganized and they were not assigned seats, but were simply told to enter the venue and find a place to sit. So they climbed up into the far reaches of the bleachers in the back of the stands. When audience members arrived to claim those seats, the two were forced to move and find other empty spaces. They tried to watch the show, but were distracted by latecomers they saw climbing the steps, invariably heading for the seats José and Andrea had been temporarily occupying.

At some point, Andrea became agitated and annoyed by the uncertain circumstances and wanted to leave, so she and José left the stadium and began to walk around the neighborhood. José said he became alarmed at her erratic behavior, the self-loathing things she was saying, and so he took her to the medical tent.

After what seemed an eternity, the ambulance started moving toward Elmhurst Hospital, a city facility about 15 minutes from the stadium. José rode up front with the driver while Philip and I stayed in the back.

Andrea's behavior was still bizarre and almost psychotic. One moment she would look at me, unfocused, as though she didn't recognize me. The next moment she would be crying and apologizing. At some point she began to rub and stroke the crotch of her jeans with her free hand, clearly attempting to masturbate. The ambulance techs discreetly pretended not to see what was happening, and I took both of her hands in mine to still them.

The tech asked us questions about medical history, any events we were aware of leading up to this episode, and so on, and we answered as best we could. When the tech asked us what medications she was on, Andrea suddenly sat bolt upright, perfectly alert, and rattled off a list of prescriptions and dosages. Apparently, unbeknownst to us, she was on several medications for depression, anxiety, and attention deficit disorder.

From the moment they're born, our children lead secret lives of their own which only grow in complexity as they age. We think we know them, but they are in fact as mysterious to us as strangers. They belong to themselves. If we're lucky, they may occasionally give us even just a glimpse into the foreign landscape of their inner lives.

We arrived at the emergency entrance of Elmhurst hospital and followed Andrea's gurney as she was wheeled inside. If you've never been in the emergency room of a New York City hospital – and I hope you have not

– you have missed one of the more Dickensian experiences still available to us in the 21st century. In triage, your disoriented daughter may have to compete for attention with a domestic abuse survivor, a gunshot victim, or the fellow who just staggered in through the sliding doors with an ax embedded in the middle of his forehead.

It was at this juncture that whatever Andrea was experiencing moved from pathos to absurdity. As she was wheeled past a bed containing an extremely elderly old gentleman with a wisp of white hair and a befuddled expression, she compounded his confusion by winking in his direction, clicking her tongue twice, pointing a shooting finger at him, and asking flirtatiously, "How ya doin' there, handsome?"

Her gurney bed was wheeled into a corner in a large antiseptic room with patients lying down or propped up in a large circle around the periphery, most gazing hopefully at their opposites, everyone waiting for someone else to make the first move, like an 8th grade dance, but with physical injuries rather than emotional ones. Unforgiving fluorescent lighting hummed and buzzed relentlessly overhead. It was around midnight by this time, so Philip took the opportunity to drive poor José home, while Andrea and I waited to see a doctor. A nurse came by regularly to check her vital signs, and I kept her hydrated with water from a nearby cooler. We didn't talk much. Andrea was still a little loopy, so we spent the time watching the misery around us with gratitude that we were only about half as bad off as everyone else. She periodically lurched to a sitting position and wretched over the side of the gurney between the mattress and the wall. It was all thin liquid, tinged with red – blood or wine? – no solid food.

After a while we were moved into an adjoining ward room almost identical to the first but, I assume, one inferno circle closer to a doctor. Philip returned from New Jersey after safely depositing José and we three continued to wait. A nurse stopped by with a laptop precariously balanced on a wheeled metal stand and keyed in our insurance particulars.

The doctor finally arrived and began asking for details about what had led up to Andrea's presence in the emergency room. Philip and I filled in what we knew, but we should have held on to José because, with Andrea still so disoriented, he was the best authority on what had happened between the time we dropped them off at the stadium entrance and the time we finally located the ambulance in the maze of Forest Hills.

The doctor did have some information gleaned from what José had told the EMTs and the attending nurse at the medical tent. He and Andrea had attended the wine tasting and then left the venue when they were unable to find satisfactory seats for the show. They wandered around the local neighborhood. At some point, they sat down on a stoop and Andrea began to cry and talk about how "bad" she was. Then she threw herself backwards, hitting the back of her head on a concrete step. I'm still not sure how the two of them made it to the medical tent, but she was retained by the staff there, who called for an ambulance due to concerns that Andrea's rambling statements indicated a desire to harm herself.

So this was basically a psychiatric hold.

Andrea was starting to become slightly more lucid, so the doctor told us that we should stay and keep an eye on her, letting the tincture of time resolve her disorientation, and that we might be able to take her home with us in a few hours. So we waited.

Hospital staffers were calm and competent, circulating easily among the patients, asking and responding to questions, checking vital signs, providing assurances that all would be well.

Suddenly, there was a raised voice from a bed in a corner of the room, just a few yards to Andrea's right. A white woman, overweight, middle-aged, with pasty, lumpy skin like cottage cheese was shouting something about her cigarettes, a carton of cigarettes, which she insisted had been stored in the metalwork beneath her gurney and had now evidently been stolen by "some niggers" on the hospital staff.

It was shocking to hear such raw hatred being spewed in such an antiseptic setting, but staffers seemed unperturbed and unruffled by the display,

indicating that such behavior was by no means unusual. My instinct was
to stay as far away from the incident as possible, but Andrea was agitated.
She wanted to get up out of the bed – "I'm gonna go over there…" – and it
was all Philip and I could do to keep her calm and focused. We reminded
her that the goal was discharge from the hospital, which would be ill served
by her jumping into an altercation with another patient.

Orderlies (how aptly named) and nurses appeared to have the situation
under control. After attempting to calm and reason with the woman, to
little effect, she was sequestered in a private enclosure clearly reserved for
this purpose. The rest of us in the ward could still hear her ugly charges
and see her through a window in the door flailing about in restraints, but
the level of disturbance in the larger room subsided and we continued to
wait.

At last, perhaps around three in the morning or so, the doctor stopped
by again and after receiving our assurances that Andrea would be safe with
us and that we were comfortable taking her home and looking after her
ourselves, discharge papers were filed.

We emerged into the damp, sticky New York summer air and got into
the car. Houses surrounding the hospital were dark, even as incoming
sirens signaled that the night was not over. Sleeping residents must have
become as inured to the sights and sounds of their neighborhood as those
in beachfront homes become accustomed to the lapping of waves onshore.

Andrea fell asleep in the backseat as we drove home. She went to bed
easily and closed her bedroom door, but we kept ours open through the
night. We were half asleep with exhaustion, but half alert with confusion
and fear. Should we have kept her home forever then, like a princess locked
in an ivory tower? Perhaps. Then everything would have been different.

But wait. The story started before that. Let me go back to an earlier
mistake I made.

Like most parents, we were ambitious for her. So when the perfect school for the subject in which she wanted to major was 3,000 miles away, in southern California, we were supportive. I wanted to keep her close by, within a 50-mile radius, preferably. But I was aware of this tendency of mine toward becoming "The Devouring Mother," the one who never wants to cut the apron strings, so I had to fight against that impulse.

When Andrea came home for Thanksgiving freshman year, Philip and I were shocked to see her coming up the gangway from the plane. We had heard of the "Freshman Fifteen," but Andrea had gained a tremendous amount of weight, at least 20 pounds, maybe more. Traveling in a baggy sweatshirt and sweatpants only accentuated the drastic change in her. We tried to quickly rearrange our faces from shock to joy at seeing her for the first time in almost three months.

If only we had withdrawn her from school then...

The State of Texas vs. ANDREA SCOTT

INDICTMENT

INTOXICATION MANSLAUGHTER

THE GRAND JURY, for the County of Travis, State of Texas, organized as such at the July Term, 2018 of the 427th Judicial District Court, presents to said Court that ANDREA SCOTT, on or about the 9th day of February, 2018, in the County of Travis, and State of Texas, did then and there operate a motor vehicle in a public place while intoxicated and, by reason of that intoxication, did cause the death of the victim, by accident and mistake, namely by: colliding a motor vehicle into and against a vehicle ridden by the victim, and ANDREA SCOTT used and exhibited a deadly weapon, namely a motor vehicle, during the commission of the offense, against the peace and dignity of the State.

The State of Texas vs. ANDREA SCOTT

INDICTMENT

ACCIDENT INVOLVING DEATH

IN THE NAME AND BY THE AUTHORITY OF THE STATE OF TEXAS

THE GRAND JURY, for the County of Travis, State of Texas, organized as such at the July Term, 2018, of the 427th Judicial District Court, presents to said Court that ANDREA SCOTT, on or about the 9th day of February, 2018, in the County of Travis, and State of Texas, did then and there drive a vehicle that became involved in an accident that was reasonably likely to result in, and did result in, the death of the victim, and ANDREA SCOTT did then and there, with knowledge that said accident had occurred, fail to immediately stop the vehicle at the scene of said accident or as close to the scene as possible, fail to immediately return to the scene of the accident, fail to immediately determine whether a person involved in said accident required aid, fail to remain at the scene of said accident until ANDREA SCOTT had given to the victim, or to a person attending or occupying the vehicle occupied by the victim, her name, her address, the registration number of the vehicle she was driving, and the name of her motor vehicle liability insurer, and fail to remain at the scene of said accident until ANDREA SCOTT had provided reasonable assistance to the victim, who was injured in said accident, against the peace and dignity of the State.

~Three~

"Never let evil talk pass your lips; say only the good things men need to hear, things that will really help them. Get rid of all bitterness, all passion and anger, harsh words, slander, and malice of every kind."

Ephesians 4:29-32

When she was in high school, Andrea wrote a poem I have framed on our wall at home. It's typical high school juvenilia, but adolescent poetry – good, bad, or indifferent – comes from the heart, because children may not always know how to think, but they know how to feel.

Open Your Eyes

What is love really?
Some say an emotion,
Others say simply an overused word.
What do I say?

What's been the force guiding the hands that penned so many lyrics?

What's been the cause of countless tears?
What's stretched people so thin they went nearly insane?
What's all around us, though we can't always see it.

Is it the look in a new mother's eyes?
Is it the home you've always known?
Is it an act of kindness from a stranger?
Is it there from birth or does it come after death?

I say that love is everything.
Love is in your family,
Love is in your friends,
Love is in everything around us.
To see it,
All you have to do is open your eyes.

One of the first things our friend and lawyer Ben said to us was, "When the press contacts you, just say, 'No comment.'"

Wait, what?

When the press contacts us? Why would the press contact us? She's just a young woman who works in a hotel. I'm just a speech-language pathologist. Philip is just an actor turned businessman turned actor again. This is not as though Matthew Broderick or Laura Bush accidentally killed someone with their cars, nothing crazy like that.

Ah, but the "press." When it bleeds, it leads, indeed.

News vans camped out on our Austin street, and ambitious newsies worked the block, talking to our neighbors, keeping an eye peeled for us. Andrea was still in jail while we tried to put bail together, so she was at least safe from the vultures. Fortunately, a neighbor called Philip and me while we were shopping at HEB and gave us a heads-up. When we got to the street, a news van was waiting at the intersection to catch us driving in, but we were walking. And perhaps we looked too old to be the parents of a 21-year old. So we were able to walk nonchalantly past, grocery bags in each hand, and then scurry into the house.

Andrea's housemate, Cole, adopted a more bold approach. "No, sorry, I don't live here," he responded to a member of the Fourth Estate, even as he locked the front door and headed for his car.

Here are just some of the news outlets and other entities that covered Mr. Boyd's death and our family's tragedy: The Associated Press, Austin Texas.gov, The Austin American-Statesman, Bicycle Austin, CBS-Austin, The Dallas Morning News, Fox 7 Austin, The Greater Austin Underage Drinking Prevention Council, Insurance-NewsNet.com, KLBJ 590AM, KVUE-ABC, KXAN-NBC, The New York Daily News, Patch, The Seattle Times, and U.S. News and World Report.

We even made it onto KEYE-Telemundo: "Arrestan a presunta responsible de atropellamiento fatal en el centro de Austin." It sounds so much more romantic in Spanish, doesn't it?

One of the other first things Ben told us was, "Andrea should disable all of her social media."

This is something that never would have occurred to me, but of course people are going to troll online to see if they can detect emanations and penumbra in Andrea's Facebook posts because, of course, no one ever says anything stupid on Facebook.

Perhaps it's a generational thing, but there is something deeply sad to me about the idea of people going on "social media" immediately after a tragedy where someone died to see if they can weigh in. It's like the virtual equivalent of all those flowers and teddy bears you see people leaving at the site of some unspeakable tragedy that happened to someone the flower- and teddy-bear-bearers didn't even know. Is there not enough joy and sorrow in their own lives to fill that void? They have to check the police scanners to see if there's something out there they can pretend to feel? There is an epidemic of loneliness in this country, and you only have to look on "social media" to see where it lives.

Ben was right. It was about four days before we could get bail together to get Andrea out of jail, and in the meantime there were 80 posts about her on her Facebook, from total strangers.

Make no mistake about it: the internet and the cruelly misnamed "social media" are out to get you. You might not think so, but you would be wrong. Today you might be part of the mob, safe on the side of righteousness, smug in your condemnation of others. But there's always tomorrow. And all the Caryns and Justyns are waiting out there to pounce on you.

Karla Caryn was clearly confused when she said, "Deport them all!"

Our daughter was born in New York.

José Justyn, obviously similarly confused, immediately jumps on KXAN's website to shout, *"You dint say its legal or not kxan! That was the first thing you point out last week on a similar news and lots of puthos said 'build that wall' what you all puthos say now??"*

Stephanie Caryn adds, *"I wonder where all the racist are now? Because she is white criminal it's okay to break the law and stay in the U.S. and supported by MY taxes, but if she had any pigmentation every one would be jumping on becoming Facebook warriors. Yeah let's make Am..."*

I could have seen more, but I chose not to.

Donna Caryn says, *"I know a white girl who killed two men driving the wrong way on I35 intoxicated who has been in prison and will remain in prison from age 17."*

This is all just racialist hysteria. I don't think that people should be excessively punished for being black or brown, but nor do I think that my white daughter should be singled out for especially severe punishment, and made an example of, just to prove that we're "color blind." What are the facts? What are the circumstances? These people are not the least bit concerned with any of that. This is The Mob.

Racquel Marie Caryn confuses me still further when she says, *"It has nothing to do with guilty or not... she still killed a man..."*

How can it have *"nothing to do with guilty or not?"*

Lynn Caryn said, *"Legal – illegal – it doesn't matter where she's from or what her last name is... what matters is that she killed someone by making a horrible choice that she can never take back. She's ruined her life and the life of the man's family."* Lynn adds later, *"The only way to end drunk driving is to prosecute everyone, EVERYONE, to the full extent of the law."*

Allison Caryn agrees, *"Omfg. Who would say such a thing. What an idiot."* (For you oldsters, like me, Omfg means "Oh my fucking god.") *"She belongs in Jail! I hope she stays in there for a long time!"*

On her own website, Allison actually feels compelled to tell us that she's "a real person." No shit. This is right up there with a colleague of mine, who when I told her that my father used to make the observation, "Every year we pass over the anniversary of our own death, but we don't know when it is," replied, "Wow. Did he say that before he died?" Yes. Yes, he said that before he died.

So, a word to the wise (including you, Jessica), comb through your online posts to make sure there's no joke or offhand remark made in there that could later be used as an "Ah-ha!" moment by someone with clearly too much time on their hands. Like "knife throwing," Jessica? Really? Under the right unhappy circumstances someone could make quite an issue out of this hobby of yours.

Christopher Justyn was so fascinated by this tragedy that he moved on from Facebook to explore Andrea's contributions to the online college writing forum Odyssey, writing, *"She admits to having severe mental and substance abuse problems in this article she wrote."*

Christopher is a Claims Specialist for State Farm.

So, another word to the wise: never admit to mental and substance abuse problems. All that talk in the media about how much we care about people with mental health issues like depression and anxiety: clearly nonsense. Your vulnerabilities will be used against you. Trolls, like sharks, can smell blood in the water.

Kelly Caryn also quotes one of Andrea's posts indicating that she is a *"Lover of beer..."*

Ah ha! So, all you lovers of beer out there: Kelly Caryn is watching you. Kelly herself loves Chanos Tacos, and knows how to pack a wound with gauze. She also thinks *"y'all need to experience the vegan chocolate at Hula Girl Shaved Ice."* Kelly clearly has a lot of important opinions, not all of them about my daughter or beer, apparently.

Larry Justyn is pissed because he thinks Andrea will receive only *"5 years probation!!! And community service."* Larry also says, *"I make a dangerous Old Fashioned."*

Careful there, Larry. How "dangerous?"

He is also a grown-ass man who paints teeny tiny models of video-game characters and is the kind of middle-aged man who cloyingly and relentlessly refers to his middle-aged wife as "my bride." Larry holds forth on his Twitter account on everything from Bell of Lost Souls to Dungeons and Dragons to Aeon of Strife, Tomb of Horrors, Lord Discordant the Chaos Space Marine, Dragonslayer, Game of Thrones, Star Trek: Deep Space Nine, Mothra-Rodan, the Noctilith Crown, Necromunda, Warhammer 40,000, the Athenian general Militiades, the Cathedral of Notre Dame, Austin bakeries, Strawberry Bingsu, Whataburger Dr. Pepper milkshakes ("why we live in Texas!"), Thai termite repellent commercials, candy corn, pogo sticks, and, of course, my daughter.

My favorite tweet of Larry's?   It's really hard to pick just one, but   I think I have to go with: *"Regarding Vigilus 2 - GW needs to have the fortitude to have Abaddon/Chaos clearly win now and then. Repeat Deus ex Machinas wear thin. The Imperium is a big place - and Imperial reversals now and then only make the Villains more credible."*

Deep. Thank you for sharing, Larry.

"I am trapped in the Phoenix airport till morning. It's eerily quiet in here. Ask me things."

Larry can't stand to be alone in his own head. It's obviously not a pleasant place to be (exacerbated, I am sure, by the Phoenix airport), which is why his mind must be constantly filled with silicone weaponry and the questions posed to him by other devotees of silicone weaponry.

He appears to be married to a woman who has been diagnosed with bipolar disorder, with a 296.7 tattoo on her arm, which is the International Classification of Diseases code for bipolar disorder. I hope nobody ever holds that against her. (See: Christopher Justyn at State Farm, above.)

Larry posts a picture of a menu board featuring Casamigos Top Shelf Margarita, Spicy Margarita, Skinny Margarita, The Margo 3-2-1 Margarita, Herradura Margarita, and The Perfect Padron over a quotation from 'Ghostbusters.' *"'Choose the form of the Destructor,' tough Austin decisions."* Over a photo of a bottle of Amaro Sibilla Italian liqueur, Larry writes, *"My year of searching Austin liquor stores has paid off. Sweet, sweet ambrosia, you are mine."* He also posts a picture of his cat Harry apparently finishing off Larry's glass of Japanese whiskey (thereby appearing to encourage and support feline intoxication) and a picture of Jell-O shots over Larry's caption of *"Now this is my kind of dinner party!"* There is also a lovely beauty shot of a bottle of Suntory whiskey, with two ice cubed glasses, arranged like a magazine ad, captioned, *"There's only one way to end a week of wargaming news."*

Ah, ain't it the truth?

A picture of a 19th century Spanish flexible rapier (a light, sharp sword used for thrusting, especially for those whose traditional swords have ceased to thrust) elicits this rapturous response from Larry, *"Ok, this is the coolest thing I've seen all week!"* Larry asks if there is *"such a thing as too many [Dungeons & Dragons] books?"*

Spoiler Alert: There is.

Larry digs through his archives and finds some of the earliest Games Workshop minis he ever bought and painted, from the mid-80s, so he's been doing this for at least 35 years. He posts a picture of a uniformed ancestor who apparently fought in World War I, but Larry's war is made entirely out of plastic. His WWI ancestor would be so proud.

Marilyn Caryn also reads the tea leaves, *"And she will be penalized with a very short sentence. For taking a life."* Elma Caryn agrees, *"She'll probably get a slap on the wrist Smh."*

That's "shaking my head" for those of you over 50. Elma is apparently shaking her head.

Tammi Caryn clearly feels secure in her own particular glass house when she writes, *"Lock her up and take away her life like she did his. That man in his forties could have been reasonably expected to live for about another 30-40 years. She should spend that time locked up. No leniency. No mercy. No second chance. Every GD drunk needs to be dealt with swiftly and with no mercy. Murderers."*

Lacey Caryn says, *"That's so sad guy lost his life and hers is over also. Terrible people can't make better decisions and not drink and drive."*

Terrible people? That's a helluva lot of terrible people, Lacey. I guarantee you know at least one or two. You might even love some of them.

Lori Lynn Caryn writes, pithily, *"Prison or death sentence."*

Candida Caryn wants us to know, *"This is what really scares me while commuting back home from my overnight job! I've reported several drunk drivers on my way to work. Now were they caught, who knows! Hopefully she doesn't get a slap on the wrist!"*

Jim Justyn knows different liberals from the ones I know when he says, *"The liberals cry but she should go to prison and never be free again!"*

Thomas L. Justyn jumps on the "Off with Her Head!" bandwagon with, *"Honestly, people who kill people should also lose there life period! Doesn't matter if they had alcohol, drugs or using mobile phone to be distracted? I'm sorry but so many Innocent lives get lost due to others poor recreational activities!!! If you lost a loved one or a family member etc you'd want an eye for an eye effect!"*

Cheryl Caryn agrees, *"Another POS who should spend her life in prison."*

Jozie Caryn is even more adamant, in all caps, *"PUT HER IN JAIL FOR LIFE THAT WAY SHE WON'T COME BACK N 9 YRS N LAUGH ABOUT IT"*

Why is the assumption that my daughter is a monster? *"Laugh about it?"* Jozie, like so many in The Mob, suffers from a corruption of the soul.

pf_college_throwaway, who obviously did not have an exam to study for, trolled all the way through all six google pages of this story to unearth the following: *"Oh man her writing online is a fucking insight. Her Odyssey online profile comes up quickly if you google her."*

Thanks for that diligence. Your writing online is also a fucking insight, pf_college_throwaway! He found this written by Andrea: *"A little background: my record with substance abuse is not exactly spotless. I won't get into the gory details, but here's the gist: I've put myself in mortal danger with my drug abuse on more than one occasion in the past, and it isn't something I'm super proud of, nor is it something I talk about a whole lot."* This is under Andrea's posting entitled, *"What Your Go-To Drink Order Says About*

You."

ODA157 was another one of those who leapt onto Andrea's Facebook profile to ferret out *"Lover of beer."* Gotcha!

Ah ha! Just like Luke Combs, Dylan Mulvaney, and Brett Kavanaugh!

Jessica Caryn very helpfully posted a screen shot of one of Andrea's profile pictures with the caption, penned by Andrea herself, *"when you realize you haven't updated your profile picture in almost a year and feel the need to confirm you still exist and haven't been incarcerated b/c like let's be real, it's only a matter of time."* Jessica's response: *"The saddest part is she knew it would come one day and didn't seem to care."*

Jessica is a realtor with young twins, who obviously is deeply certain that they will never make a stupid, perhaps deadly mistake. I hope she's right.

BurrDurrMurrDurr also found the entry unearthed by Jessica Caryn above (it's always helpful to have more than one ghoul on the case), to which BurrDurr added, *"Can't make this up."*

Well, yes you can, BurrDurr. She did make it up. It was a joke. But if you comb through someone's Facebook profile looking for naughtiness, bad jokes, false bravado, and downright lying, you will surely find it. Speaking of which, BurrDurr, why do you include "MurrDurr" as part of your handle? Under the right circumstances, that could be very telling, couldn't it? "MurrDurr." "MurDur." "MurDer." "Murder." Kinda makes you go, "Hmmmmmm...."

Mona Caryn is rallying the peasants with pitchforks: *"Hey I am hoping we can get some people to show up to court as [the victim's] brother lives out of state. I want to make sure we have a presence there since I may be the only one at the court dates. I've never done anything like this so any help we can get would be great!!! Feb 26 courtroom 299 9:30am"*

Thanks, Mona. Turns out Mona also works for State Farm (what is it with the ghoulish State Farm agents online?), so she doesn't like it when bad things happen to people and her employer has to pay out. Time for a new slogan? "Like a good neighbor, State Farm is there..." They sure are.

winux_xp wonders idly, *"Is there any proof that this is actually her (besides her name)?"* To which Blacky_McBlackerson helpfully replies, *"Tattoo."*

Jordan Peterson's Rule for Life #6 is: "Set your house in perfect order before you criticize the world," which is a variation on Jesus' admonition in John 8:4, "He that is without sin among you, let him first cast a stone at her." Amen. The temptation to judge is great.

But lest you think that everyone out there is a Madame DeFarge wannabe, cackling and knitting at the guillotine, there is the virtual equivalent of those people who leave flowers and teddy bears. I still worry about them. I wonder why they feel the need to be concerned with the tragedies of strangers, but I was pleasantly surprised at some of the genuine sympathy and empathy on display.

Clyde Justyn saw *"Just a normal young adult who made a very bad choice, now must deal with the consequences of her actions."*

In a similar vein, Manuel Justyn said, *"Wow poor woman The bad decisions are expensive in the life. Her life is broken"*

Delia Cardenas Caryn said, *"Very sad, that one decision changed the lives of many. Prayers for both families."*

Rene Justyn adds, *"Sad for the family of the man she killed. And sad for her and her family. What a waste of a life. Please kids don't drink and drive."*

Bubba Justyn says, *"She's got some bad days coming! Or years!"*

And then there was Erv Justyn, *"Man did she ever ruin her life. It's sad."*

And John Eric Justyn, *"2 lives, over"*

And Wanda Caryn came with *"Prayers for the innocent victim & family."*

Cherissa Caryn holds out hope, *"Sometimes it takes a big event (or several) in order for a person to make wiser choices."*

Diana Caryn says, *"regardless of color or race i don't think anybody should go to jail for 1st offense drunk driving when bars and stores are allowed to sell it...but i think extensive probation and counseling should be there..."*

And then there was this interesting exchange on a UT Austin forum: First, "redsooz" writes, *"I mean, alcohol impairs judgment."*

But then "madstbh" weighs in with, *"It makes you say stupid things, dance like an idiot, call your ex, etc. Even when you're shitfaced, as an adult, you should at least know that you can't drive drunk."*

And this prompts "redsooz" to reply, *"I'm not saying alcohol is an excuse or justification. But the same mechanism that makes you hit on your boss or dance with a lampshade on your head impairs your judgement of how impaired you are, or whether you should drive. This is why so many intelligent, reasonable, and otherwise responsible adults end up with DWIs. Somehow people end up thinking that they are the exception to the rule and that they'll be ok."* Then "redsooz" goes on to describe himself as *"an otherwise responsible, intelligent, and somewhat reasonable adult who went to prison for drunk driving (and who is now 8 years sober)."*

"madstbh" then relents a little in light of this shared confidence, *"Congrats on your sobriety! I suppose that I was quick to judge. I do have loved ones who have gotten DWIs; sometimes I just forget that everyone tries to be good."*

Wow. Not only did this exchange bring tears to my eyes, it was also a historic moment. This marked the first time that anyone has ever changed his mind about something on the internet. Here's to "redsooz" and "madstbh." You guys should meet for a drink. (Sorry. Too soon?)

foxendpapers and LegendaryWanderer also had a lively exchange:

foxendpapers: *"There's a huge difference between choices that may affect your own well-being and choices that have the potential to kill innocent people. Don't drink and drive, folks. You can do all the drugs you want as long as you're not driving."*

LegendaryWanderer replied: *"Oh we all know it's wrong, and I don't mean to give off the impression that doing so is excusable. It's not like people don't know not to drink and drive. Everyone has seen or heard some story of someone dying and it is illegal on top of that. People know not to do a lot of bad things. In the end though humans are flawed creatures that give in to impulse over rational thinking more than we would like to admit. Humans aren't perfectly rational actors, especially when intoxicated."*

itonlytakes11 said, *"God, how incredibly tragic. One decision to drink and drive ended an innocent person's life and changed hers forever. So awful."*

But letsgetmolecular was not about to let itonlytakes11 get away with that rare moment of empathy for both parties: *"Hate to be a cynic but odds are if she did it then, she probably made that 'one decision' many times."*

tennismenace3 also tried to come to the rescue with: *"She also has lots of random people commenting on every single thing on her profile. Kind of trashy thing to do IMO, kicking someone when they're down."*

But once again, foxendpapers will have none of it: *"Maybe if her friends had kicked her a bit when she was posting her 'Obligatory first [legal] drink' and joking about how she 'miss[es] the sweet taste of wrongdoing' she wouldn't have become the drunk that crushed someone to death with her car. I have no problem with kicking people who are down because their selfishness killed an innocent person."*

I do applaud the use of brackets to sequester some portions of text that do not appear in the original, in order to maintain the appropriate tense. foxendpapers is obviously a lover of the language and comes by his handle honestly. (Foxing refers to the spots of discoloration that often appear on the pages of older books, and endpapers are the blank pages in the front and back.) However, foxendpapers, it should be "she wouldn't have become the drunk *who* crushed someone to death with her car." Just so you know.

However, tennismenace3 does not back down. Go, tennismenace3! *"If you ever make a mistake I'll be sure to taunt you about it then."*

foxendpapers rises to the challenge: *"Driving while drunk isn't a 'mis-*

take.' It's a choice. If I ever make a decision that results in someone's death, and which I only made by breaking the law, violating common sense, and ignoring a lifetime of PSAs, feel free to taunt away."

foxendpapers is still obviously secure in the certain knowledge that he will never make a stupid mistake, and that no one he loves will ever make a stupid mistake. And I actually do hope he's right. I really do. And I greatly appreciate the Oxford comma. ;-)

Even as liquor ads urge patrons to "drink responsibly," the primary objective is still to sell booze. And people do stupid stuff because it's easy to delude ourselves into thinking that the worst will not happen to us. The CDC estimates that there are still more than 34 million cigarette smokers in the United States, one in 10 Americans. No one can accuse any of those people of being ignorant of the effects of cigarette smoking. And yet.

But tennismenace3 just won't lie down. Foxendpapers. Tennismenace3. I think this could be the start of a beautiful friendship. *"Do you know the definition of a mistake..."*

foxendpapers snaps back: *"Yup. When someone claims that rape or domestic violence was just a 'mistake,' do you nod your head then too?"*

Wow. I think that's something of a false equivalence. So deliberate violent sexual assault and deliberately beating your life partner are now conflated with making a fatal error in judgment... when your judgment is impaired? Clearly, my daughter is a monster. How did I never see it?

tennismenace3 has to fold at this point, quivering beneath the majesty of foxendpapers' searing intellect, perhaps just "another apse in the cathedral of his mind," as one might say (of Peter Buttigieg). *"I'm not saying I approve of the mistake or that it's trivial, I'm just saying there's no need to harass the person. The justice system will take care of them."*

Sorry, tennismenace3. Thanks for the effort. But game, set, match goes to foxendpapers.

But tennismenace3 does have one great advantage over most of these other posters and poseurs: an awareness that he is young, and that life is short, but also long. And that he might make a fatal decision one day. Or someone he loves might make a stupid mistake. That not everything is within his control. tennismenace3 has some tools for life from which foxendpapers could greatly benefit. Humility. Wisdom. And some healthy fear, trembling, and uncertainty.

Perhaps foxendpapers will skate through life with all of his prejudices confirmed and all of his dreams fulfilled. Perhaps his life will be charmed, and he will congratulate himself that it was all his doing. I genuinely hope so. I'm not kidding. I really do. I wish that for everyone. I certainly wished it for me, for my husband, for my daughter, for our friends and relatives.

But the odds are greatly against it. And a little humility, and a little fear and trembling, go a long way.

What all the Caryns and Justyns haven't realized (yet), while some others have, is that we are all just one moment, one choice, one decision, left turn, heartbeat, blink, thought, one phone call from being brought to our knees, every single one of us.

As someone I know once wrote:

> *I say that love is everything.*
> *Love is in your family,*
> *Love is in your friends,*

Love is in everything around us.
To see it,
All you have to do is open your eyes.

"It requires more courage to suffer than to die."

Napoleon Bonaparte

I think often, almost daily, at least weekly, of the other people affected by this event. There are ripple effects to any tragedy, like the rings expanding out from a stone thrown into a still lake. The friends, the families, the co-workers, people who have suffered from similar events who read about this in the paper, see it on television, and the old pain is conjured up, the wound opened. My stomach still clenches when I see a Jeep on the road, especially a silver Jeep. I feel a pang at car commercials featuring joyful teenagers reaching up to grasp that first set of keys dangled by doting parents, that first taste of freedom and early adulthood.

Whenever I fly, I look around at the airport employees at check-in, TSA, clerking the shops and cafés, and I wonder if they've ever been here at work when a plane went down from this place of origin. Do they wonder if they greeted any of the victims, secured their tags to luggage, sold them coffee or candy bars?

I've thought the same sorts of things whenever we've bought a car. It's the melancholy, morbid streak in me, but I can't be the only person who thinks these thoughts. "What do we have to do to get you in the car today?" the smiling salesman will say, and I wonder if he's ever wondered if any of the cars he's sold through his long career have killed somebody.

Of course, it isn't the cars that kill, it's people. Accidents don't just happen, they're caused.

There was a young woman, a witness after the fact, who lived in the apartment building adjacent to the incident site. The sound of the impact had awakened her, and she had the sense that the noise she heard was serious enough for her to investigate. I often think about the horror she must have felt when she discovered Mr. Boyd's lifeless, mangled body. She must have been in her pajamas or nightgown, if she slept in those. She probably didn't get dressed, but most likely wrapped herself in a coat and quickly slipped her feet into a pair of shoes. (On "House Hunters," clients often scoff at fireplaces they find in Texas homes, as though wondering when and why they would ever need one, but it can get pretty nippy in Texas during the winter.)

She must have averted her eyes from the scene and dialed 911 on her cellphone, her voice trembling and breaking as she gave the operator her address and the nature of her emergency, because it was her emergency now. Maybe the operator offered to stay on the line with her until help arrived. Or maybe, while she waited, she texted a friend or her parents, to alert them to her situation. I can imagine her just standing there alone with Mr. Boyd, in the dark on that deserted road, clutching her coat around her, shivering from cold and shock, hoping she would wake up any second in her warm bed.

Did anyone come along before the police arrived, driving up or down Red River while she was waiting there? Did she have to wave them around the scene, or did they stop, too, to see what had happened?

What is she doing right now? How often does she think about this incident, describe it to new friends and co-workers? Does she wonder what the outcome of the incident was? Does she Google it from time to time?

Then the police arrived, and emergency medical services. The EMTs must have had to wait for the police to take photographs before transporting Mr. Boyd's body to St. David's Medical Center, where he was officially pronounced dead.

Meanwhile, the police remaining at the scene had set up flares to divert traffic. Austin is famous for its traffic, and I35 in both directions becomes the world's largest parking lot during rush hour, lunch hour, any hour. Many use the parallel Red River as an alternative route to avoid the jams, but their plans would be thwarted that morning.

The officers photographing the debris then encircled each piece of scooter debris with fluorescent green spray paint and sprayed symbolic markings next to them ("S," "G," "M10," "M11,"). We learned later from one of the accident reconstruction experts that there is no official labeling convention for these markings; every team just makes it up as they go along. So we assumed "G" stood for "glass," "M" perhaps for "motor scooter." I don't know what "S" could have been.

As he was taken to the hospital, the police must have secured Mr. Boyd's wallet, keys, and phone, in order to make an identification. They were only steps from his apartment, so they may have entered right away. Do the police have to get a warrant before entering the home of an accident victim without permission? Did they knock first, to see if anyone else was home, or if there was a dog inside? Or had other residents of the building emerged, hearing the commotion, people who were able to tell the officers a little of what they knew about Mr. Boyd?

How did they find his half-brother, who lived out of state? Was there some indication on his phone that this was his closest connection? Did they look back at recent phone and text history to find someone with whom he was frequently and recently in contact? What was it like for the first recipient to get that 3:00 a.m. phone call? Did his brother have to wake up his wife to tell her what had happened? Did he then go online to make travel arrangements to Texas? If the planes were all full on that short notice, did he contact the airline directly and explain the situation? Do airlines keep a couple of seats back on standby for just such emergencies?

When he arrived in Texas and made his way to the hospital morgue, what did he find when he got there? Was the scene what we see in movies and television, where someone peels back the sheet or opens the cooling drawer and the identification is made? What condition could Mr. Boyd's body possibly have been in? What was his brother confronted with?

It doesn't bear thinking about. And yet I will never stop thinking about it.

And what other thoughts and questions torture me in those dark hours of the soul?

I go back to those moments right before the impact.

We've never found out exactly what happened in those last seconds, because Andrea doesn't remember and Mr. Boyd is not here to tell us.

Did he pull out in front of her without seeing or hearing her? Or because he had pulled out at that hour so many times before, and by this time, after so many uneventful trips, did he not bother to listen or to look over his left shoulder? Or had he just pulled out, and then heard the approaching vehicle behind him, but thought to himself, "Well, they see me." But was he visible? Was his rear bike light working?

And was there that moment, that moment of horror or resignation, when the sound was so close behind him, bearing down on him, that he suddenly realized, "No, they don't see me. They haven't seen me. They can't see me. This might be it." Did he swerve to the right, or was it too late? Was he frozen in place by the inevitability of impact? Did his life, in fact, flash before his eyes?

And what did he see? What did he think? What did he feel?

These are the flashbacks that will accompany me for the rest of my life. Flashbacks of something I never even experienced, but cannot help imagining. This is now a well-worn groove in my brain that will never go away, and will probably be my own last thought as I leave this world.

If I could have traded places with Mr. Boyd, I would have. I still would. But I can't. And so we pick up our burdens and carry them up the hill, for what choice do we have?

THE STATE OF TEXAS   IN THE DISTRICT COURT
MUNICIPAL COURT OF COUNTY OF TRAVIS
SEARCH WARRANT

The State of Texas to any Peace Officer of the State of Texas, Greetings

Whereas, the affiant whose name appears on the affidavit attached hereto is a Peace Officer under the laws of the State of Texas and did heretofore this day subscribe and swear to said affidavit before me. Now you are commanded to enter the suspected place and premise described in said affidavit: 2012 Jeep Wrangler SUV, Silver and to search for the personal property described in said affidavit and to seize the same and bring it before me as follows:

Any forensic evidence to include DNA trace evidence, fingerprints, hair, or skin, and any property and papers from the interior of the 2012 Jeep Wrangler that would provide the identity of the driver/operator of the motor vehicle at the time of the offense. Any fingerprints, hair, skin, or DNA trace evidence from the exterior of the 2012 Jeep Wrangler that would provide the identity of the driver/operator of the vehicle.

Any fingerprints, hair, skin, or DNA trace evidence from the exterior of the 2012 Jeep Wrangler that would provide the identity of the person struck on a 1996 Yamaha Moped/Scooter, Maroon.

The Sensory Diagnostic Module, Powertrain Control Module, Restraint Control Module, Airbag Control Module, and any and all data or information, digital, electronic, or otherwise, contained therein.

Such data may contain information about the speed, throttle position, engine revolutions per minute, seat belt use, airbag deployment, and/or braking application of the vehicle.

Issued at 4:14 PM on this 13th day of February, 2018

THE STATE OF TEXAS   IN THE DISTRICT COURT
MUNICIPAL COURT COUNTY OF TRAVIS

RETURN AND INVENTORY

The undersigned Affiant, being a Peace Officer under the laws of Texas, on oath certifies that the foregoing Warrant came to hand and that it was executed on the 14th day of February, 2018, by making the search directed therein and seizing the following described property:

Insurance Card
Prescription receipts
Photographs
Interior and exterior Latent prints
DNA sample/swab

"Wisdom comes to us when it can no longer do any good."
                Gabriel Garcia Marquez, "Love in the Time of Cholera"

Mothers Against Drunk Driving (MADD) was founded in California in 1980 by Candace Lightner after her 13-year old daughter Cari was killed by a drunk driver.

With chapters in every U.S. state and in Canada, the organization's mission is "to end drunk driving, help fight drugged driving, support the victims of these violent crimes, and prevent underage drinking."

Among the statistics cited on MADD's website are these:

On average, every two minutes someone is injured in a drunk driving accident.

On average, every 51 minutes, someone is killed.

Two out of three people will be impacted by a drunk driving crash in their lifetimes.

The average drunk driver has driven drunk 80 times before a first arrest, and on any given day, your family shares the roadways with more than 2 million drunk drivers who have had three or more prior convictions.

MADD is lobbying for the installation of Ignition Interlocks as standard equipment in all new cars, just as seat belts and air bags have become. An ignition interlock is about the size of a cell phone and is wired into the ignition system of a vehicle. It can be required by the Court for offenders to use in order to drive to and from work and on other essential errands as part of a restricted driver's license.

This would, of course, add an additional charge to the cost of a new vehicle. But we build distractions into cars in the form of radios, phone jacks, and multiple entertainment screens. Why not an ignition interlock?

Another one of MADD's key initiatives is the Victim Impact Panel, available in every state:

"The purpose of the Victim Impact Panel (VIP) program is to help drunk

and drugged driving offenders to recognize and internalize the lasting and long-term effects of substance-impaired driving. The classes seek to create an empathy and understanding of the tragedy, leave a permanent impression that leads to changes in thinking and behavior and prevents future offenses.

"At a VIP, victims, survivors and others impacted by substance-impaired driving crashes speak briefly about the crash in which they were injured and/or a loved one was killed or injured. They share a first-person account of how the crash impacts their lives.

"They do not blame or judge. They simply tell their stories, describing how their lives and the lives of their families and friends were affected by the crash."

Offenders customarily attend a VIP by order of a judge, usually as part of the sentence following a DUI conviction. But Andrea and Philip attended a local session just a couple of weeks after the accident. This was just a first step in our daughter's and our family's long – lifelong – process of coming to grips with the enormity of this event, and our acclimation to a new life, brutally severed from the old one.

"Chances are, if it's not you, it's going to be someone you love. If not today, then tomorrow." https://www.madd.org/

"Keaton always said, 'I don't believe in God, but I'm afraid of Him.' Well I believe in God. And the only thing that scares me... is Keyser Soze."

Verbal Kint (Kevin Spacey) in Christopher McQuarrie
and Bryan Singer's "The Usual Suspects"

When she could talk about it, all Andrea said was, "I swear, I didn't see anything. I felt a 'bump' and then the car sounded funny and the steering wheel didn't work right, but I'd been smelling gasoline for weeks, and I hadn't had time to take it into the shop, so I just thought whatever was wrong with the car was finally coming back to bite me for ignoring it for so long."

She had finished work at the Westin front desk at 11:30 p.m. on Thursday, February 8, 2018, and was planning to head home to spend the evening with the dog, order something for delivery to eat. But a co-worker she considered a friend had just gone through a bad break-up and begged Andrea to come out drinking with her and some other friends, so Andrea, wanting to show support, reluctantly relented.

She went briefly to the friend's apartment, and then met other co-workers for a pub crawl to two gay bars. Andrea recalls having a shot of tequila and a Long Island Ice Tea at each place, for a total of four drinks, more if the Long Island Ice Teas were strong, which they usually are (vodka, rum, gin, tequila, and triple sec). She felt fine to drive, she said, and none of her friends expressed any concern when she walked back to the parking lot next to the hotel to head home.

The two and a half miles from The Westin to the corner of Red River and Dean Keeton were uneventful. (Fun fact: Dean Keeton, formerly 26th Street, was renamed for Werdner Page Keeton, a popular Dean of the University of Texas Law School, working at UT from 1949 to 1974, and became the name of Gabriel Byrne's character in 1995's "The Usual Suspects.")

The traffic light at Red River and Dean Keeton is notoriously lengthy (in a city known for long light cycles), and our family had often joked, while sitting at this light, about sending out change-of-address postcards: "I guess we live here now." Andrea stopped and waited, for nothing. It was three o'clock on a Friday morning and there had been no other cars on the road, as there were none in sight at the light. She considered simply looking both ways, checking for other cars (especially police cars), and going through the light, rather than waiting. But, in the end, she waited for the green. Like a good girl.

She felt buoyant, exhilarated. Not normally a particularly social person, she had enjoyed going out with friends much more than she had anticipated. Life was good. She had a job, co-workers she enjoyed, friends, a boyfriend, a great dog waiting for her at home. When the Dean Keeton light turned green, she put her foot on the gas.

If she had carefully run that light, she would have been ten, fifteen, twenty seconds earlier up Red River, and I would not be writing this book.

About the sensationalized reports in the media that she had thought Mr. Boyd was "road kill," she told me that she didn't really think that at all. She didn't think anything, she said. After the impact, her mind was a blank. But the police officer was patient and clearly wanted her to say something, to fill in the gaps, so she thought about the times driving home at night when she had seen nocturnal animals lumbering and waddling across the road in her headlights, and so she speculated that this might have been what happened. She wanted to be able to give the nice police officer something.

She was 30 seconds from home at the time of impact, so she turned right onto our street and then a wide left into our driveway, hitting the neighbor's fence because the front axle had been compromised by the motor scooter affixed to the car's chassis. She then backed up, righted the car, pulled into the driveway, got out of the Jeep, and went into the house without stopping to examine the car for damage. She got into a colorful onesie and, without even brushing her teeth, crawled into bed with the dog.

Fifteen minutes later the police were at the door and she opened it, stepping out then into the rest of her life.

"Cometh the hour, cometh the Man."

John 4:23

By July of 2018, Philip and I had both expressed concerns about continuing to have our friend Ben representing Andrea. On appearance days, the commute back and forth between the center of his practice in Dallas and the courthouse in Austin was a hardship for him, with traffic on I-35 frequently coming to its customary halt in Temple, and then again in Round Rock, then in Austin. But more than that, we feared for the sake of our longstanding friendship of more than 40 years. If the outcome for Andrea was dire, which it almost certainly would be, we didn't want to blame Ben, even subconsciously.

Where to turn for a lawyer recommendation? We had received solicitations from criminal defense attorneys in the mail just days after the accident, which put me off. Our tragedy had become their opportunity.

Our neighbor Cal, whose fence Andrea had taken out on her wide turn into our driveway, was a lawyer, focusing primarily on corporate and real estate law, but he was wired into the Austin legal scene and had been so kind and understanding about the fence (our insurance company replaced it with an even better, more trendy model). He recommended Austin's Kevin Lawford immediately, and then the next day came back with an additional recommendation: Richard Peters of Georgetown, who had coached Cal's son in baseball.

Philip was back in New Jersey, so Andrea and I headed to Georgetown first, to speak with Richard Peters. I white-knuckled my way up I-35. My reflexes were never very good, even when I was much younger, but motorists today drive as though playing a video game, zipping in and out between cars and lanes, with only inches between their bumpers and those of the cars they're cutting off. Most of them are on their phones at the same time. We were newly schooled in the fragility of life, the awesome power and possibility of a split second, so the recklessness around me was more unnerving than usual.

We arrived at Mr. Peters' office, cheek-by-jowl with the County Court-house. It was an old brick foursquare with an historic air. We climbed the outside stairs to the second floor and entered the waiting area.

The office was impressive, spectacular. The long waiting area across the building's second floor front formed an open platform overlooking the ground floor downstairs, accessed by an iron spiral staircase. Andrea and I looked over the balcony and saw Mr. Peters' office directly in front of us down the stairs, a large aquarium-style cube consisting of two-story floor to ceiling interior windows. His secretary sat in a small area downstairs to our right. She came upstairs to greet us and ask if we could use a couple of cold drinks, returning with the beverages and to tell us that Mr. Peters would be with us shortly.

While we waited, we perused the walls, all festooned with various trib-utes to Mr. Peters and his career: plaques, certificates, awards, citations, magazine features, newspaper stories, personal correspondence, tax-de-ductible sports memorabilia in glass cases. Fanned out on one side table were a dozen mint-condition copies of a lawyerly magazine with Mr. Peters featured on the cover and a glowing article inside. The number was about a decade old, so Mr. Peters had clearly bought every issue and kept them carefully preserved for this purpose.

One letter on the wall was from a former client, reading along the lines of "Deer Mr Peters, I jus wannid to think you fer all yer hlep wif my cayse. I gotta lot les tyme then a buncha the gize in heer what dun the same think I dun."

Another letter was from a former juror who noted that Mr. Peters was annoying and relentless "like a buzzing bee who won't be swatted away," but that his annoyingness had been effective because she had voted in his favor just to shut him up.

The room was like a shrine. I briefly considered genuflecting.

Mr. Peters himself came up the iron staircase to meet us. He was a tightly built, stocky man, mid-60s, wearing a gleaming white shirt and suspenders, a barrel-chested bantam rooster with a cocky walk and a firm, assertive handshake. He said that he wanted to speak with Andrea alone, and that he would call me in when they were ready. So she joined him downstairs in the fishbowl while I continued my tour of the reliquary.

They were in there for a long time. I understood that she was an adult, and the client, but she was also a terrified 21-year old young woman, and I didn't understand why I couldn't sit in from the beginning of our consultation.

When I was at last invited to join them, the office was decorated in much the same self-reverential style as the waiting area. Mr. Peters sat behind a large carved mahogany desk, with more tributes and sports memorabilia adorning the floor-to-ceiling brick wall that rose two floors behind him. Andrea and I sat in green leather club chairs facing him, and I clutched the chair arms for support.

Mr. Peters led with, "Well, we're looking at a maximum here of 40 years in prison," and my heart rose to my throat. This was indisputably true. The maximum for the manslaughter charge was 20 years, and after a controversial and somewhat similar Austin case that had taken place six years before, the maximum penalty for leaving the scene had been raised from 10 years to 20. You could say that Mr. Peters was just stating the facts and not attempting in any way to sugarcoat what was clearly a very serious situation. There are many countries in the world where life is cheap, but the United States takes loss of life seriously, and the negligent taking of a life very seriously. So perhaps he was simply no-nonsense.

But it didn't feel like that. It felt aggressive and manipulative, and as though he was trying to scare the shit out of me. And it worked. My stomach dropped and I felt as though I might vomit. I wanted to jump out of my skin, run, vaporize.

He also told us that it was a pity the accident hadn't happened in Williamson County, where Georgetown is located, just north of Austin.

"In Williamson County, people are more understanding of driving while intoxicated, having mostly done it themselves. In Travis County, it's the main focus of law enforcement and the judicial system, and there is less empathy than there would be up here."

Mr. Peters said that he wanted to get started right away, that he might be able to have the case thrown out altogether. I didn't see how that would be possible. Andrea had been legally drunk and had struck and killed Mr. Boyd. I felt that the best we could hope for would be some extenuating circumstances that might ultimately reduce her sentence: the lighting on the road, her distractions, Mr. Boyd's visibility, the mercy of the jury and the judge.

He would charge us a flat fee of $100,000.00 and would begin work as soon as the funds were received. I blanched at the amount and the timeline, and said that it would be very difficult for my husband and me to put our hands on that amount of cash within a brief window. We had just scraped together $17,500.00, our 10%, for the bail bondsman. At that, Mr. Peters suggested a payment plan of two $50,000.00 installments to be paid over a period of, say, four months. I said I would have to speak with my husband to determine if that would be feasible.

Having settled on an amount and fee schedule, Mr. Peters wanted to make sure I understood that this payment would be non-refundable. If he were to have the case thrown out in the first week of negotiations with the prosecution, or if they were to offer what he felt to be a reasonable plea bargain, he would urge Andrea to accept the plea and the decision would be entirely up to her as the client, not to my husband and me. In the event of a quick plea bargain, he explained, the $100,000.00 would still be his, not pro-rated in any way. No backsies!

He seemed very concerned with hammering home to me this issue of the $100,000.00 being unaffected by any early resolution of Andrea's case, and I immediately began to question what incentive he would have to pursue the case to a more favorable resolution. Could he convince Andrea that settling for 10 years, eight years, four years in prison would be preferable to placing the case before a judge and jury? Wouldn't it be in his best financial interest to wrap this thing up as quickly as possible, regardless of the criminal penalty to my daughter?

Just then, a young man in his mid-twenties appeared on the other side of the glass wall, grinning in at us. Mr. Peters burst into a wide smile and jumped up from his desk, excusing himself as he went out the door, put his arm around the young man's shoulder, and escorted him down the hall and around the corner.

Andrea and I looked at each other anxiously. I couldn't know what she was thinking, didn't know what to say. Our friend Ben had offered to handle our case for the "friends and family" discount rate of $15,000.00. Surely Mr. Peters' fee meant that he was a "better" lawyer, more experienced, more well-connected on the local legal scene. He certainly had constructed a shrine to himself to encourage that very assumption.

Before we could say a word to one another, Mr. Peters was back, buoyant with paternal pride. "That was my son," he said, seating himself back down behind the desk. "He just got a fabulous college coaching job up in Michigan, and the whole family is getting together in town this weekend for a celebration barbecue."

"Is he waiting for you?" I asked, "I don't want to keep you from your family."

"Oh, no, no, no, that's all right. He'll wait," he assured me, smiling. "Now. Where were we?" he asked. "So tell me. Are you speaking with other lawyers?"

I hadn't been expecting this question. Was this typical in attorney interviews? Caught off guard I stammered, "Well, yes, we were also referred to a Kevin Lawford in Austin, but we haven't spoken with him yet."

At this, Mr. Peters spun around in his chair to the laptop computer on the sideboard behind him and, to my astonishment, did a Google search for Mr. Lawford.

"I've never heard of this young man," he said dismissively. He kept referring to Kevin as "this young man." "Well, all I can tell you is that this young man cannot offer the same level of defense expertise I can." Peters also began telling us about an associate he would bring in as co-counsel, a certified criminal law expert, and "far superior to any co-counsel this young man might have access to," he said, with a wave over his shoulder toward Kevin's profile page smiling back at us from his computer screen.

"Well," I said, "we have a lot to think about and discuss," I said, rising from my chair, "and I don't want to keep you from your son any longer."

Andrea and Peters both stood up, and we shook hands all around. I appreciatively indicated all of the baseball swag and made a small talk joke about the infield fly rule, then assured Mr. Peters that we would be in touch shortly, after my husband, Andrea, and I had a chance to discuss the matter. He showed us out to the iron staircase, we said our last farewells, and then he hurried around the corner to celebrate his son's good fortune.

Andrea and I climbed the interior stairs up and then the exterior stairs down, and walked across the hot, gravelly parking lot. "Well," I said. "Forty years."

A few days later we went to the west side of downtown Austin, the Legal District, to meet with Kevin Lawford. His office provided a stark contrast to that of Richard Peters. It was a shared space in an old Victorian home. There was a geriatric office dog with a white muzzle who belonged to one of the attorneys, and she wandered around through the offices accepting snacks and affection where she could find them.

Kevin came down the winding wooden staircase to meet us, and I assumed that he too would want to speak with Andrea alone first, so I remained seated as they headed up the stairs. Kevin stopped on the bottom step and looked at me quizzically. "Don't you want to speak with her privately first?" I asked. "Oh, no," he said, beckoning to me with a wave of his hand, "come on up."

His office was spartan: just a large wooden desk with a chair, a couple of leather club chairs for clients, a banker's lamp, a long sideboard against one wall. There were two framed certificates on the otherwise bare walls: one a law school diploma and the other some sort of military veteran discharge certificate, I think. The diploma was hanging a little crooked and I had to continue to fight the urge to stand up and right it.

Kevin, like Peters, was serious, but affable and warm, like Fred Rogers. He wore glasses and a beard and was thinner than his pictures online, and we later learned that he was a cancer survivor, having been diagnosed with esophageal cancer a while back. He was married, with young children, so the cancer was a wake-up call for him to lead a healthier lifestyle. He offered us some pecans from a brown paper bag, and nibbled on them as we spoke, sometimes scooping out a half a handful and shooting them from his palm into his mouth, head thrown back.

Kevin spoke gravely about our situation, but he was not an alarmist. He later introduced us to his co-counsel, Daniel Freed, the criminal law expert. Daniel was stockier than Kevin, more solid and put together in a well-tailored suit, with salt and pepper hair elegantly coifed. As we got to know them better, Kevin and Daniel became our version of "good cop/bad cop," with Kevin much more relaxed, almost disheveled, sometimes even goofy, while Daniel was more conservative and stern. Kevin's aw-shucks personality was ideal for appealing to a jury, his colleagues, the judge. Daniel would occasionally almost crack a smile over some absurdity, lifting one corner of his mouth a fraction, which was the equivalent of a guffaw from someone so buttoned up and with such a restrained and cautious view of the world.

Kevin told us that, while he normally charged a flat fee for a case like this, he would prefer to bill us hourly, because the case might be complex and would probably involve contracting with an investigator and an accident reconstruction expert.

This fee structure provided Kevin with incentives diametrically opposed to those in Richard Peters' proposed agreement. Where Peters' flat fee encouraged an early settlement, Kevin's proposal favored stretching the case out as long as possible, inflating and extending billable hours. It would certainly be easier to pay the fees over time. Whichever route we chose, trust would be an important factor.

Andrea liked both of our options: Richard Peters and Kevin Lawford. I leaned toward Kevin because he didn't attempt to frighten me, which I appreciated, as I was already frightened enough. Kevin was also in Austin, while Mr. Peters was up in Georgetown. And there was something about Mr. Peters' arrogance vs. Kevin's evident humility that just rubbed me the wrong way. Would that sort of blustering and strutting prove to be persuasive or grating with a jury and a judge? I had no way of knowing.

I wished that Philip had been there for the interviews. He has a much more keen eye for character, while I tend to simply take people at face value. We spoke via FaceTime and I detailed both interviews, trying to be as neutral as possible in my descriptions of both men and their respective styles.

Philip bristled when I described Mr. Peters' crowing about his son's accomplishments and good fortune, and the family celebrations they were about to enjoy. He thought it tone deaf of the man to share with us his evident life satisfaction at precisely the moment we were all going through the worst period in our lives.

In the end, we decided that Kevin was the way to go, and Andrea agreed.

I sent Mr. Peters an email advising him that we had decided to go in another direction, and to thank him for his time and expertise. I received an email in return pleading his case and asking why we had gone with another attorney. He made me uncomfortable, again, asking me to engage in a back-and-forth about our decision, so I explained simply in another email that Mr. Lawford was in Austin, steps from our courthouse, and I just felt that his proximity to us and his familiarity with the Austin legal environment and its players would be a better fit. Then I closed my laptop and got on our treadmill to work off some anxiety.

My cell phone rang, and I didn't recognize the number, so I let it go to voicemail. When the voicemail dinged, I listened, still walking on the treadmill, and it was Mr. Peters calling to tell me that he too had an office in Austin, which he had neglected to tell me about. He and his wife had moved to Austin some years back in order to send their son to a prestigious private school there (again with the celebration of his own family; Philip would have popped a vein), and so he maintained an office in Austin as well as Georgetown. "So if you would still prefer me..." he averred that the geography would pose no problem.

I then assumed that he had asked us up to Georgetown for our first meeting, rather than coming down to us in Austin, because he was eager for us to see his monument to himself, and this realization further failed to endear him to me.

Once again, the man was making me uncomfortable. I didn't understand why he seemed so desperate to secure our case. Was it because most of the criminally accused have little money with which to defend themselves, while we looked as though we might have deep pockets? (We didn't. We don't.) Did he need the business? The iconography festooning every wall and flat surface of his office would seem to indicate that he should be much in demand, not needful of our custom.

I continued to walk on the treadmill, troubled, and dreading having to reach out to this man again. But before I could begin to formulate another response, my phone rang again from the same number, and Mr. Peters left yet another voicemail. I don't recall what the thesis statement of this last message was, but it only served to alienate me further. We had consulted, considered, deliberated, and made our decision. This continued outreach was becoming unseemly, embarrassing, bordering on harassment. I didn't respond further, and the entire episode left a bad taste in my mouth.

We found out some years later that Mr. Peters passed away in 2021, on my birthday as a matter of fact, more than a year before our case was finally settled. He was evidently a much-loved husband, father, and grandfather, and a pillar of his church community. We will never know how circumstances would have unfolded if we had chosen him to represent us. Life is full of choices between doors. Walking through one automatically precludes walking through another, and there is so often no turning back. We live by free will, but also by fate, and the stronger of these is fate.

Legal Services Agreement

This contract is entered into by and between the Kevin Lawford Law Office, hereinafter referred to as Primary Counsel, and you, hereinafter referred to as Client.

Client, having been charged with Intoxication Manslaughter, a felony in Travis County, TX, and further, being in need of legal advice, hereby employs the above named Counsel under the following conditions.

Counsel will represent Client by advising and counseling, investigating the law and the facts, representing the client through a trial by the judge or jury, and/or if advisable, negotiating an agreed settlement with the prosecuting attorney or agencies.

In consideration of said Counsels' representation, Client agrees to pay Counsels' hourly rate in the amount of $400.00/hour for Primary Counsel and $350.00/hour for Secondary Counsel. All fees and expenses are to be paid at the Firm's office in a timely manner according to the following terms: Deposit a retainer of $30,000.00 on the 16th day of July, 2018, and thereafter retainer can be replenished by check, wire transfer, or credit card. Joint Counsel Fees (joint discussion of Counsel and when Counsels are working TOGETHER for Client) shall NOT exceed $650.00/hour (*except time after case placed on a jury docket or in jury trial). Retainer balance shall be renewed in $15,000.00 increments, when balance falls below $2,000.00.

Each thirty (30) to sixty (60) day period, an accounting of attorney time and services charges shall be conducted and communicated to Client.

Expenses to be considered may be those including investigators, experts, transcripts, court fees or our court costs, bail bonds, scientific tests, professional printing, photographs, or other expenses that Counsel considers necessary to the proper defense of the Client.

If representation in a Jury Trial should become necessary, a Retainer balance in Primary Attorney's trust account for Client shall be at a min-

imum $50,000.00. Additional sums shall be delivered to counsel where said amount in Trust drops below $10,000.00. Additionally, Counsels' fee shall be $450.00/hour EACH ATTY after the case is moved to a trial docket and during Trial.

Failure to pay any of the payments agreed to in this agreement will constitute a material breach of the agreement by the Client and may be grounds for The Law Office to withdraw as attorney of record from this case.

SIGNED AND AGREED TO in Austin, Travis County, Texas, on this the 16th day of July, 2018.

~Four~

TRAVIS COUNTY PRETRIAL SERVICES
RULES AND AGREEMENT TO COMPLY WITH PORTABLE
ALCOHOL MONITORING PROGRAM

I, the undersigned, have received a copy of the rules requiring my compliance with the Portable Alcohol Monitoring Program. The rules and conditions of the program are clearly stated below and any violation of these rules may possibly result in a warrant being issued for my arrest.

I will not violate any federal, state, or local laws and understand that my re-arrest may result in a change in the conditions of my bond or a revocation of my bond.

I will refrain from disorderly conduct, abusive language, or disturbing the peace while present at the office of the department.

I will abstain from the use of all alcoholic beverages, drugs, narcotics, and controlled substances or other intoxicants, unless lawfully prescribed by a licensed physician or dentist, and submit to drug tests. [Added by hand: "Do not use products containing alcohol (mouthwash, cough syrup)."]

I will comply with any and all conditions attached to my bond by the judge including but not limited to installation of the interlock device, alcohol counseling, urinalysis, etc.

I will appear in Court on all dates and times as required.

I am ordered as a condition of bond to obtain a portable alcohol monitoring device, and to use it with the frequency as set by the Court (i.e., provide a breath sample during the required testing window).

I understand that, unless otherwise directed, I must provide four [Changed by hand to "three"] samples per day on the portable alcohol monitoring device (one between each of the following timeframes: 7AM-9AM, 5PM-7PM, 10PM-12AM), and I may not allow anyone else to use the device. I understand that I may not obstruct or cover the camera on the portable alcohol monitoring device, and that I must be dressed appropriately when using the portable alcohol monitoring device.

I understand that the device is portable and may be taken with me for the purposes of providing a sample during a required test window for which I am not at home (e.g., place of employment, out of town trip, etc.).

It is my responsibility to contact the vendor to obtain the portable alcohol monitoring device by the deadline set by the Court. I will notify my interlock officer when I have obtained the device, and I will not tamper with or allow others to tamper with the device.

It is my responsibility to pay for the installation and calibration fees of the portable alcohol monitoring device. Once I have obtained the device, I must keep up with regular appointments with the vendor at intervals specified by the monitoring authority. I am also aware that frequent missed or rescheduled appointments may result in a warrant issued for my arrest.

The ignition interlock officer will be contacting me to discuss calibration reports if violations are detected, and it is my responsibility and in my best interest to return calls in a timely manner. Therefore, it is important that the ignition interlock officer have all numbers where I can be reached or a message left as well as my current address at all times. Should I have a "fail," I am aware it is required that I submit a validating re-test and that failure to do so will result in a violation.

I understand that I am responsible for all fees associated with the condition of the portable alcohol monitoring device.

If I fail to comply with any of my bond conditions and have made no attempt to remain in contact with the ignition interlock officer, I will have violated bond and a warrant will be issued for my arrest.

"For I know the plans I have for you,' declares the Lord, 'plans to prosper you and not to harm you, plans to give you hope and a future.'"

Jeremiah 29:11

Andrea was such an easy baby, an easy kid. She was the best kind of companion: funny, smart, just a joy to hang around with.

And hang around we did.

Our Lamaze coach told Philip and me that whenever I woke up in the middle of the night during pregnancy, that would be when the baby would wake up when she arrived. For Andrea, that was 3:00 a.m. and, by golly, she was up for the day. So it was true for us that the days were long – very, very long. But the years, indeed, were short.

She was a late baby. I was 42 years old when she was born. I had never really thought about having children, and Philip and I had never really talked about it.

We had been married for a little more than eight years when I had a fibroidectomy to remove benign tumors in my uterus. My surgeon was the formidable Nellie Schlacter. She was from Costa Rica, but her accent was vaguely German, in keeping with the surname. Her accent made you listen up.

My hemoglobin level was extremely low prior to surgery (just four grams per deciliter, where a normal range is between 12 and 15), so I asked her if I should try to find A-negative friends and relatives willing to donate blood for me. Dr. Schlacter's eyes narrowed, and in her thickest, most ominous Joseph Mengele intonations she said, "No. When it comes to blood... you have no friends."

Turns out I had to wait a while and build up that hemoglobin count on my own.

The other thing Dr. Schlacter told me was that fibroids grow back and, at age 40, I had no time to waste if Philip and I wanted to start a family.

But we were a family, weren't we? I had him, he had me. We had two cats.

By this time, Philip and I had been together for over nine years. He was an actor, with a survival job at Citibank. I had worked in theater administration off and on for over 16 years, first at Circle Repertory Company (home of Lanford Wilson, Marshall Mason, Jeff Daniels, William Hurt, Patricia Wettig, among so many others), then the Manhattan Theatre Club, then Playwrights Horizons (Wendy Wasserstein, A.R. Gurney, Christopher Durang, William Finn), eventually landing at the Shubert Organization where I worked for the brilliant playwright and director James Lapine.

Work is work. You show up early and stay late, at least if you're me. The best part of working in theater is the product. And the people. Everyone I worked with was bright, funny, passionate about what they were doing, endlessly amusing and entertaining, hard-working, and crazy talented. And sometimes just plain crazy. I slept until 9:00 a.m., stayed up late at the theater every night, wore black to work, and talked to famous people on the telephone almost every day. (I once had a hilarious 20-minute phone conversation with Wallace Shawn about which I literally remember absolutely nothing because I spent the entire time thinking, "I can't believe Wally Shawn is talking to me! 'Incontheevable!'").

Why would we want to start a "family?" Why would I want to trade all that in just to have someone vomit on my shoulder?

So I went home from Dr. Schlacter's office ready to have the obligatory conversation, which I was confident would be brief and satisfactory.

I don't even particularly like children. I now work in education, and it makes me tired when bubbly, hopeful, idealistic young teachers explain their reason for going into the field. "I just love children!" they squeal. It makes me want to slap them silly. What an absurd thing to say. Would anyone say, "I just love adults!" Of course not. Some adults, to be sure. But "adults?" I don't know about you, but I do not love adults. I can think of a lot more adults I don't like, just off the top of my head, than I can think of adults I do.

So do I like children? Some children. Sometimes. Do I love children? I can count on the fingers of one hand the children I have ever actually loved. But I am capable of liking them, under the right circumstances. But let's face it: children are people, adults in training, and not very good at it at this point. I think we tend to romanticize childhood, and I have too much respect for the children in my charge to do that to them. It's the same thing we do when we anthropomorphize other animals. Aren't bears cute? Hell, no! Bears are fucking scary, that's what they are. Wild, unpredictable, often hungry, and much faster than you think. (Just like children, come to think of it.)

Similarly, when we attribute to children all the goodness and innocence in the world, we do them a disservice. They are certain to disappoint, just as anything romanticized will. Hasn't everyone read "Lord of the Flies" by now?

Some of the children I work with are just assholes. They're assholes now, they'll certainly be assholes in adolescence, and then they'll be assholes when they grow up. Assholes have to come from somewhere, and given the number of adult assholes there are in the world, they had to get their starts sometime.

You'll hear people on occasion make the trite observation that Adolph Hitler was once a child. So was Pol Pot. So was Joseph Stalin. So was Mohammed Atta. So was Jeffrey Dahmer. So was Ted Bundy. So was Jeffrey Epstein. People note this banality with wonder, as though it's an original thought, and as though they can't imagine how those dear, innocent darlings went from being toddlers to being what they became. What kind of journey could that possibly have entailed?

The answer is as simple as it is obvious. There was no journey. I guarantee you that little Pol's (or is it little Pot's?) and little Joe's and little Adolph's and little Mo's and little Jeffrey's and little Ted's and little other Jeffrey's kindergarten teachers all knew right from the get-go that they were all wretched little assholes, doomed to be assholes for the rest of their lives, and to inflict their assholesomeness on countless millions.

That driver behind you stuck in traffic who got out of his car and made you roll down your window so he could call you a "cunt" for letting some poor bastard trying to pull out from a side street merge in front of you? He's not a cherub gone horribly awry. He was an asshole in utero.

So all of this is by way of explaining my general attitude toward "motherhood," if you will, prior to the conversation. Why build your own jerk when there are so many out there already waiting for you? Every single day.

So Philip and I had the talk. I was confident of the outcome. We would get this out of our systems and we could continue with our fascinating lives.

And then, after a slight pause, my wonderful, strong, courageous, beautiful husband said, "I think we should go for it."

And I burst into tears.

"If there's no alternative, there's no problem."

James Burnham, Philosopher and Political Theorist

If you allow this to happen to you, killing someone with your car, your every movement will be monitored. The GPS ankle bracelet will immediately report the slightest infraction, including any attempt to cut it off or otherwise disable it. Each week, you will meet with your friendly PreTrial Services Liaison Officer to review the previous week's movements and to lock in next week's schedule for monitoring.

He will know if you are late for work. "If it doesn't bother your employer," Mark told Andrea, "it doesn't bother me. But it should bother you."

You won't walk the dog when the dog has to go. You will walk the dog when you said you would walk the dog, when you are expected to walk the dog, when you told Mark you would walk the dog, when you are required to walk the dog. And Mark will know when you walk the dog. And where.

Like to surf? Forget it. Coffee with friends? No can do. Need a Brazilian? Use duct tape and a hand mirror. Your life now belongs to the state. You are effectively institutionalized. And binge-watching Netflix is really only fun when it's your choice.

And when you do go someplace, as prearranged, you must obtain signed proof that you were there. Andrea was too mortified to take the dog to the vet, because she loved the people at the vet, and they loved her and the dog, and she didn't want them to know what was happening with her. She was ashamed. You will be ashamed.

Her father and I took the dog to the vet.

Would you like to see what your life will look like? It's rather bleak and repetitive. Work. Home. Preapproved appointments. Wash. Rinse. Repeat.

Here is a sample weekly schedule preview of your life:

Travis County Pretrial Services

WEEKLY SCHEDULE REVIEWED WITH PRETRIAL LIAISON OFFICER

Time	Thu 7-5-18	Fri 7-6-18	Sat 7-7-18	Sun 7-8-18	Mon 7-9-18	Tue 7-10-18	Wed 7-11-18	Thu 7-12-18
AM 1:00								
2:00								
3:00								
4:00	Leave 5AM	Leave 5AM	Leave 5AM	Leave 5AM	Leave 5AM	Leave 5AM	Leave 5AM	Leave 5AM
5:00	walk dog	walk dog	walk dog	walk dog	walk dog	walk dog	walk dog	walk dog
6:00	Home 6AM	Home 6AM	Home 6AM	Home 6AM	Home 6AM	Home 6AM	Home 6AM	Home 6AM
7:00								
8:00				Leave 8:30AM				
9:00				WORK 9:00AM-5:30PM	Leave 9:30AM			
10:00					WORK 10:00AM-6:30PM			Leave 10:30AM
11:00		Leave 11:30AM					Leave 11:30AM	Psych Appt 11:30AM
NOON	Leave 12:00PM	WORK 12PM-8:30PM					WORK 12PM-8:30PM	

Time	Thu 7-5-18	Fri 7-6-18	Sat 7-7-18	Sun 7-8-18	Mon 7-9-18	Tue 7-10-18	Wed 7-11-18	Thu 7-12-18
PM 1:00	Therapy Appt 1 PM							Therapy Appt 1 PM
2:00	Attorney Appt 2 PM					Leave 2:30PM		
3:00	PreTrial Svcs Review 3 PM					WORK 3PM- 11:30		PreTrial Svcs Review 3 PM
4:00	Home 3:45PM							Home 4:30 PM
5:00								
6:00				Home 6PM				
7:00	Leave 7:30PM				Home 7:30PM			
8:00	AA Meeting 8 PM							
9:00	Home 9PM	Home 9PM					Home 9PM	
10:00	walk dog	walk dog	walk dog	walk dog			walk dog	walk dog
11:00								
MID-NIGHT						Home 12AM walk dog		

Is this how you want to spend your 20s? I didn't think so.

Andrea had to have a CAT scan (to rule out the possibility of a seizure event, secondary to family history, contributing to the incident) and this was while she had both the GPS and alcohol monitors on, one on each ankle for that "Papillon" look), so special arrangements had to be made with the Court to have the monitors removed, have the CAT scan, and then have both monitors reinstalled. Or attached. Or applied.

These monitors are provided by third party vendors and cost about six bucks a day, at this writing, to "rent," payable by the defendant. That's right; that's $4,380.00 a year you don't get to spend on something you might actually want. The vendor for the alcohol monitor, in a wicked bit of irony or cruelty (and because God needs the laughs), is located in an industrial park in north Austin, right next door to a bartending school.

The vendor for the GPS monitor was located in west central Austin, near all the courthouses and lawyer offices, in the basement of a grand old antebellum Victorian, now chopped up and converted into sad little mildew-smelling office spaces with green carpeting, worn in the high traffic areas and buckled in places from the damp. The parking lot is in the back of the building, through a porte cochere, where five narrow, steep concrete steps lead down into a basement which must have once been used for cold storage. Or as a murder room. Duck as you enter, so you don't hit your head.

The steps are so old and shallow that you have to place each foot on a diagonal, almost sideways, in order to step down without pitching forward. There is a drain set into the stone in the middle of the bottom landing. The door is heavy and made of wood, thick with decades of chipped and peeling green paint. Inside, two young, pretty Latinas sit behind large steel grey desks, awaiting their clients. I hope they have guns in those drawers, because this is not a Hallmark store, and their clientele are not coming in to buy snow globes and wrapping paper. There are a few metal chairs in the waiting area, and a table topped with a bowl of sad-looking lifesaver peppermints which must be crawling with the residue of urine hands.

Andrea and I are like unicorns in this environment, as though we got lost on a college tour and somehow wandered into a Stephen King novel. While we waited, one of the young ladies attended to another client, who was in the process of having his house arrest monitor affixed. He was grizzled and tousled, wearing a dirty grey sweat-stained tee shirt and torn jeans. His eyes were rheumy and bloodshot, and his teeth were yellow and widely spaced, his nose and cheeks a road map of broken blood vessels. He looked to be any age between fifty and seventy, but was probably closer to forty. Maybe thirty. He cursed graphically and colorfully while this young woman knelt at his feet, attempting to satisfy his demands for the exact positioning and tightness of the monitor. When she was finished, he stomped out and up the narrow stairs, still complaining.

"And another satisfied customer!" I beamed, hoping to lighten the mood. But before we could commiserate with the agent, our desperado came back, furiously stomping down the steps and bursting through the door, spewing a hail of obscenities. "Goddam son of a motherfucking cunting bitch, this goddam fucking ass-eating thing is too fucking tight! You have to fix it! And you have to move it around to the other side of my ankle, so it doesn't rub up against the bone! It wasn't this tight the last time!"

Andrea and I shot each other a look with a grimace and raised eyebrows. "The last time?" Clearly, whatever lesson there was to be learned, our friend had not learned it.

The young lady looked to us for unspoken permission to handle this gentleman first. "It's okay, we're in no rush," I told her. He sat while she knelt down again with her skate key and adjusted the monitor, inserting her finger between the bracelet and his scabby ankle to make sure that the fit was loose enough to satisfy his tender sensibilities, but tight enough so that he couldn't slip it off over his foot and return to whatever mischief had gotten him here in the first place. He huffed and puffed, but finally stood up and made his exit once again. On the way out of the parking lot, he tore through the port cochere at about sixty miles an hour.

Andrea leaned over and whispered to me, "Most of the people wearing these things are sex offenders." She had done her internet research.

Question: Why did New Jersey get all the toxic waste and California all the lawyers?

Answer: New Jersey got to pick first.

CITATION
THE STATE OF TEXAS

PLAINTIFF ON BEHALF OF
THE ESTATE OF THE VICTIM, DECEASED
vs.
ANDREA SCOTT and PHILIP SCOTT

YOU HAVE BEEN SUED. You may employ an attorney. If you or your attorney do not file a written answer with the clerk who issued this citation by 10:00 A.M. following the expiration of twenty days after you were served this citation and petition, a default judgment may be taken against you.

PLAINTIFF'S ORIGINAL PETITION
AND REQUEST FOR DISCLOSURE

PLAINTIFF, on behalf of the ESTATE OF THE DECEASED hereby files this suit against ANDREA SCOTT and PHILIP SCOTT, and for cause of action would respectfully show as follows:

LEVEL 3 CASE AND CLAIM FOR RELIEF
Pursuant to Texas Rule of Civil Procedure 47(c)(5), the Plaintiff, on behalf of the Estate of the Deceased, seeks monetary relief of over $1,000,000.

PARTIES
PLAINTIFF is an individual residing in the USA. He is the half-brother of the DECEASED at the time of the death of his death (sic). The DE-

CEASED'S domicile was Travis County, Texas, at the time of his death. PLAINTIFF, as an heir and pursuant to a family agreement, brings this action on behalf of the Estate of DECEASED.

FACTS

On or about February 19 (sic), 2018, the Deceased was driving a "scooter" motorcycle Northbound on Red River Street. The Driver was driving a Jeep vehicle behind the Deceased. Due to the speed of the vehicle at which (sic) the Driver was driving, and because of her impairment due to her drinking alcohol before, she ran into the back of the scooter the Deceased was riding.

The force of the impact caused the Deceased to suffer serious injuries.

Those injuries resulted in his death. Specifically, it is hereby alleged that Defendant Driver was negligent in the following respects:

in failing to maintain a safe and proper distance from the Deceased;

in failing to maintain a proper lookout;

in failing to apply her brakes in a timely manner;

in causing the vehicle to strike the Deceased rather than braking;

in failing to maintain proper attention to the driving conditions surrounding her;

in failing to control the speed at which she was driving;

in failing to take timely evasive action to avoid hitting the Deceased;

in driving her vehicle when she was intoxicated; and

in engaging in other acts of negligence.

NEGLIGENCE OF DEFENDANT OWNER

At the time of the collision, Defendant Owner was the owner of the vehicle operated by Defendant Driver. Prior to the collision, Defendant Owner knowingly permitted Defendant Driver to use said vehicle for the purpose of operating it on the public streets and highways. At the time of said operation, Defendant Driver was incompetent and unfit to safely operate a motor vehicle on the public streets and highways. Defendant Owner knew or, in the exercise of ordinary care, should have known that Defendant Driver was an incompetent and unfit driver and would create an unreasonable risk of danger to persons such as the Deceased.

Defendant Owner's actions and omissions, as described in above, constituted negligence and were in heedless and reckless disregard for the rights, welfare and safety of persons likely to be affected, such as the Deceased. Such negligence was the proximate cause of the collision in question and the resulting damages to the Deceased and his Estate, and Plaintiff, as representative of the Estate of the Deceased, is entitled to recover her (sic) damages from Defendant Owner, in addition to Defendant Driver.

TRIAL BY JURY

Plaintiff, on behalf of the Estate of the Deceased, demands a trial by jury.

"We believe in one God the Father Almighty, Maker of heaven and earth, and of all things visible and invisible."

The Nicene Creed

The writer Dennis Potter, author of the deliciously surreal "Pennies from Heaven" and "The Singing Detective," once said something to the effect that if he thought that all that we can see is all that there is, he simply would not be able to go on.

There is apparently a theory in physics called the "block theory" of the universe. I'll get it wrong, because I'm not a theoretical physicist (and, please, don't all you theoretical physicists out there send me hate mail), but it seems to be about everything happening at once, all the time, and every possibility of every outcome existing somewhere, and it makes time travel theoretically possible. At least, that's what it sounds like to me, but it's one of those ideas that is so big and unruly that you can't think about it without your head hurting. Like black holes. Or thinking about a universe that is ever-expanding and so expanding into what; what's on the other side of it? And how rich would the Kardashians be if any of them actually had any sort of talent?

Anyway, what I take away from the block theory of the universe and "The Singing Detective" is that there is so much more going on than that which we poor mortals are able to perceive.

I say this because – and if this doesn't give you goosebumps, nothing will – ever since she was about 10 years old, Andrea has said to me periodically, "Someday I'm going to kill somebody."

She hasn't said it malevolently or gleefully, or even sadly or mournfully. And she hasn't exactly said it with an absence of feeling, resignedly. But she's said it as just a statement of fact, the way your child might tell you that kangaroos are marsupials, or that Ethan threw up during P.E. today at school, as though she just knows it to be a fact, that's all. That's just the way it is. "I'm going to kill somebody someday." Simple as that.

Andrea comes by this second sight honestly. My father's aunt Esther was quite a character. She was no-nonsense. She never married. She didn't think people should get married; they should just have children. But she didn't do that either. She took care of her ever-expanding extended family.

And she knew when everyone was going to die.

My father left me a picture of his father's family. Well, actually, I stole it when he was still alive, because he kept it in a drawer and I wanted it on the wall where I could see it every day because it had such resonance for me. It must have been taken around 1913 or so. In the picture, my father's grandmother is a stern, hatchet-faced woman in a white starched blouse and dark skirt. His grandfather is also seated, hands like ham hocks resting on his knees, one of them clutching a straw hat, which must have been a prop. He didn't look like the sort of fellow who wore straw hats. He looked like the kinda guy who might know what happened to Jimmy Hoffa.

The children are standing, arrayed around the parents: Emil, Esther, Eino (my grandfather), Elsie, and Haiki. Emil, standing straight and wearing a tie, is in his role as the oldest child, the one who made the Atlantic crossing from Finland as an infant with his mother. Eino is in a sailor suit, holding his mother's hand in her lap, his head lightly cocked to one side, his white blond hair swept off his forehead. Elsie looks worried with her furrowed brow, as she always did, even as an old lady, carrying unseen burdens. Haiki, the youngest, is in short pants with a bowl-shaped haircut, just wanting this peculiar ritual to be over so that he could get out of this stiff outfit and run around the studio, prying into the photographer's equipment.

And then there's Esther, the second to oldest, probably about 10 in this picture, a bow in her long blonde hair. She is the only one with a slight, sardonic smile for the camera, clearly aware that this is not how her family ever looks in real life. Her eyes are burning with intensity, with wit and humor, ferocity and determination.

She sees past the camera lens, beyond the photographer and the room and the city, straight out to the block universe. "I see what the cat sees," Shirley Jackson wrote. And so does Esther.

When Esther was old (I only knew her when she was old, of course), my parents and I took the bus up from D.C. to the family's old railroad apartment on 48th Street in Manhattan. By that time, Esther and Elsie were living there with my bachelor uncles Bob and Eddie.

I had a blanket – a blankie – pink flannel with a satin border. While I sucked the thumb of my left hand, I would hold the smooth corner of the blanket in my right hand and rub it between the first knuckle of my index finger and the inner side of my thumb, so much so that I wore a hole through the fabric, separating away a couple of inches of the satin trim. I derived so much comfort from that blanket that when my mother washed it I would cry the entire time. And when she hung it on the clothes line to dry, I would stand in the yard holding on to the damp dangling corner, sucking my thumb, waiting for the blessed release of evaporation.

At a certain point it became time to break me of the blankie habit. I don't know whether my mother forgot the blanket by accident or deliberately, as a way of forcing the issue, but we arrived at Port Authority bus terminal for our visit sans blankie.

I was devastated, inconsolable. If this was a purposeful decision, my poor mother must have regretted it when she saw my reaction. Aunt Esther, ever resourceful, simply cut a hole for my thumb in the corner of one of my Uncle Bob's blankets, and I was thus soothed and mollified. "I got my big toe stuck in the hole in that blanket for years afterwards," my uncle would lament.

The last time we visited that Hell's Kitchen apartment, Esther said to my parents, "It's too bad you couldn't have come up a couple of weeks later. You could have been here for the funeral." A couple of weeks later? "Who's funeral?" my father asked. Esther answered simply, with a shrug, as though the answer should be self-evident. "Mine."

Two weeks later she dropped dead in the bathroom. The block universe.

We had a poltergeist in the house when my mother and I were living with our friends the Mitchells in Hawaii, while my father was in Vietnam in 1967-68. There were three adolescent girls in the house – a popular target for poltergeists – Pam and I turned 14 while Lisa turned 13.

This poltergeist would turn lights on and off, move lights and shadows across walls and windows, rattle doorknobs, knock things off shelves and tables. Poltergeists are not harmful, just restless, agitated, like the hormones that set them in motion.

Andrea showed early signs of having sensitivity to the unseen. Once, when I was reading her to sleep in her room, I was sitting on the side of the bed facing her, and she was gazing up at me, listening. I noticed that every once in a while she would tilt her head slightly to one side, looking over my shoulder up past me into the corner of the room, where the walls met the corner of the ceiling behind me. She would smile and then shift her head and her gaze back to me and listen, then tilt her head again, smile upwards, then rock back and look at me again.

Finally, she smiled quizzically and said, "Mommy? Who is that?" "Who's who?" I asked.

"Right there," she said, "who are those people?"

I shifted to look around over my shoulder and when I turned back around I found her expression still serene. "I'm sorry, honey," I said, "I don't see anybody." She didn't question it further, just shrugged and continued to listen to the story. Whoever they were, they were certainly benign, and she seemed to enjoy their presence. Fear of ghosts is completely irrational. The dead can't hurt you.

It's only the living we have cause to fear.

When she was a little older, perhaps five or six, Philip and I discussed buying Andrea a bike for Christmas. She was old enough to start to learn to ride, at least with training wheels.

I have a checkered history with the bicycle. I love to ride, but when I was 12 years old I fell off my bike and broke my elbow. This was at Sangley

Point Naval Air Station in the Philippines, so I had to be airlifted in a World War II vintage plane to Subic Bay Naval Air Station where there was an orthopedic surgeon. It was one of those old planes with a wide center aisle and metal-tube-and-canvas seats racked along the sides, with straps extending from the bulkheads to loop over your shoulders, the kind of plane people jump out of more often than they land in.

I had been following friends around a corner of a sidewalk when I cut the corner too short and my back tire slid off the sidewalk and pulled the bike up short, sending me flying over the handlebars and onto the sidewalk in front of the steps up to the base hospital where my father worked as a hospital corpsman, a medic.

Lying on the ground, I tried to get up, but my right forearm stayed flat on the concrete while my shoulder and bicep lifted a couple of inches, which certainly seemed wrong. My friend Bill Koestler ran back and knelt down next to me, so he must have seen my elbow sticking out in a compound fracture, but he didn't flinch. He took off his jacket and attempted to wrap it around my arm, which remains the most chivalrous gesture I've ever experienced. By that time, hospital staff had emerged from the building and I was carefully lifted to my feet and led inside for X-rays.

While I was sedated and readied to be air-evacuated, my father went to the base legal counsel's office, where my mother worked, to break the news to her.

When the accident happened, my mother had been waiting at home for me with a grilled cheese sandwich ready for my lunch. When I failed to arrive, she assumed that I had decided to spend the afternoon with friends, and perhaps she mourned the days when she was a larger presence in my life than my peers. I still often think about her tipping the cold sandwich into the garbage can and going back to work. I so wish I could sit down with her right now and share that grilled cheese sandwich.

My father walked into my mother's office, which was unusual. She was sitting at her desk, with her feet entwined in the legs of her desk chair. She must have known something was up. My father paced back and forth in her office a couple of times, then stopped and said, "Now, don't get excited…"

Which, of course, is exactly the wrong thing to say. My mother almost fell flat on her face trying to jump up from her chair with her legs wrapped around one another.

It was one of the worst days of my parents' lives. My mother was a very anxious person and never got over the trauma. When I next wanted to ride a bike, she was frantic with worry. But she was frantic with worry most of the time. She died five days before Andrea's second birthday, so Andrea has no conscious memory of her, but the love my mother felt for that child for those two years is still there somewhere, I'm sure, safe inside a heart that remembers. At any rate, Philip and I never discussed the planned bike purchase around Andrea, to preserve the surprise.

One day, shortly before Christmas, Andrea and I were in the living room playing a board game on the coffee table. Suddenly, as though she had just heard someone call her name, she looked up to her right and knit her brows, appearing to be listening intently. Then she mouthed a few words I couldn't make out, shook and tilted her head quizzically, mouthed a few more words. I watched this pantomime with interest, trying to figure out what she was doing. She looked as though she could hear something I could not. Finally, after a couple of minutes of this dumb show, her forehead softened, she nodded, and turned back to me.

"Grandma doesn't want me to have a bicycle," she relayed to me matter-of-factly, and then turned her attention back to the board game.

"Oh. Okay," was my stilted reply. I looked at the space to Andrea's right, into which she had been communicating, but I saw and heard nothing.

We didn't get her the bicycle.

Memory and emotions are closely linked with our sense of smell, more so than any other sense. It was the aroma of the madeleines, not their appearance, that sent Proust hurtling back in time.

My mother was very attached to her cologne, Norell, partly because it worked well with her chemistry and people always remarked on it, and partly because I had given her that first bottle and, like my father, I wasn't a great giver of gifts, so she cherished it inordinately. It was so easy to make my mother happy. I wish my father and I had thought to do it more often.

That fragrance comes back to me powerfully sometimes. It's real, as real as if my mother were right beside me. For some reason, I smell it most often when I'm alone in the car, and I talk to her then, asking her to guide me. She's trying to reach me somehow, with a message, and I try to be open to it. Sometimes it would also hit me on the second floor landing of our home in Englewood, a home she never saw. But she was there. I would be heading down the stairs when a powerful gust of Norell would pull me up short.

I don't ever really feel my father's presence. He's probably too busy reading. His attachment to the corporeal world was always tenuous, and I don't think he was particularly reluctant to "shuffle off this mortal coil." My mother remains more present, a slender hand on my shoulder, the redolence of love.

And so this familial history might help to explain what happened to me one morning in the wake of Andrea's accident.

Our attorney told us that Mr. Boyd had lived in the White Sapphire apartment complex, about 200 yards south of us on Red River. It was just one of the many sad, cynical, filthy apartment complexes clustered around the university, designed to appeal to students who don't care about living in squalor. When your life is circumscribed by textbooks and ramen noodles eaten straight out of the pot, your external surroundings become secondary, almost insignificant. Slumlords thrive on this indifference to the creature comforts. I had passed by the White Sapphire hundreds of times, of course, but had never given it a thought.

Until one day shortly after the incident when I took Giacomo out for his morning walk. We usually didn't make it any further south than Lex Lane, but on this day he suddenly jerked me across the road and headed down toward the apartments. This might have been a case of me subconsciously guiding the Ouija board planchette, but it certainly didn't feel like it. Giacomo seemed to know exactly where he was going, and he was determined to take me there. He pulled me across the White Sapphire parking lot and toward the building.

There were three levels of units, formed into a fishhook shape, a long back row of apartments turning twice at the right end to form a shorter front row facing the street. Cement walkways fronted the doors and windows on all three levels, with metal staircases at either end. All unit doors opened to the outside, like a motel.

Giacomo pulled me along the first floor row toward the back corner, a dark cul de sac of units shaded from the street and the sun, and we stopped in front of the farthest apartment, tucked in the back under the staircase, across from the common laundry room. The door read 104, and next to it was a single dark window. To the right of the window, propped against the red wooden fence that marked the perimeter of the property, there was a stack of common belongings, a familiar sight during transition times at the end of university semesters. A worn mattress, a couple of ladderback chairs with broken spindles, a trash can holding a dusty electric fan, a couple of grey throw pillows, a lamp with a torn shade, some cardboard boxes. These were clearly earmarked to either make the trek to the next temporary lodging, or to be added to the debris next to the parking lot dumpster for bulk collection day.

Giacomo sniffed around the door saddle and the seam of the door frame, moving on to the household belongings. I had an uncanny feeling as I stood there, as though this moment was important. The interior blinds were open, so I leaned over and peered in.

The apartment was empty. There was a small living area just inside the door, with a pony wall running from left to right about ten feet inside and a tiny galley kitchen just beyond. A hallway to the left of the kitchenette led back to a bathroom door, I assumed, on the right, and the open bedroom door straight ahead. There was a glimmer of light from the bedroom, indicating sliding doors to a small patio area just beyond. The entire place could not have been more than 350 square feet. This was when I thought I might know what the dog knew.

I reached out and took ahold of the door knob. I tried turning it, but I knew it must be locked. Still, I held onto the knob. I squeezed it tight, then held it loosely in my hand, as if I lived here and was just leaving or coming back home. I wanted to feel something. I had already felt so many things: sadness, guilt, remorse, despair, fear. But I wanted to feel something else, something bigger, something infinite, some connection, perhaps some understanding. Maybe I wanted to be magically transported back through time and space so that I could stay his hand as he reached for his keys that early morning. Wait. Don't go yet. Let's just wait here together for a minute. Sit down. Tell me about you. Tell me your story. Where have you been? Why are you here? Where are you going?

But I felt nothing. Just emptiness. Whatever I wanted was either gone or beyond my capacity for communion. Perhaps I was just too old, too tired, too mired in this all too real world to be able to reach beyond it. All I felt was a door knob in my hand. And then just an empty hand as I let go. Then Giacomo and I both turned away and continued on our walk.

Of course, months later, when we finally saw the accident report, it turned out that Mr. Boyd had indeed lived in apartment 104. I was not surprised, but it was a long time before I could bring myself to tell anyone about my and Giacomo's walk that lonely morning, and I still don't understand it.

Who's funeral? "Mine." "Grandma doesn't want me to have a bicycle." Apartment 104. "I'm going to kill somebody someday."

The block universe.

"No more war, no more plague, only the dazed silence that follows the ceasing of the heavy guns; noiseless houses with the shades drawn, empty streets, the dead cold light of tomorrow. Now there would be time for everything."
                    Katherine Anne Porter, "Pale Horse, Pale Rider"

At the urging of our first attorney, we had hired what was referred to as an "accident reconstruction expert," to the tune of $2,000.00. This was a person who would, we were told, painstakingly investigate the physical circumstances of what had happened that night on that almost-deserted road. How was the lighting, what was the condition of the road bed, the bike, the car? Was the bike taillight working? How fast was the car going? Was Mr. Boyd wearing dark clothing, no helmet? What mitigating factors might have contributed to the accident?

There was a large illuminated sign on the lawn of the Lutheran Church on the right of Red River, between Mr. Boyd's apartment and our street, and there were moments when the entire sign would flash bright white before displaying its next offering. For a while, I nursed the notion that perhaps Andrea had been momentarily blinded by that flashing brightness and didn't see Mr. Boyd on the road, particularly if his rear light had not been working. Or perhaps he was blinded and swerved into her path, or the flashing triggered his epilepsy. So it was all worth exploring.

But this so-called "accident reconstruction" turned out to be a colossal waste of time and money. In the end, all we got were outdated aerial photographs that showed an inaccurate topography, a list of impenetrable measurements with no key or reference, and new yellow spray painted markings next to the police's fluorescent green spray painted markings that were already there.

Nice work if you can get it.

Here is part of one of the documents we spent $2,000.00 on:

Date: Saturday, May 26 23:07:48 GMT+08.00 2018

Method: Radial with Angle

Units: F

Project Note:

Point	X	Y	Z	Type	Name	Note
	1	0	0	0 point		Origin
	2	-62.46	-41.61	1.8 Point		pole
	3	-40.17	47.26	1.38 Point		pole
	4	-34.24	76.83	1.57 Point		pole
	5	-117.06	-375.84	-2.62 Point		yy

This goes on for another 95 rows, but I will spare you that insult. There was no helpful narrative to accompany and illuminate this data, so we were left with meaningless numbers.

There was a picture of our Jeep, with which we were already quite familiar. There were specs on the victim's scooter, a Yamaha Riva Razz described as "a nice little scooter" with "a tiny physical stature" and a "single speed design." The color, ironically, was "Deep Red Cocktail 2."

The only useful information the accident reconstruction "expert" left us with was the elusive accident report. Philip had signed up on the police website to be notified when the accident report was available, but was never contacted before the notification alert had expired. We had been unable to get ahold of it, but somehow a total stranger was able to obtain this information. But the accident report also didn't tell us anything we didn't already know.

Much later, when the gay bars Andrea had visited that night were brought into the civil suit with us, their attorney – unlike our first "investigator" – was able to discover that Mr. Boyd was being treated for active epilepsy and had been advised by his doctor not to drive, that he had never had his vehicle inspected. But none of that matters, as it turns out, if you've been driving drunk. Perhaps those factors might have been important if Andrea had been killed and Mr. Boyd had survived, his culpability and contributions to the incident might have been issues to be considered then. But this was not the case, and it's unseemly to blame the victim, because he has suffered enough.

"....the seahorses themselves were so arch, so antic and heraldic, and armored in the husks of insects. It was the seahorses themselves that she wanted to see as soon as she took her eyes away, and that she wanted to see even when she was looking at them. The wanting never subsided. "

Marilynne Robinson, "Housekeeping"

I first felt her moving in my 20th week of pregnancy while lying on my stomach on the beach at Shangri La Resort in Playa Del Carmen, Mexico. I thought I had felt her before that, I wasn't certain, but friends assured me that "when it happens, you'll know." It turns out that what I had been feeling up to then was probably just gas moving through my intestines, or the little shifts and shufflings that our internal organs make around one another, especially when trying to accommodate an alien being. But when I was on that beach and felt that little fluttering deep inside, like a butterfly's wings, I knew that was her.

She was a transverse breech with her head under my left ribs and her feet under my right. In the middle of the night, when I was close to term and got up to pee, I had to waddle to the bathroom bow-legged because she had often moved down into position, taking a deep dive toward the cervix, so I thought she might be ready to make her debut. But by morning she had bobbed all the way back up so that at times it felt as though she was just below my collar bone. My doctor speculated that my fibroids had grown back and that they were probably obstructing her route, so he suggested a Caesarean. He advised me to stay within 20 minutes of the hospital, in the event that my water broke and she collapsed onto the umbilical cord, cutting off her oxygen supply.

I was on the good side of the little curtain during the procedure, the side without the blood and guts. Philip was not so lucky. This was a routine day for them, so my two doctors talked about cars while they cut me open, started pulling things out, things still connected to me somehow, and laid on a metal tray everything that didn't look like a baby. Sometimes they would pull something out of me and say, "no, that's not it," before either shoving it back in or setting it on the tray for later. Finally, they found what they were looking for and then apparently just shoved everything else back in rather unceremoniously and stapled me together like a mortgage application. For the next several days, I could feel my internal organs sliding around each other, trying to get back to their original positions, politely saying, "Excuse me, pardon me, coming through, sorry about that, my fault entirely."

Her eyes were like her father's, long and almond shaped. They didn't quite fit yet on her tiny face, so the corners wrapped around to the sides a little bit, like RayBans. They put one of those little knit hats on her and swaddled her in one of those ubiquitous little blue- and red-striped receiving blankets. (Who manufactures those things? They are unchanged across generations of babies. I wish I owned stock.)

I was in a semi-private room with a 14-year old girl who had just given birth to a son. She was attended by a huge extended family, including the baby's paternal grandfather who had come to sign the birth certificate because his son, the baby's father, was only 13 years old. My side of the curtain was very quiet, with Philip my only visitor. By contrast, the happy family on the other side of the curtain celebrated endlessly, even ordering in pizza. I think about that family often. At this writing, I am about to turn 65, Andrea about to turn 23. Meanwhile, somewhere, that mother is 37, that father 36, and their son is 23. They must all be great friends. In fact, those parents might be grandparents by now.

From the beginning, I could not get Andrea to "latch on." Instead she chewed my nipples until they were ragged, bloody stumps. Who could blame her? She was hungry, and I was dry. A kindly nurse offered formula, and I gladly accepted. By that time, I couldn't bear to have Andrea any-where near my nipples. They looked and felt as though I had taken a cheese grater to them.

Later, the Lactation Nurse (or The LactoNazi, as I will always think of her) stopped in and asked how the breastfeeding was going. When I told her that I was not able to breastfeed and that a nurse was kind enough to offer me formula for my hungry baby, The LactoNazi's face turned red and her neck veins bulged. "Who was it?!" she demanded to know. Well, I wasn't going to narc on my Florence Nightingale, so I said that I didn't know.

With that The LactoNazi asked to examine my breasts and, when I opened my gown (and without asking for "consent," I might add), she grabbed my poor udder around the areola and gave a powerful squeeze. I flinched from the pain.

Sure enough, a single tiny drop of off-white, syrupy liquid oozed from my chewed flesh. The LactoNazi was triumphant. And then she stomped off. I never saw her again, thank God.

I have met many breastfeeding mothers in my travels, and some of them appear to me to be quite normal. Others, however, are strange and smug, as though they've accomplished something no one else ever has. Like climbing Everest (the first time). Or sitting all the way through "Dirty Grandpa." I don't mind mothers breastfeeding in public. I would hate to eat or breastfeed in a public bathroom. I don't even like to go to the bathroom in a public bathroom. But they don't have to act as though they're better than everyone else, or that their kids are going to be taller, healthier, stronger, thinner, prettier, nicer, smarter, richer, and just all around better.

Some will tell you stories about how they were in an aisle in Walmart when someone's infant in a neighboring aisle began to cry, and their own breast milk shot across the room like a water cannon. As though that's some sort of accomplishment. Instead of it just being weird that you're shooting bodily fluid all over a linoleum floor, like some sort of demented Jackson Pollock.

Breastfeeding women are like vegans. If you don't know that someone is a breastfeeder or a vegan, it's because you haven't known them for more than 20 seconds. And they're like that girl in 7th grade who lorded it over you because she sprouted breasts before you did, as though that makes her more of a woman. I'm afraid the "I'm more of a woman than you are" impulse in some women just never goes away.

Still, I felt guilty, because of the Cult of the Cow, so when I got Andrea home, I pumped. I pumped and I pumped and I pumped. And after hours and hours of pumping, and stringing out my breasts until I could swing them over my head like a lasso, I finally gave up. My old college boyfriend made me feel better about not being able to breastfeed when he pointed out that formula is "brain food." We were all raised on it in the 1950s, and he was one of the smartest people I know. And I'll let you in on a little secret: I happen to know (because I peeked at my file in high school) that my measured IQ is 148 (for all the good it's done me). And I owe it all to infant formula.

The popularity of breastfeeding saw a rapid rise in about the middle of the 1990s. Know what else has been increasing exponentially over the past 25 years? Autism spectrum disorder and life-threatening peanut allergies.

Let me be clear. Unlike the anti-vaccine hysterics, I am not saying that there is a causal relationship here or even a correlation. We would need several well-designed, replicable, randomized trials to draw any of those conclusions.

Ahm jus' sayin' is all.

Anyway, after four days in the hospital (mothers of first children want to go home right away, while mothers with children at home want to stay in the hospital longer), the hospital people, who up to now had seemed perfectly reasonable human beings, just let us take her home. In a cab. Just like that. Granted, she was bundled up and cushioned like a Faberge egg, and strapped into a car seat, but still. It's not as though they knew anything about us but for the fact that we had eschewed birth control at least once, so we were clearly irresponsible.

My boss had told me that I wouldn't return to work. "They never do," he said. But I loved my job and I admired my boss. Why would I leave a job that hundreds, thousands of ambitious theater nerds would kill for?

Let me tell you why.

Let me tell you about my daughter. Maybe she's like you. Maybe she's like someone you love. All I know is that she is nothing like what you'll find if you Google her.

Billing Statement and Current Trust Balance

05/20/2019	Investigator's research into Jeep Wrangler EDR (Event Data Recorder, aka "Black Box") and crash picture. Research into blood vials and blood draw issues. Email drafted and sent to Attorneys regarding findings and proceedings.	$93.75
06/25/2019	Attorneys watch SFST (Standardized Field Sobriety Tests) video, read confession transcript, prepare for meeting with family. Meet with family.	$2,457.00
06/26/2019	Attorneys meet with accident reconstruction expert at Starbucks.	$1,124.50
07/11/2019	Attorneys hold conference call with Client regarding hiring of accident reconstruction expert.	$325.00
07/25/2019	Expert witness fee for accident reconstruction.	$5,000.00
07/26/2019	Attorneys in court. Asked Judge for ex parte order to inspect and photo prior blood vial. Prepared emails to prosecution and emails with attachments to accident reconstruction expert.	$1,950.00
08/26/2019	Confirmation and collection of requested information for accident reconstruction expert, plus half hour phone call to him.	$1,200.00
10/16/2019	Prepare expert's findings and notes for email regarding progress to later be emailed to Defendant.	$1,200.00

This is just a sample from many lengthy quarterly statements. (How many Starbucks lattés can you buy for $1,124.50?) Note that, as indicated above on July 11, you will be charged several hundreds of dollars for a phone call designed to convince you to hire yet another expensive expert who, in turn, will hold several expensive meetings and phone calls on your behalf.

If a lawyer takes a bowel movement on your time, he will charge you for it.

We just paid the balance of every invoice they sent us, and you will too, because you will just want to keep yourself or your child out of prison.

I believe that our total in all attorney fees by the time of the disposition of Andrea's case was $90,000.00, in increments of $30,000.00 as the well began to run dry, although Philip thinks there might have been one additional payment, which would take the total up to $120,000.00, but we're not exactly sure. It was like paying for college. We just kept writing checks until the invoices stopped coming.

And so will you.

~Five~

"Let's be scared together.
Let's pretend that nothing
... is awful;
There's nothing to fear,
so stay right here.
I love you."

William Finn, "Falsettoland"

James Lapine was right. It didn't take me long to realize that I couldn't leave my baby daughter with someone else. I just wanted to look at her all day long. I sat with her on the sofa, my legs stretched out, Andrea in my lap looking up at me. Hours could go by, she would fall asleep, and we would stay there, just being together. She was then and she remains today the most beautiful thing I have ever seen.

I'm glad that this was before the advent of the cell phone, because if I could have talked all day to friends at work, I probably would have. But it was just me and her, all day long, while Philip was at work. I talked to her, and she gurgled, and I talked some more.

Five days after Andrea was born, I was sitting at our dining room table with her in my lap when Philip walked in the door early. It was a lovely surprise, but before I could say anything he walked across the room wordlessly and picked her up out of my arms, clutching her to his chest. Then, "Your dad died today," he said.

I think he must have been worried that I might leap up out of the chair and drop Andrea, but I was just stunned. I think I just said, "Oh." I don't think I even cried just then.

Weeks later we ran into our friend Ed in Grand Army Plaza, and when I told him that my father had died just five days after Andrea was born, without ever having seen her, Ed said in a hushed voice, "They traded places. I've heard of that before."

My father had been diagnosed with bladder cancer two years earlier, but I was still surprised that he died when he did. Giving birth to a daughter, losing a father. It just seems as though two such momentous events should be spaced further apart. How does more than one life-altering event happen at the same time, when there are all those long stretches when nothing much seems to happen at all? It just didn't make sense.

My mother had told him the previous Friday that Andrea had arrived, and that we were both fine. And she told him the baby's name, with "Madeleine" and my maiden name sandwiched between the first and the last. She said that a tear ran down his face before he composed himself and said wryly, "Those names don't go together." Then she said that he turned over on his side and went to sleep. Those might have been the last words he ever said.

My pregnancy was charmed. I never felt better in my life. I didn't even gain that much weight, just 21 pounds, and it turned out that eight of those were another human.

Post-pregnancy was a bit more problematic. I don't know whether the hormones were a factor, my inability to breastfeed, my father's death, or all three, but I believe I suffered from postpartum depression.

Estimates vary, because most women are never reported to have suffered, and I was one of those, but it is believed that anywhere from 20 to 30% of women in the U.S. will present with some symptoms of postpartum depression, and probably many more, largely due to that underreporting.

After years of stimulating and creative adult company, I was suddenly alone all day with an infant. As my friend Erin observed when she went shopping with a friend of hers who was a new mom, "I realized that it was possible, in fact, to physically die of boredom."

I thought a lot about taking myself over to the subway at Grand Army Plaza and throwing myself onto the tracks in front of an oncoming train. But I hated the thought of doing that to the engineer, and anyone else who might be around, and I wrestled with whether or not to take Andrea with me. On the one hand, I didn't want to leave Philip saddled with an infant he didn't have the time or wherewithal to take care of on his own. On the other hand, he would make such an attractive widower: a handsome man with a decent income and the world's most adorable motherless baby. Maybe that was the move. Yeah, leave her here and go alone.

I wrestled with this conundrum all day long some days, until Philip came home from work, and then I would be distracted for the evening by his company, only to return to the same dilemma the next morning when he went back to work.

I developed a form of agoraphobia. The world just seemed suddenly so massive. Had the sky always been this vast? I would take Andrea out in her stroller to lull her to sleep, and my shoulders would hunch as soon as I stepped out of our lobby, as if the world were pressing down on me.

I started shoplifting from Barnes & Noble. I would wheel in with Andrea in her stroller, and find myself slipping a book into the diaper bag hanging over the carriage handle. I never stole children's books, because that would have implicated Andrea as an accessory. And I always bought other books while I was there. I guess I must have figured that no one would suspect me of having something stolen in my bag if I were at the cash register paying for other books.

I think most shoplifting is a symptom of some sort of mental disturbance. I read that Lizzie Borden got caught shoplifting long after her trial. Perhaps, after getting away with murdering her parents, she was subconsciously crying out to be nabbed for something, at least.

I never read any of the books I shoplifted. Years later I donated them to Symposia, a community bookstore in Hoboken, New Jersey. I figured that someone should benefit from them. I probably should have just returned them to the shelves at Barnes & Noble, but after all those years I might have just thrown off their inventory system. I only realized that I must have been suffering from postpartum depression when Andrea was about 10 months old, and then only because the fog began to lift. You know how, when you get sick, really sick, it doesn't take very long before you forget what it felt like to feel well? I didn't recognize what I had been dealing with until it started going away and I thought, "Oh, yeah, this is what normal felt like."

But anyway, sorry. I was going to tell you about her. About Andrea.

When she was tiny, I was holding a sleeping Andrea on my shoulder when, without thinking, I said to Philip, "I never thought I could love anyone this much."

He immediately looked stricken, crestfallen, abandoned. "You love her more than you love me, don't you?" he asked tremulously. I scrambled to cover up my faux pas. "I mean," I said, "you know, honey, love isn't like a mountain or a pyramid with just one person at the top and everyone else somewhere down below." I gestured wildly, outlining a pyramid with my hands and shaking my head. "No! It's... it's... it's like a pool," now doing a breast stroke in the air to simulate the glowing, flat surface of a serene lake. "Yeah, that's it. Like a pool of warm, soothing water, with all of our loved ones sharing the same warm, enveloping experience of..." By this time he was smirking at my feeble attempts to backtrack. I felt duped. "Why?" I asked suspiciously. "Do you love her more than you love me?"

He snorted at me derisively, "Of course!" he said. And so we were agreed.

She was just fun to be with. I was always tired, but never bored. She didn't sleep well. New parents still ask me when Andrea started sleeping through the night and I always reply, "I'll let you know." She had night terrors sometimes and would wake up screaming and crying. On those occasions, the only thing that would calm her down was an episode or two of "Barney." I don't care if people think the show was lame, low tech. And I wouldn't care if Barney went on to become the pimp for a Tantric sex brothel. To this day, I won't let anyone say a negative word about that ridiculous, purple, singing dinosaur. He got us through many a middle-of-the-night.

She walked at 10 months and started talking early. When she was still in her crib, there was someone shouting outside on the street, and Andrea stood up and said, "Mommy. Someone is louding!" For the first few years of her life, I thought my name was "Maaaaaah-Mee! Cu-Meeeeeeee-Yer!" which she could shorten to "Mommycmere." "Mommycmere." "Mommycmere."

And I was always there.

"It gets a whole lot more complicated when you have kids. The most terrifying day of your life is the day the first one is born. Your life as you know it... is gone. Never to return. But they learn how to walk and they learn how to talk... and you want to be with them. And they turn out to be the most delightful people you will ever meet in your life."

Bob Harris (Bill Murray) in
Sofia Coppola's "Lost in Translation"

Not long after her first sentence came her first paragraph. Philip had disassembled her crib and put it away, because she was almost able to climb out of it, so we wanted to be proactive. We replaced it with a twin mattress on the floor, so that even if she rolled off, she would only topple about six inches onto the padded rug. When I walked into her room to check out the new arrangement, Andrea was sitting on the mattress, bouncing gently. With clear pride in her newfound maturity, she said to me, "No more crib. Daddy lipped it! Put it up inna attic. Andrea not need anymore. Andrea big girl, sleep in new bed."

We sang "Kidz Bop" songs in the car on the way to preschool each morning, and Andrea made up a story about "The Sun's Little Brother." The Sun was tired one morning and couldn't rise to shine, so her brave little brother took over, just for one day.

I wrote this email to a friend on May 25, 1997, when Andrea was 13 months old:

Yesterday, while visiting my mother downstairs, Andrea took off for the kitchen before I had the gate up and, when I cautioned her to come back here she said, "No," which I have a feeling we'll be hearing a great deal over the next two decades. She also said it a couple of times as she tried to push me away from barring her path to my mother's television controls and then – and this was really funny, and just a fluke, I'm sure – she spelled it out for me. "No, no, N-O!" The incredible, emphatic, spelling baby.

Then, on June 3, 1997, 14 months old:

Words, words, words. We now have DADA, MAMA, ITE (for light), OOK (for look), the ever-popular NO, as well as, I am almost certain, something approximating BALL and something akin to DODIE for her little pink and white terrycloth dolly. We also almost have a YEAH, but this is greatly eclipsed by the all-purpose NO, which she uses to hilarious effect, especially when she does actually want something. "Do you want some juice?" "NO," she says, as her lips part and she pulls the cup toward her mouth. "Do you want a bath tonight?" "NO," she says, as her arms reach up to be picked up for her bath. Damn. I pity da fool. I pity da fool who takes her off our hands.

Once, when we were visiting my in-laws over in the Orkney Islands of Scotland, where my mother-in-law came from, we went to a restaurant on the island of Westray. Andrea must have been about four years old by that time. When we wandered around past the fields before dinner at sunset, a bevy of cows came meandering over toward us at the fence, assuming we were the farmers, come to feed them. After they had gathered like a bovine chorus, we chatted them up a little bit. Suddenly, one Elsie let her bladder loose and flooded the ground between her legs. "Mommy! Is that what they do?!" Andrea asked, scandalized. "Well, yes, you don't see a Ladies Room around here, do you?"

That evening, in the restaurant dining room, we spotted a little girl around Andrea's age sitting at a neighboring table. The two girls kept eyeing one another, each waiting for the other to make the first move. "Why don't you just go on over and introduce yourself?" I asked Andrea. "I think she wants to meet you." With that, my shy little daughter did what few adults can muster the sand to do nowadays. She slipped off her chair, walked across the room, and in a tiny voice said in a rush, "Hi-my-name's-Andrea-what's-yours?"

It was the bravest thing I had ever seen anyone do.

Andrea started kindergarten on Thursday, September 6, 2001 at a little "cooperative" school in Hoboken, New Jersey, Frank Sinatra's hometown, just across the Hudson River from Manhattan.

The parents waited nervously outside the classroom for the door to open on Day One, while the kids made themselves comfortably familiar with one another by sitting on the floor and comparing the skinned knee scabs accumulated throughout the summer. I was surprised and happy to see Jason in their number, the little guy we had met at the North Bergen pool who had already formed a tiny crush on Andrea. She and he would have a built-in friend to start the year with.

Any parent who has ever left their child off at kindergarten the first day knows that feeling, the combination of guilt for leaving them in someone else's care, to nervousness and anxiety, to hope for a golden future stretching out before them, with today representing only the first paving stone.

My mother told me that she cried all day after dropping me off at nursery school for the first time, when I was four years old. When she called the school mid-morning to check on my welfare, she was told that I was having the time of my life, laughing and playing and reveling in a landscape of other four-year olds. She was relieved, but hung up the phone and kept on crying. I was already starting to leave her behind.

After I dropped Andrea off the following Tuesday on her fourth day of kindergarten, I got back into the car and turned on "Curtis and Kuby," the ABC radio morning show featuring sparring partners conservative Guardian Angel Curtis Sliwa and progressive attorney Ron Kuby. The breaking news was that a "light plane" had flown into one of the World Trade Center buildings.

I have to confess that my first thought was, God forgive me, "It sounds as though someone got killed, but at least we might not have to hear any more about Gary Condit and Chandra Levy."

It had been the Summer of Chandra Levy. The 24-year old had been an intern at the Federal Bureau of Prisons in Washington, D.C., and had disappeared in May of that year. The chief suspect, at least as far as the media were concerned, was a 53-year old California congressman named Gary Condit. The story had dominated the airwaves for months. Only fresh bad news would demote it from the headlines. This "light plane" accident had potential.

I drove out of Hoboken and up onto Boulevard East in Weehawken, along the Jersey Palisades, with a view of the Hudson River and Manhattan. Both sides of the street, the river side and the far side, were lined with spectators looking toward lower Manhattan, mouths agape. At the first stop light, I looked over my right shoulder out the car window toward the Twin Towers across the water. A tremendous gash was visible about three-quarters of the way up one of the buildings, with an enormous and distended cloud of black and grey smoke billowing out into the crisp September morning.

This was no "light plane."

The light changed and I turned around and continued up Boulevard East. Curtis and Kuby were interviewing an eye witness in a nearby high rise who had seen the plane go into the side of the building. Suddenly, the crowd of spectators to my left began shouting, pointing, and running across the street into traffic toward the river side. I pulled over to the side of the road just in time to hear the witness on the radio screaming, "Oh, my God! Oh, my God! Another plane!"

I leapt out of the car and looked across the roof toward the towers. Now both were engulfed in fire and smoke, both severed with flames. Shaking, I grabbed my cell phone and called Philip. "Something's happening," I said. "Turn on the TV. The World Trade Centers are on fire. I'm coming home." It didn't occur to me to turn back for Andrea. She was safe at school. I had to get home. I moved slowly up the Boulevard, dodging dazed pedestrians wandering heedlessly into the road, cell phones out, some crying into them.

I made my way home and found Philip watching the events unfolding on television. "You have to call your parents right now," I said. My in-laws were at home in Orkney, probably puttering in the garden. When they came in for lunch, they would turn on the TV and panic if they had not heard from us. Philip was able to reach them right before we all lost cell phone service. While he was on the phone, I watched on television as the first tower collapsed slowly straight down into a billowing base of dust and concrete that spread out for blocks. It didn't look real, more like special effects in a movie. "What just happened?" I said aloud.

Philip is much more savvy than I am about the ways of the world, people and their motivations. He can figure out the trajectory and endings of movies just 20 minutes in, based on character clues, directorial hints. When we heard that another plane had gone down in a field near Shanksville, Pennsylvania, Philip's face tightened and he said, "Those people knew." I didn't understand what he meant until much later, but he could instantly picture the surge, the courage, the uprising. Of all that we had to process that day, Philip knew this: it had taken Americans less than an hour and 17 minutes to start fighting back.

Andrea's school had reached out to us, to all the parents, to urge us to leave them in school for the day and pick them up at dismissal as usual. They were all safe, and needed that sense of normalcy. The towers could not be seen from the school, except from windows in the 8th grade classrooms, and it was felt that those students were old enough and mature enough to start talking about what was happening, to confront it. The Head of School advised us to keep the televisions off when the children came home. She explained that young children are not able to understand that a single incident can be replayed over and over again. "They're inclined to think that it's a new terrible event happening each time."

Our friend Joe was stuck in the city when the bridges and tunnels shut down, so he asked us to pick up his 2nd grade daughter Katie from her Jersey City school when we picked up Andrea. So Katie stayed with us that night, and Joe walked back to Jersey across the George Washington Bridge the next day.

The country was in shock, and people were kinder to one another, at least for a while. The 20th century was officially over and the 21st century had begun. Andrea's century.

Accident Reconstruction Engineering Associates, Inc.

Pre-Bill Worksheet

07/29/2019	Office investigation. Open file. Preliminary review.	$750.00
08/20/2019	Office investigation. Review file. Look for vehicle data.	$600.00
08/22/2019	Field investigation. Inspect scene. Review photos. Analyze aerial photos.	$1,050.00
09/03/2019	Telephone. Telephone conference.	$330.00
10/01/2019	Office investigation. Reducing survey data and plotting.	$1,050.00
10/03/2019	Office investigation. Working on survey data and drawing.	$750.00
10/04/2019	Field investigation. Re-inspection of accident site.	$600.00

When we discussed with Kevin and Daniel whether or not to hire another accident reconstruction expert, after the first debacle, Daniel told us a persuasive anecdote from his law school years. He and his fellow law students participated in moot court sessions designed to allow them to practice their courtroom presentation skills. Moot court jurors are like focus group participants, providing valuable feedback to these budding attorneys on what worked and what didn't.

After one session, Daniel was interviewing and debriefing one of the juror participants, and he asked her why she found in favor of his opposition. "Because," she said, "they had more witnesses than you did."

So for that juror, and perhaps for many others, there is persuasion in sheer numbers.

In our case, Andrea and Mr. Boyd were the only two people present at the incident. Kevin and Daniel had not yet decided whether or not they would put Andrea on the stand in the event of a trial. Because Mr. Boyd could not testify and Andrea could not remember, we had no witnesses at all.

So we bought one.

"What nobody understood about David, with the possible exception of Greta, was that he had suffered a very serious loss in his life. Two losses, in fact. Two very dear children: Emily and Nicholas. It was true that these days there happened to be two very dear grown-ups who were also named Emily and Nicholas, but they weren't the same people. It was just as if those children had died. He'd been in mourning ever since."

"French Braid" by Anne Tyler

One day when she was just 18 months old, Andrea and I were at our favorite playground in West New York when she walked up to a couple of boys who looked to be about 12 or 13 years old, and she stared at them in her little baby way and they began to make polite conversation with her. One of them lost interest early and wandered off, but the other one, who seemed like a very sweet boy, sat on a bench and talked with her for a few minutes. Then he looked up at me and said, "She has beautiful eyes. She's going to be really pretty."

And suddenly I thought, "You get away from her you, you, you... you adolescent, you! When she's 17 you'll be 29 or 30!" Yeah, and she would have beautiful eyes and be really pretty. And I was terrified.

Before he had children of his own, Jerry Seinfeld used to muse, "I see people traveling with children. And I ask myself... why?" Just as you can never wade into the same river twice, because both you and the river have changed and moved on, so you can never travel with the same child twice. We flew back and forth across the Atlantic every year when Andrea was growing up, to visit my in-laws, and she was an amazing traveler each and every time, even as a baby.

You know the drill. Boarding passengers look daggers at you as they search for seats as far away as possible from the potentially relentlessly explosive baby. But at the end of every flight, those same passengers would stop by our seats beaming, "What a wonderful little girl!" they would say, squeezing her chubby little legs. "What a perfect little traveler."

By 19 months, Andrea's vocabulary included toes, bear, beer (uh oh), cracker, teeth, boo-boo, bath, juice, kitty-cat, Daddy, Mommy, wow, oh my, sock, shoe, NO, ball, book, door, dog, doggie, all gone, all done, bib, quack-quack, nose, ear, hand, eye, bye, keys, bag, hot, tail, owl, boo, night-ie, monkey, towel, mouth, banana, grandma (eh-ma), Elmo, egg, cheese, lion, apple, chew, moon, camel, mine, more, papaya, boy (uh oh), beak, drawer, tissue, Barney, mirror, and an approximation of her name (ee-ah). By the time children hit 50 words, it's impossible to keep track of the explosion of vocabulary that follows. The flood gates open and commu-nication pours forth. At a certain point she began to repeat every word I said, so if I had still been writing them down as she said them, I would have basically been recording my own vocabulary.

Her favorite TV shows were "Barney" at 4pm and "The Big Comfy Couch" at 4:30, which she referred to as "The Big Comfy Ouch." Once we were out for a walk (and it always struck me as funny to be out for a stroll and a chat with someone so short), when I looked at my watch and found it to be 4:10. "Uh oh," I said, "We'd better get back home. Your show is coming on." She looked up at me and said, "Barney." "I'm afraid not," I said. "It's already 4:10. 'Barney' will be over by the time we get home." She took this in, we walked a few more paces, and she looked up at me and said solemnly, "Ouch."

She liked to watch "Arthur" and read the books with me, and she referred to D.W. as "Double." In one of her books, "D.W. All Wet," D.W. is at first afraid of the water at the beach, but by the end is shouting, "Can we come back tomorrow?!" Andrea loved to turn back to that page when the book was over to call out something like, "Come back, Amado!"

At two years old her favorite food was Stouffers' Mac 'n' Cheese for virtually every meal. At lunchtime every day she would cry out, "Mac 'n' cheese! Mac 'n' cheese! Mac 'n' cheese!" Then one day, inexplicably, when Philip informed her that her mac 'n' cheese was almost ready, she advised him, "No mac 'n' cheese, Daddy." When he expressed his surprise and said to her, "Wait a minute. Is this the same baby I've known for the past two years?" she replied grandly, "Not any more, Daddy!"

At two years of age she also told her first joke. We had given her a little wristwatch sent to us by "Highlights" magazine and when I said to her, "Hey, Andrea! Mommy's watch says 7:15; what does your watch say?" she replied, "Tick, tock, tick, tock, tick, tock."

There was a time when she would rather read or be read to than eat or sleep. She liked a series of books about a character called Hattie Rabbit by a writer named Dick Gackenbach. I always read her the names of authors because my father taught me to read by author. If you read something you like, read everything by that author. Same with the directors and screenwriters of movies. Always take note, and then see everything they direct and write.

Andrea thought the name Dick Gackenbach was hilarious, loved to say it, loved it when I said it. It never got old. One day I read her a new book: "Harold and the Purple Crayon" by Crockett Johnson. She also found the name Crockett Johnson hilarious, but not as funny as Dick Gackenbach. So every time I prefaced our reading with, "'Harold and the Purple Crayon' by Crockett Johnson," she would respond joyfully, "Dick Gackenbach!"

She was simply a delightful little girl. We took her to the park once and she started walking around saying, "Where could it be? Mommy, Daddy, where could it be?" We never found out what "it" was, but she seemed so determined to find it. Once I put her on one of those old free rides they used to have in the entranceway of stores like Caldor, and as soon as it started moving she said, very solemnly and with a straight face, "I'm having too much fun." It was hilarious because, as I say, this wasn't said with jubilance at all, but very seriously.

Once she said something funny at the dinner table – I don't remember what it was – and when Philip and I laughed, she crowed, "I'M FUNNY!"

She made me cry sometimes, too. After my mother died, just five days shy of Andrea's second birthday, she would say, "Want to go see Grandma," and sometimes used her doll Dodie as her surrogate. "Dodie misses Grandma," she would tell me. Yes, I know. Me, too.

When she was in about 2nd grade, she and her classmates were tasked with coming up with an "invention." Andrea's was the T-Hat. She had noticed that, in cold weather, she and her friends got runny noses when they were playing outside at recess and after school, and there wasn't always access to tissues, unless a mom or a teacher had the forethought.

Enter the T-Hat, or Tissue-Hat. She jobbed me in to crochet a red hat out of yarn, with ear flaps and braided strands to tie under the chin. She then punched a couple of holes in the bottom of a box of Kleenex, threaded a strand of yarn through them and then through the top of the crocheted hat, tying the strands on the inside. Voila! The T-Hat! A box of tissues affixed to the top of a winter hat. No wad of tissues in the pocket that ends up shredded in the washing machine. No fumbling in mom's purse. When your nose starts to run, just reach up to the top of your head and grab a tissue. Her prototype was somewhat crude, but some enterprising and visionary entrepreneur will figure out how to mass produce a practical model. Elon Musk? I only hope Andrea gets a piece of the action.

All of the children in her class were introduced to the "recorder" wooden flute as a first musical instrument, designed to lead to a fascination with music that would extend to more serious exploration of more serious instruments. When we offered to provide Andrea with a guitar or a piano to continue her musical journey, she informed us that, "No, Mommy. I want to be the one with the stick. The one who makes everyone right!" So she wanted to move right up to maestra, with no intermediate stops. She wanted to be in charge as an entry level position, but life doesn't work that way.

She's an "old soul" as they say, with a compassionate heart. American Girl Place opened in New York City in 2003, when Andrea was seven years old, so she and I were the perfect target audience for a hundred dollar doll with a vast wardrobe and matching accessories.

When Andrea and I took the escalator up to the Bitty Baby floor, we were greeted with a wall of perfectly aligned stacked boxes, each featuring a perfect vinyl doll: neutral expression, somewhat beady eyes, button noses, rosebud lips, a demographically various range of skin hues.

Disturbing the aggressively symmetrical display, a jarring visual anomaly, was one doll that had obviously shifted during transit. This one had somehow come unmoored from the back of the box, no longer upheld by those coated wire ties, the untwisting of which takes up most of every parent's Christmas morning. This doll had settled down below the heart-shaped window, with only one eye showing. Clearly, this would be the last doll to be adopted, for if there was one flaw, there might be many.

This was the doll Andrea chose, and for exactly that reason. "Nobody else would want her, Mommy. She needed a home."

Andrea was precocious, but not in an annoying way. She wasn't a little smart ass, like so many children brighter than their years. She just didn't miss a thing, still doesn't.

My friends Tracey and Paul have a daughter six months older than Andrea, and had struggled to expand their family, enduring several miscarriages and fertility treatments. When Andrea was about seven years old, Tracey was finally bringing another baby to term.

Andrea and I were going for a visit, she in her car seat and me in the driver's seat of our gold Saturn station wagon (christened "Blondie" by Andrea). On the way, our eyes met in the rear view mirror as we chatted happily about the afternoon to come.

"I'm so relieved that they're finally having another baby soon. They've been trying to have another baby since Briana was born."

There was a pause that I should have found ominous, and then Andrea drawled quizzically, "Mommy.... how do you try to have a baby?"

And there it was. The yawning maw to the conversation no parent looks forward to having, especially with a 2nd grader.

I didn't want to lie. I never lied to her. (Even when she insisted that she wanted to know whether Santa Claus is real and I took her at her word and told her. Then she cried inconsolably for hours. Why did I tell her? I still wish I could take it back.) But I was determined not to lie to her now.

So I told her. But not in graphic, Amy Schumer/Candace Bushnell/Chelsea Handler detail. I simply gave her the CliffsNotes version, as clinical and sterile as possible, light on the specifics, heavy on the miracle.

There was another ominous pause before she asked me in a voice dripping with disgust, "And do you and Daddy do this at home?"

Well, yes, most of the time. Most other venues are frowned upon.

My favorite Andrea story is one she pretends to be embarrassed about and tired of hearing, but I suspect that she secretly revels in it. We went to the Museum of Modern Art, MOMA, one day when she was maybe about six years old, I think. Philip and I took her everywhere with us, calling her "The Portable Friend."

We wandered the exhibition rooms and I chatted with her about some of the paintings. As we were walking past the door of an oval room in the center of the building, I glanced in and there, illuminated in the dark against the far wall, was Van Gogh's "Starry Night," a painting reproduced on posters, coasters, tea towels, tea cozies, tee shirts, handbags, scarves, shower curtains, beach towels, and refrigerator magnets the world over.

"Andrea!" I gasped, taking her hand. "Come quick!" I pulled her into the room and into a semi-circle of fellow-worshipers, all standing, hushed. We stood there for a few moments, just looking, and the pattern remained the same. People would start to walk by the door, glance in, there would be a gasp, and they would slip quietly into the room as unworthy supplicants to bask in the presence of greatness.

As we stood there, all of us such sophisticated New Yorkers, humbled for once in our lives, I struggled to think of something I could say to this small child that would have resonance for a six-year-old. I couldn't tell her about the ear thing, obviously. Or the theory that the luminescence around the stars was the result of a visual disorder secondary to lead poisoning from

Vincent licking his paintbrushes into a fine point between strokes. What's an idea that's relatively easy for a young child to wrap her head around?

I know! They're obsessed with age, always breaking it down to four, four and a half, four and three quarters. I leaned over, close to her ear in the hushed room. "Andrea," I whispered, "do you realize that this painting is more than one hundred years old?"

She took a moment to digest this impressive factoid, and then, in her loudest, jaded 1st grade voice she asserted, "Well, gee, Mommy! It must be dry by now!"

All over the room I heard the titters and stifled guffaws of investment bankers, writers, not-for-profit managers, web developers, and fashion consultants, all of us united in our appreciation of this perfect observation. The painting was, in fact, absolutely dry.

She hates it when I tell that story.

By the time Andrea was in 3rd grade, one of her classmates listened to an exchange of ours at the cubbies in the classroom one morning as backpacks were being stowed. The little girl looked back and forth between us before telling me, "She talks like you." And she did. It was like having coffee with a 37-year old, as her teacher told me that year, adding "In one way or another, Andrea will make her living by writing."

We moved to Tenafly, New Jersey in 2006, just as Andrea was entering 5th grade. It was an idyllic time. We were within walking distance of Stillman Elementary School, so every morning was like an episode of the old "Andy Griffith Show." We walked to school, picking up new friends along the way, and I would be eagerly waiting for her outside at afternoon dismissal. We were the right people in the right place at the right time. Life was good. Breathing was easy.

Middle school was a trial, all hormones and raging emotions and cocky attitude. I always feel for them at that age, and they're my favorite age to work with. Too old to be coddled, too young to be given real responsibility. They're trying to invent themselves, but they don't yet know what they want to be. If you want to make a table or a cake, you have some picture in your mind of what you want the finished product to look like. But these kids, at this age, they're creating something blind. Should I do this or that, be this or that, think this or that, want this or that?

She broke up with her best friend in 6th grade because the other girl had developed breasts and Andrea had not, and the other girl started waving her dick around about it, if that isn't physically or metaphorically impossible. Again, what is it about girls and breasts? Why does that become the determining factor of womanhood? I've always had fairly small breasts, and they seem to suit my body. I've always been perfectly satisfied with them. And now that I'm older, I'm glad that gravity hasn't been able to have its way with me the way it has with some other women, whose nipples are now residing approximately three inches below their kneecaps. Mine are still surprisingly perky. Humble little breasts who know their place, and stay there.

But back to middle school. No. On second thought, the less said, the better.

High school was its own nightmare. The hallways of Tenafly High School smell like pizza, anxiety, and feet. Every summer, when the kids are finally gone, the custodians throw the doors open and leave them open all day long all summer long while they scrape away the accumulated grime and sweat and desperation of the preceding academic year.

THS is like any other middle-to-upper middle class suburban school, a "public" school in a "private" town, you might say. There is sex. There are drugs. There is rock and roll. Every generation of teenagers believes it has discovered something new, something their tiresome old parents would never dream of. But sex has been around since Adam and Eve, and some estimates say that the earliest brewery was built 3500 B.C. Opium consumption started around 2500 B.C. So, before Cain flipped out and killed Abel in a fit of pique, they were probably getting high together behind their parents' garage.

Andrea was no different from most of her peers. She smoked pot and she drank. We told her, as most parents do, "If you find yourself in a bad way, just call us to come get you, no questions asked." And one night, in senior year, she did. "Mom? Remember when you told me that I could call you anytime..."

"Where are you?" I interrupted. And we went and got her.

They practice being adults before they're ready, because if they wait until they're ready, it will be too late. And, as parents, we all walk that fine line. You want to protect them from their worst impulses, but you also want to give them enough freedom so that they can make some mistakes, learn from them, make fewer mistakes, and learn from those.

We've heard about "Helicopter Parents" for years, those parents who hover so much that their children never learn any coping skills and are thus totally unprepared for real life. Now we hear of "Lawnmower Parents." These are the ones who want to mow down all obstacles in their children's paths, so that they never have to encounter an adult problem. So what should we do? Do we want our children to be "safe," or do we want them to be "competent?" The answer is "both," but the rules and the path are by no means clear. Perhaps I was naïve. I never smoked pot. I didn't drink in high school. I was exposed to pot in college, of course, and then I could be a smart aleck about it. I was out with my parents in Annapolis one day, and we walked past a doorway on State Circle out of which wafted that unmistakable, spicy, pungent odor. I smirked, as kids in their 20s are wont to do when schooling their parochial parents.

"That's marijuana," I said sagely. "I went to college."

"I know," my father replied drily. "I was in Vietnam." Checkmate.

So, yes, I was naïve when it came to my daughter and drug consumption. She was a member of Teen Pep at the high school, and then a Peer Leader. These are the students charged with counseling the younger students not to engage in drinking, drugs, and early sex. Of course, the Peers themselves all indulge in drinking, drugs, and early sex. There are basically two types of parents: those who know their kids are up to mischief, and those who don't know their kids are up to mischief. But there is basically only one kind of kid. Maybe yours is a saint or a choirboy, but mine wasn't. And most aren't.

I had a wisdom tooth removed when I was in my 50s. It was the first day I really felt old. Up until then I had been in possession of all 32 of my teeth, like a 25-year old. This was the beginning of the end, I felt. My dentist gave me a prescription for a heavy duty pain killer, an opiate, but he urged me not to fill it unless I absolutely, positively needed it. And then to only take as much as I absolutely, positively needed. And then, when I didn't need it anymore, he urged me to throw it away immediately.

He explained that this was because kids in town routinely raided their parents' medicine cabinets (or other parents' medicine cabinets) for the good stuff, and then either sold it or took it to parties, where everything is placed in a big bowl on a coffee table and everyone is urged to help themselves.

He scared the bejeebers out of me.

My family has a high pain threshold. My father could walk around with his leg hanging off by a thread, and he would still go to work. When he was a kid, he broke his wrist playing stickball, so his folks took him to the doctor. "When did you break the other one?" the doctor asked him. "I never broke the other one," my father, replied. "Oh, yes you did," said the doctor. My father never knew. He just carried on.

I never filled that prescription.

Andrea had a rough time, personally, in high school, but she kept it inside, hid it from us, never opened up. She struggled with anxiety, as all Tenafly kids do. These families are self-selected to live in a town with a good school system. They buy onesies for their infants that read, "Harvard," "Yale," and "Princeton." Kids call out to each other in the hallway at college application time, "How many did you apply to?" "Ten!" "Fifteen!" "Twenty!" "Twenty-five!"

In my day, I applied to a college, I got in, and I went. Those days are gone. Now it's standard operating procedure for kids to apply to at least fifteen: five "Reaches" (e.g., Harvard, Yale, Princeton), five in the student's individual zone (e.g., Bard, Emerson, Lafayette), and five "Safeties" (e.g., Rutgers, Montclair, Bergen Community).

As a result, I have students who tell me that they must do well on a state-mandated 3rd grade standardized test because "I have to get into Cornell," and kids who pull out all their eyelashes and bite their nails up to the elbow. Anxiety is the common cold of the 21st century, especially in high performing high schools.

When the Varsity Blues college cheating scandal broke in March 2019, most of the nation was outraged. But I could almost hear parents all over Tenafly slapping their foreheads and saying to one another, "Wait, what? Can you really do that? I didn't know you could do that!" Here they'd been spending all this money on tutors and Kumon and test prep camp, when all the while they could have just resorted to good old fashioned bribery? Why didn't you say so?

Andrea developed an eating disorder in high school. It didn't look like what we thought an eating disorder looked like, if we had thought about eating disorders at all. She went down to the basement at night, around 10:00 p.m., and worked out for two, three hours at a time. We thought she was just staying in shape. We thought she was healthy. She looked great. I couldn't believe she belonged to me. I was a fat kid, my husband was a fat kid. Andrea looked like the cover of "Self" magazine.

Things went bad during her junior year. I dropped her off at school one day in November, and later that morning received an email from her French teacher expressing concern because my daughter had already missed one day that week and now was missing another. My heart was in my throat when I called Andrea's cell phone. "Where are you?" I asked when she answered. "At school," she said. "Where are you?" I asked again, and there was a pause. "I'm at home."

I sent her straight back to school. I was frightened and angry. It didn't occur to me that she might be frightened, too. I thought it was teenage malingering, but it was probably much more than that. I didn't see it, probably because I didn't want to see it. When they're little, their behavior is more predictable. And they don't hide as much. When they're sad, they generally look sad. When they're angry, they usually act angry. When they're scared, they tell you how scared they are. But even before they hit adolescence, there comes a break between their interior and exterior lives. They start to live within, the way adults do. But we're so accustomed to seeing the child we can read instantly. We aren't looking for the person underneath. Or, at least, I wasn't.

She became defiant junior year, at least when it came to me. She and her father could still connect, but there was nothing about me she liked. I couldn't suggest any course of action to her, because the surest way to turn her against something was for me to be in favor of it. I was afraid to speak around her, because she would snap back, or come back with some withering response. If I said "up," she said "down." If I said "black," she said, "white." I thought that perhaps she was getting herself ready to leave home after high school, because it's easier to reject than to separate. So if she distanced herself from me now, perhaps it wouldn't hurt so much when it was time to go. Senior year was much better for her, but only a little better for me. I was like a beaten dog by that time, so accustomed to her withering disdain.

"There are more tears shed over answered prayers than unanswered ones."
St. Teresa of Avila

We started looking at colleges during her sophomore year, a year earlier than most, as I was so enthusiastic about it. I knew she would just love the college experience, one's only chance, really, to basically live in a village inhabited almost entirely by people your own age, with similar interests, the opportunity to make friends for a lifetime. My own experience at Hofstra University on Long Island had been pleasant enough, but not transformational. Hofstra was then, and perhaps still is, largely a commuter school. Most of the students with whom I had classes got in their cars at the end of the day and headed back home to Massapequa or Elmont. Those of us who lived on campus were a small, tight band. But I lost track of almost all of them after graduation. Of the two college friends with whom I remained close for years afterwards, one moved to California and passed away in 2002. The other committed suicide in 2011.

I wanted something different for Andrea, a real community of oddballs for her to bond with on the Island of Misfit Toys.

Initially, I drew a circle around Tenafly with about a 50-mile radius. I liked The College of New Jersey, while Rutgers seemed way too big, and you had to take a bus to get anywhere on campus. SUNY Purchase was ugly, with its Brutalist architecture. She liked NYU, but had never liked New York City itself (too loud, too dirty), and since that's where they keep NYU, it seemed a non-starter. The infrastructure at Sarah Lawrence was crumbling (window frames, door saddles; where does all the money go?). We both liked Bard, Vassar, and Wesleyan. I liked Trinity, the most beautiful campus we had seen, but she hated the drive out through South Hartford. When I stopped for gas and was getting out to buy a candy bar I asked her if she wanted to come with me and she said, "I am not getting out of this car here."

Gradually, the 50-mile radius widened. Friends of ours warned us,

"Don't let her go too far away to college." But my rationale was, "If you lived in New Mexico, and your kid got into Harvard, you would let her go, wouldn't you?"

So we looked at Ithaca College, Susquehanna University, Lehigh, Emerson, Boston College, Boston University, Tufts. She flew out to Oberlin where she observed, "Everyone here is a lesbian, so I might be popular."

By this time, in the summer before her senior year, Andrea had settled on screenwriting as her preferred major, so the search now extended to southern California, and my cherished 50-mile radius was completely thrown out the window.

Law Offices of Insurance Company

July 20, 2018

Dear Mr. and Ms. Scott:

Your insurance company has referred the civil lawsuit filed against you to our office. We will file the appropriate response on your behalf, and will take all other actions necessary to defend you. I will be the attorney primarily responsible for your case. Pursuant to your insurance policy, my services will be provided at no cost to you. Please be aware that all attorneys and staff of this office are salaried employees of the Insurance Company.

In defending you, it is my job to see that this lawsuit is resolved in your best interests. To do my job well, I will need your assistance in defending this lawsuit. This will include information about the facts and other witnesses to the events on which the lawsuit is based. You may be required to answer oral and written questions from the plaintiff, and to provide documents relevant to the case. I ask that you complete and return to my office the enclosed Questionnaire.

It is very important that you discuss this lawsuit only with individuals affiliated with my office or with your insurance company or your personal attorney.

If you are a member of any online social networking site, please be aware that everything you post on the site could be subject to disclosure during this lawsuit. Do not post anything regarding your case in any status updates, wall posts, or in any messages or photographs.

It is my understanding that your insurance policy states that your insurance company can settle the claim against you, at its own expense, whenever it wishes. At some point, the insurance company may ask me to enter into a settlement within your policy limits. Such a settlement would not require any financial contribution from you.

I will keep you informed of the status of your case. This includes anything that I think might create or significantly increase a real possibility of some personal risk to you.

The majority of cases never go to trial before a judge or jury. If your case cannot be settled, we will proceed to trial and defend you. What is expected of you at trial will be explained to you at that time.

Please let me know immediately if you have any questions or concerns about the case or my representation.

I look forward to working with you.

Sincerely,

I still walked on eggshells around Andrea at times, and some of my skittishness from her junior year has persisted for me to this day. She had an old rag rug in her room a few years ago, just a blue/grey thing we had had for years, and that didn't match any of her furniture. At the time, she was into black and white patterns, black and white florals, clean lines. Her furniture was white, school folders, notebooks, and binders with black and white patterns. I saw a rug in a catalog that was exactly her style, and it was on sale! So I bought it, and switched out the old rug while she was at school.

She had a fit. What I saw as a thoughtful gift, she saw as an imposition, an intrusion, me attempting to decorate her room, a violation of boundaries.

We had a painful and absurd conversation in front of her therapist when she went for eating disorder therapy at the Renfrew Center. Her father and I were brought in for a family therapy session. At the time, we were planning to buy a King size bed for her room. She objected, saying that a King was too big. "How can a bed be too big?" I thought. It's just more room to sleep and flop around in. Who doesn't want more room? She wanted a Queen. "A King will make the room too small," was her reasoning. "It's only a foot wider," I argued, "That's about six square feet more bed and less floor. Just six square feet."

I think I knew even then that this conversation, and all of these conversations going back to high school, were really just about control, about her trying to assert her independence and wrest control from us, in general, and from me in particular. Eating disorders are about anxiety and control. And absurd, reductionist arguments about rugs and bed width are about anxiety and control.

When she was little, Andrea, as most children do, drew a lot of pictures of her family and her home. In all of the early pictures, her cats are tiny, Andrea is small, Philip is medium-sized, and I loom large. I am always the largest figure, the largest character, the largest presence in the picture. I'm not a domineering person; I'm soft, really. Yielding. Accommodating. Agreeable. But I'm sure that's not how I appeared to her all those years, because plans were mine. We did what I wanted us to do when I wanted us to do it, went where I wanted us to go, bought what I wanted us to buy, ate what I wanted us to eat, wore what I wanted us to wear. I try to imagine how that must feel. There is an element of safety and security, to be sure, in having someone else always make the decisions. But it is infantilizing, which is okay when you actually are an infant, but not so much when you're 14, 16, 18, 20. She had to defeat me, to slay me, in order to become herself.

I still feel it, as I'm sure she does. I was visiting her recently, and she had been working so hard and for such long hours that she was down to just a couple of pairs of underwear. Her laundry hampers were full, and she was running out of clean business casual. So one day, while she was at work, I spent the entire day washing, drying, folding, ironing, stacking, and hanging up her laundry. I could only hope that she would see it as a favor, a helping hand, a gesture of love, and not an infringement on her turf. But I was nervous. Those high school and college years have left a permanent psychic scar, and I will never do anything for her again without worrying that my gesture is unwelcome.

But she was grateful when she came home, relieved to have the help. And so that was a moment for us when a mother could offer and a child could accept. And that has been something to build on.

~Six~

"The past is never dead. It's not even past."

William Faulkner, "Requiem for a Nun"

Once when Andrea was shopping for a cognitive behavioral therapist to help her deal with issues of anxiety and depression as well as an eating disorder, she found a wonderful clinical social worker called Brenda Stern who, as part of her intake process, wanted to speak with me privately.

I had never sought or participated in talk therapy. I come from a pick-yourself-up-by-your-bootstraps family, and it would never have occurred to me to discuss my most private thoughts and feelings with a relative stranger. I have friends and family I confide in, but those are reciprocal relationships. I open up to them, and they open up to me. But just telling everything to a disinterested party? Paying someone to listen? Having them judge me? I had no interest in that.

In a scant hour, Brenda managed to get under my skin. Not in a negative way, but in a self-revelatory way. Somehow I found myself confiding in her about my need for control, a product of my own anxiety. I am a person who has to make sure that things are done, and that things are done correctly. My house looks as though nobody lives there. Yes, there are personal touches, pictures, paintings, books, a basket of crochet yarn, pillows, incense, decorative touches. But everything is exactly where it belongs at all times. If something is pulled out and used, it is also put away again. Vacuuming is a Zen experience for me.

Somehow, through the Black Magic of clinical social work, Brenda managed to wrest easily from me my most shameful memory of raising my daughter. No, I didn't hit her, or yell at her, or blame her for something she didn't do. I didn't show up late to pick her up from school or ask her why she got that B in gym when she had an A in everything else. I never called her fat or ugly or stupid. I didn't dis' her friends or her boyfriends. I never dropped her off at a New Jersey Turnpike rest stop and tell her not to come home until she was ready to say she was sorry. I didn't lock her in a closet or stub out cigarettes on the inside of her forearms.

No. It was worse than that.

One day, when she was little, perhaps six or seven years old, she made her own bed. I'm sure I praised her. I'm almost sure I did. But you would have to ask her, because she has a much sharper memory of the incident than I do. And it was a creditable job of bed-making, I'm sure. For a six-year old. But because of my own sickness, because of my own need for that level of perfection, that standard I expect from myself, after praising her efforts, yes, you guessed it. I unmade that bed and then showed her how it should really be done.

If I could take back a single act I have ever committed in my life, it might be that. Why did I have to do that? What type of rigid insecurity in a 48-year old woman does it take to unmake a bed just made by an aspirational six-year old, and then remake it... better? How could I possibly have made it better than she did? I didn't.

I don't remember actually seeing this, but when I think back on this incident, and consider how acutely my adult daughter remembers it, all I can see is her little fallen face, disappointed in herself for disappointing me.

The question from Brenda Stern was "What would happen?" "What do you mean?" I asked her.

"What would happen if you didn't do everything? If you didn't fix everything? Didn't anticipate every need? If you didn't smooth everything over, tidy everything up, put everything away, make sure that all was done the way it was supposed to be done?"

I was speechless. I think I sputtered and flushed. The thought had never occurred to me. My breathing quickened and became more shallow. It was unthinkable. Even a single chink in the armor could lead to absolute chaos. It was the Broken Windows Theory. Once you allow even a little laxity in standards, chaos is the inevitable result. It's not often we have our entire worldview challenged so comprehensively.

Brenda nodded sagely. "We don't come from nothin'," she said.

Andrea,

I spoke to our engineer expert, George Coltrane, several times in the last several weeks about both progress and fee status (his hourly fee is billed against the $5,000.00 retainer we sent him). He has depleted the retainer and as we consider replenishing it, I wanted to discuss his progress thus far. In our discussions, Mr. Coltrane said he originally hoped to assist us to clear up two problem areas for our benefit. First, he made attempts to find evidence to support the argument for the lack of conspicuity of Mr. Boyd and his Yamaha Jazz Scooter. The thrust here is to show the likelihood that you would have had a difficult time seeing the Scooter and Mr. Boyd prior to the collision. Second, Mr. Coltrane wanted to assist our defense position by analyzing the scene to 'normalize' the fact that you did not believe you had hit someone, and certainly did not have reason to notice a scooter stuck to the bottom of your car.

Mr. Coltrane has reviewed a number of items including: visiting the scene, plotting points on a survey CAD diagram [computer-aided design], and multiple discussions with us. After reviewing much of the Police Department notes and descriptions, it was the opinion of Mr. Coltrane that the plots and maps of items sloppily recorded by the investigators opened up the possibility that Mr. Boyd pulled out of Duquesne Street (where he resided in an apartment just off Red River Street) and into the immediate path of the Jeep. Mr. Coltrane has replotted the CAD and replaced evidence and debris on his CAD map to show that the collision more likely occurred closer to Duquesne Street and not Harrison as the police have theorized. This is important because you would have had a shorter time to react if you had indeed seen Mr. Boyd. Moving the collision closer south to Duquesne is better for us arguing that you had little to no time to spot the scooter.

Mr. Coltrane was initially concerned that the evidence suggested that Mr. Boyd flew onto the hood after the collision. After reviewing additional reports and the autopsy he is now confident that Mr. Boyd did not go over the front of the jeep onto the hood. The obvious concern from our perspective is if Mr. Boyd went over the hood for any period of time, your failure to see him would compromise our version of events. Our argument supporting the difficulty to spot Mr. Boyd is consistent with facts and some speculation as follows: that Mr. Boyd was wearing dark, non-illuminating clothes at night, did not have on a helmet, and was riding a small-wheeled scooter all with potentially a non-working taillight.

Mr. Coltrane's remaining objectives are to verify that it is possible you reasonably did not hear or recognize that a scooter was stuck under your moving jeep (noise assessment) and assess whether a determination can be made that the Scooter tail light was or was not working at the time of the collision. Finally, Mr. Coltrane is to download and evaluate information contained in the Jeep's "black box."

As of October 8, 2019, our $5,000.00 retainer for Mr. Coltrane's time has been exhausted... in fact his time involved has slightly exceeded it. I would like to continue Mr. Coltrane's work, but want to let you know where we are with his investigation thus far. I do believe that this has helped considerably and will continue to do so.

Please let me know by means of email, phone or text your comments or suggestions.

Thank you,

Kevin Lawford

sisu (noun): Characterized by extraordinary determination, courage, and resolve in the face of extreme adversity. An action mindset which enables individuals to see beyond their present limitations and into what might still be. An almost magical quality. Taking action against the odds and reaching beyond known capacities. An integral element of Finnish culture and national character, and a universal capacity for which the potential exists within all people.

We don't come from nuthin'. So where did Andrea come from? Philip's father's parents were a machinist and a nurse, respectively, worked hard all their lives, and managed to send their older son to MIT to become a chemical engineer. This was certainly the proudest achievement of their lives. She was a poor sleeper, and he would probably have become a MAGA hat wearer. They ended their days in a trailer park in semi-rural Delaware.

Philip's mother's parents were from the Orkney Islands. He was first a sea captain, then the custodian in a primary school, and she was a stormy redhead. Andrea takes after my mother-in-law in virtually all things. They're both beautiful and willful. "It's like raising my own mother-in-law," I complained to Philip one day, and he replied, "How do you think I feel?"

But if Philip wants to draw a direct line between his family's heritage and our daughter, he can write his own damn book.

Coltrane Engineering Associates, Inc.

October 8, 2019

This investigation is intended to present an explanation of the accident based on:

The lack of conspicuity of the moped and rider The limited time the two were visible to the driver

The difficulty of sensing that Mr. Boyd and the scooter were under her vehicle

The conspicuity of the moped and rider are dependent upon several factors:

The rider

Mr. Boyd was wearing dark clothing.

Mr. Boyd was not wearing a helmet (which is often light colored and containing reflective materials).

Mr. Boyd was in a seated position (which reduces his visible cross section).

The vehicle

The moped was visible only from the rear. The moped is only about 39 inches high.

The moped is 23 years old, its lighting system is questionable.

The environment

The artificial lighting in the 2300 block of Red River is principally from streetlights on the west side of the street.

The area where the collision is believed to have happened is under a copse of trees.

The sky was cloudy with no moon.

The amount of time the driver had to see Mr. Boyd would be the time required for the moped to travel from the Red River intersection with Duquesne to the point of impact. Determining this time requires knowledge of:

The performance of the moped (its acceleration and top speed)

The distance the moped traveled from start to impact

The speed of the driver's vehicle prior to impact

The ability of the driver to sense that Mr. Boyd and the moped were under her vehicle is influenced by at least the following:

Neither Mr. Boyd nor the moped would be visible to the driver once under the vehicle.

Any noise made by the dragging of the moped could be masked by other ambient noise. Since the weather was cool, it is likely that the windows on the vehicle would be up and the heater on. It is also possible that the radio or other music system was on.

The investigation of the above factors would involve consideration of the following:

An inspection of the moped for any evidence that would describe the condition of the vehicle's lighting at collision.

Determining if the Jeep's airbag control system recorded any data for the event. This could establish the speed of the Jeep just prior to collision.

Determining the performance of the moped by testing a similar vehicle. This would provide the time required for the moped to travel from Duquesne Street to the point of impact. This is the time window the driver had to see the moped.

"Men at some time are masters of their fates;
The fault, dear Brutus, is not in our stars,
But in ourselves, that we are underlings."

Cassius in "Julius Caesar," (Act I, Scene 2)
William Shakespeare

My mother's father was a factory worker, a "fabricator," in Baltimore who became a farmer in Pasadena, Maryland, and then a sheriff in Anne Arundel County, back when Maryland was the most corrupt one-party state in the Union (long since eclipsed by New Jersey and Illinois). He was one of the founders of the local Democratic Club, which seemed to be less about politics and more about a chance for a lot of like-minded people to get together weekly, play some darts and cards, drink, and spin lies.

My grandfather Wilmer, "Willie" as he was known, was purported to be a handsome young man, but by the time I met him he looked to be a grandfather from Central Casting. Jowly, a large gut, and a Santa twinkle in his eye. His children adored him because he was not the disciplinarian in the house. That role fell to my grandmother, Mary. She bore him six girls and one boy, with my mother the youngest.

My grandmother was good at an old-fashioned turn of phrase. When she saw someone with a very toothy grin, she would observe that he made her nervous because "every time he smiles I'm afraid he's going to swallow his ears." At the look of my size 10 shoes she remarked that I "would have been six feet tall if God hadn't turned up so much of you for feet."

Willie was apparently something of a rogue from time to time before and throughout their long marriage. My mother recalled that one of her older sisters told of sitting down to dinner with the family one evening when the wall phone rang. One of my aunts answered it and was simply told to "tell Willie that Sarah had a boy." My aunt hung up the phone, returned to the table, and relayed the message. My grandparents said nothing in response, but the quiet speculation among the children was that they probably had a half-brother they never met. Or maybe they did. Anne Arundel County was thinly populated in the 1920s, and everyone pretty much knew everyone else. Sarah's boy must have been close by.

It is not known if my grandparents ever spoke of this phone message at some later time, but they stayed married to the end, and seemed utterly devoted to one another.

My maternal grandparents buried their only son, John, who died of diphtheria on his fifth birthday. Every year for the rest of their lives they sat in the parlor where he was laid out, on the anniversary of his birth and his death, and they wept. "He must be an old man by now," my 80-year old grandmother would say. She continued to picture him, not as the five-year old boy he had been, but as someone else, somewhere else, growing up, growing older.

These same grandparents saw one of their six daughters hospitalized as an adult to the end of her life with what was probably undiagnosed schizophrenia. Irene had always been "nasty," my mother said. She set herself apart from the rest of her family, and always felt superior to them. She was institutionalized not long after giving birth to my cousin Peter, when her nascent psychological problems may have been exacerbated by post-partum depression. At one point, she was periodically furloughed home, but that ended when my mother's oldest sister walked in on Irene beating up my grandparents. They never told anyone, because they loved her, of course, and didn't want her sent away forever. But she was sent away forever.

And that's just some of Andrea's white trash legacy.

My mother was born on September 13, 1929 in the back bedroom of a small two-story farmhouse in Pasadena, Maryland, about 1,200 square feet, with no indoor plumbing. There was an outhouse about 10 yards outside the back door. Beyond that there was a barn, and beyond that, "the shit pit" where, presumably, the feces of both humans and other animals eventually found its way. My grandparents raised six girls in that house, but not all at the same time. My grandmother bore children across a span of more than two decades, and was probably eligible for admission to the Stretch Mark Hall of Fame. My Aunt Cassie, the oldest, was old enough to be my mother's mother, and had a son, Jerry, who was only two years younger than my mother.

When Jerry was born, my mother must have thought that he was a new sibling vying for her parents' attention. When she was about five and Jerry three, Jerry's father, my uncle Harry, was in the habit of bringing home a toy for Jerry every other Friday, on payday. After a while, Cassie and Harry began to notice that the toys were disappearing as quickly as they were brought home. Where were they all going? When one of the dogs crawled under the porch and dragged out a stuffed rabbit, further digging uncovered a veritable toy graveyard under my grandparents' porch. My jealous little mother had been systematically burying all the pretty play-things of that pesky interloper. I can just picture her, with her determined and vengeful little freckled face, patiently digging away early every other Saturday morning.

My mother had a photographic memory. When my grandfather discovered this, when she was just a child, he saw an opportunity.

It may be hard to believe now, in the age of Netflix bingeing, Hulu, Facebook, Fortnite, and our endless ability to entertain ourselves with YouTube and TikTok, but there was a time not all that long ago when people had to amuse themselves by going to events like carnivals and county fairs. My mother was a superstar. Once you finished ogling the Siamese Twins, the Two-Headed Snake, and the Yak Woman, you could marvel at my mother's memory.

Little Morva Agnes could look for a few seconds at this morning's headline on the newspaper, then turn around and spell the headline backwards and forwards, no matter how long the text. She could spell anything backwards after just looking at it for a few seconds. It may not sound like much, but I have newspaper clippings indicating that this was a pretty big deal at the time. She won a few bucks here and there, which my grandfather graciously shared with her. He would sit her on his lap and give her all the "old, wrinkly, crinkly" dollar bills, saving the crisper ones for himself. "I wasn't fooled," she said. "I knew that was my money, not his." But she adored him anyway.

She graduated as valedictorian of the Glen Burnie High School class of 1946 and went to work for the Maryland State Parole Department. When I was in my high school sex education unit in health class I wondered: if people can only get syphilis from other people, how does the first person get it? And it was my mother who was able to tell me that it's a sheep-carried disease. The easiest way to be denied parole, my mother told me, was to be caught "fraternizing" with the livestock at the prison farm. Now there's an image you'll never get out of your head.

My parents met on New Year's Eve 1950 in Annapolis, Maryland. My father was a hospital corpsman, a medic, stationed on the Reina Mercedes, a station ship used as quarters for seamen assigned to duty at the Naval Academy. He loved that ship, loved all of his ships, and kept pictures of them in his wallet for the rest of his life, the way other people keep family photos.

He and his Navy buddies were way too cool to go to anything as lame as the New Year's Eve party at the Fleet Reserve Club down on the Annapolis dock. They planned to play pinochle onboard, drinking and smoking in the New Year, like real men. But their fourth player didn't show up, so they were at a loss. Oh, well. Might as well wander over to the stupid party and see what's going on.

When my father and his two buddies walked into the Fleet Reserve, my mother saw him from across the room, turned to her best friend, and said, indicating my father, "He's cute. I think I'll marry him."

They were married three and a half months later. Two weeks after that, my father went to Korea for a year's deployment. He had received his orders two weeks before the wedding and had said to my mother, "I suppose you won't want to marry me now," his future being so uncertain.

"Oh, no!" she said. "I'll still marry you!"

And so, on April 20, 1951, they were married in the tiny chapel on the naval support base at North Severn in Annapolis. (After they were both gone, I found a piece of paper in my mother's belongings stating that her divorce from her first husband had been finalized earlier that same day. We all have our secrets.)

They had known each other for less than four months, and now my father was going away for at least a year, perhaps never to return.

My mother's sister Alice, my favorite aunt, was four years older, but she and my mother could have been twins. The only factor that separated them was weight. My mother had been very heavy as a teenager, but had lost a tremendous amount of weight between her junior and senior years of high school (the dream!), and returned for her last year in high school to find that most of her classmates didn't recognize her. She had kept the weight off into adulthood, but still carried about 20 pounds more than my aunt.

So now she waited for her new husband to return from the Korean "police action." My mother was a worrier like me, ruminating about everything, so she dropped a lot of weight while my father was overseas. When he returned, and she met him at the Baltimore train station, my father looked at her quizzically and asked, "Alice, what are you doing here? Where's Morva?"

"Oh, my God," my mother thought. "I'm married to a man who doesn't recognize me."

And so they began to become reacquainted when my father posted to his new orders in Norfolk, Virginia.

I don't know if my mother ever actually wanted to have a family, but after they had been married a little over two years, my father told her that he thought it would be a good idea.

As a family, all three of us, we were always getting snagged on things, sleeves on doorknobs, that sort of thing. My mother would start to stand up and find some part of herself snagged on the sofa. I would start down the stairs, only to be pulled sharply back, with some fold of my sweatshirt looped on some part of the banister. My mother always told me that my father got up to go to the bathroom one night while they were living in Norfolk, snagged his boxers on the bedpost, they were ripped off, and nine months later I was born in the Naval Academy Hospital, overlooking the Severn River.

Plaintiff's First Interrogatories to Defendant

State her full and complete name, any nicknames she has used, or been known by, date of birth, her present home address, telephone number, and, if different, her complete home address and telephone number at the time of the collision in question.

Did the Defendant make a report in writing to any other person or organization in reference to the collision in question? If so, please state:

The identity of the person preparing each such report;

The identity of the person(s) or organization(s) for which the report(s) were prepared; and

The identity of the present custodian of copies of each such report.

At the time the collision in question occurred, was the Defendant employed? If so, please state the following as to such employment:

The identity of each employer, including their complete name(s) and address(es);

The identity of the person who was the Defendant's immediate supervisor in reference to services performed;

The beginning and ending dates of the Defendant's employment or present status of employment; and

What the Defendant's job position and duties were with respect to each employment.

Please list each state that has issued the Defendant a motor vehicle driver's license in the last five (5) years, including those licenses that may have now expired or been canceled, withdrawn, suspended, surrendered, or revoked, listing the name of each issuing state and the approximate date of issuance and status for each license held.

Please state each and every address where the Defendant has resided in the last ten (10) years, setting forth the approximate dates of your residence at each such address.

Describe in your own words how the collision in question occurred and state specifically and in detail what the claim or position of the Defendant will be regarding any cause or contributing cause of the collision, including a statement in detail of the facts or information upon which this contention is based. [Attorney's note: "Objection – we will plead the 5th."]

If you believe Thomas Boyd's acts or omissions caused or contributed to the collision in question, or to his injuries, please describe the basis for your position, including any evidence or statements that support your position. [Attorney's note: "Objection – we will plead the 5th."]

Give the dates, times, and places together with the names and addresses of persons and organizations that have provided drug or alcohol counseling or treatment to the Defendant in the past five (5) years.

Specify all mechanical or other defects, if any, of the vehicle the Defendant was driving which caused or contributed to the collision made the basis of this suit, including, but not limited to, all components of the vehicle which were inoperable, defective, or otherwise in need of repair.

State where the Defendant had been just prior to the collision, including any and all premises and for profit establishments from where you purchased and/or consumed alcohol, where the Defendant was going at the time of the collision, and the purpose of the trip that the Defendant was on at the time of the collision. [Attorney's note: "Objection – we will plead the 5th."]

State the manner in which any alcohol consumed by you on the day of the incident was provided to or purchased by you, including as part of your answer the person(s) and or premises owner/occupier who supplied or made available any alcohol to you, and the manner of any consideration you provided in exchange for the alcohol, be it by cash, credit, or bank card (identifying the type and bank issuer), or other means. [Attorney's note: "Objection – we will plead the 5th."]

"For what we know must be, and is as common as any the most vulgar thing to sense.... whose common theme is death of fathers."

Claudius to Hamlet, (Act 1, Scene 2)
William Shakespeare

My father was born in a tiny apartment above a grocery store in Jersey City, New Jersey. His father was a local truck driver, and his mother stayed home and raised three more children, two boys and a girl.

His parents were barely 20 when he was born, so I suspect that there might have been a shotgun involved, and possibly a lot of screaming and crying and rending of garments. His parents were both born on the same street in the Lower East Side of Manhattan, but his father's family was from Finland, his mother's family from Sicily, and I doubt if their shared experience as immigrants had broadened their minds so much that these two clans were ready to jump into the gene pool together. But my grandparents Eino and Julia jumped into that pool. And on December 20, 1925, my grandmother gave birth to Billy.

I don't know much about my father's childhood, just little anecdotes here and there. His parents did something unusual for the time. They split up and got divorced. I'm not sure how old the kids were. Young, I think. My grandmother took Florence, the youngest, and the only girl. The boys – my father, Vinnie, and Bob – stayed with their father.

He was a drunk, my grandfather was, and one of my father's earliest memories was having to drag his father out of bars on payday nights and take him home before he spent all the family's money. They adored him, though, those three boys, and always referred to him as "The Old Man" even after they had long outlived him.

They moved a lot, my father said. Whenever the rent was due. Their rent in those days hovered around $30.00 a month, and so they moved from Bank Street to Christopher Street to West 48th. My father played stickball in the street for "The Jane Street Pioneers." Instead of bases, they marked out the "diamond" by corners and fire hydrants and manhole covers. Every week, everyone in the neighborhood went to their local movie house that much later became the Lucille Lortel off-Broadway theater. My father and his friends called it "The Dump." "You goin' down The Dump tomorrow?" He watched a 12-part weekly mystery serial once, but missed Episode 11. When the killer was revealed in the 12th installment, my father had never seen the character before. He must have been introduced in the 11th.

I walked along Christopher Street with my father one day and we stopped outside his old building. Thirty dollars a month, I thought. "Do you know how much an apartment in that building commands today?" I asked him. "Probably about three thousand dollars. Maybe more."

My father just gave me an ironic smile and a shrug and said, "It's the same plumbing."

The 48th Street apartment was a "railroad," three rooms in a row, with doors from the hallway into the front room and the back room, which was the kitchen. The bathroom was off the kitchen with a wall-mounted tank and a chain over the toilet to pull for flushing. The bathtub was in the kitchen with a door laid across the top of it so that the tub doubled as a dining table. There were ten people and a dog living in that apartment for a time: my father, his Finnish grandmother, his father, my father's aunts Esther and Elsie, his uncles Emil and Henry, my father's two brothers – Vinnie and Bob – and his cousin Eddie (Elsie's boy).

During the winter, they closed off the front room so that they wouldn't have to heat it. Ten people and a dog in two rooms. My father used to put on his coat and hat and gloves and go into the frozen front room to sit in the window and read for hours by the streetlamp. He blamed this habit for his early need for glasses, and in later years there was never enough reading light to satisfy him. Whenever he walked into the room and found me reading, he would say, "Why are you reading in the dark? Do you have enough light? Why don't you turn on another light in here?" Never enough light.

Like his own father, mine was an autodidact. The Old Man would sit at the table for meals, a long, heavy knife laid across the pages of a book, reading and chewing, reading and chewing. When the clear plexiglass cookbook holder was invented, my father marveled at how The Old Man would have loved it, being able to prop his book up behind that clear screen so that he never had to stop reading.

My father was born four years before the stock market crash, so the family had nothing, and my father's formative years from ages five to about 16 were lived in the shadow of The Great Depression. Everything had to be divided into ten portions, no matter what. It was their own form of familial rationing. Once a month my grandfather would splurge on a chocolate cake. He didn't like chocolate cake, but the treat would nevertheless be scrupulously divided into ten equal pieces. The children would all wolf theirs down, hardly tasting it, and then sit around my grandfather, greedily eyeing the tenth piece, anxious to see who would be the lucky recipient of The Old Man's largess this month.

Everyone called my father "Billy." "My big brother Billy." When they were kids, my father sent away for a rocket ship kit called "The Aurora Borealis," and put it together in the cold front room of the apartment. Vinnie and Bob and Eddie were so excited! They alerted all the neighborhood kids, "My big brother Billy is going to shoot off a rocket this afternoon!" "My big brother Billy! My big brother Billy!"

Of course, the Aurora Borealis sputtered and fizzled in the middle of 48th Street, but my father's reputation for integrity remained undiminished in the neighborhood. He was adventurous, and that went a long way in the Hell's Kitchen of the 1930s.

My father went to Harran High, which later became the John Jay College of Criminal Justice, but he dropped out to join the Navy. (Notable alumni of Harran High include first Puerto Rican-American U.S. Congressman Herman Badillo, Soviet Spy David Greenglass, actors Edd Byrnes and Robert Mitchum, and William Hamalainen.) After his first enlistment expired, my father returned to Harran and got his diploma, but slept through the graduation ceremony, and then reenlisted.

He had always been a lackadaisical student, preferring to read widely and deeply on his own. There were only two teachers he ever talked about favorably. One was an English teacher who cannily spurred on her students by sending them home with copies of "Madame Bovary" while urging them, with a wink, to "try to overlook the dirty parts." It was probably the only book many of them ever read cover-to-cover. I hope they weren't too disappointed.

My father once spent the better part of a school week at the Polo Grounds watching the New York Giants play ball. When he returned to school, "Madame Bovary" looked at him sternly over her glasses and called him up to her desk at the front of the room.

"William," she said, "you missed a lot of school last week." "Yes, ma'am."

There was a pregnant pause before a sly smile passed her lips. "Did you have fun?" she asked him.

Momentarily taken aback, my father finally mustered, "Yes, ma'am."

Her neutral expression returned. "Good." she said. "You may return to your seat."

And nothing more was said about it.

The only other story my father told from his school days was about a math teacher who, on the first day of class, took a piece of chalk and then, starting from the right frame of the window, began to draw a chalk line at eye level horizontally across the walls and around the room. He drew across posters and blackboards, the calendar, and the door, into each corner, across a map of the world and the Periodic Table of the Elements, all the way around to the left frame of the window. At that point, he raised the sash with one hand and threw the piece of chalk out the window.

Turning around to face his bewildered audience he announced, "That, ladies and gentlemen, is infinity."

My father was Google before there was Google.

When I was a kid, we lived in Washington, D.C., and my father worked at the Naval Dispensary downtown, mostly nights and weekends. On the evenings he was home, the phone would often ring during dinner, and my father would answer.

"Hello. Yeah. Leslie Howard. Sure. Bye."

Then he would return to the table and pick up his fork. "Who was that?" my mother would ask.

"Oh, just one of the guys at work. They were talking and couldn't remember who played Ashley Wilkes in 'Gone with the Wind.'"

This was a common occurrence throughout my life, wherever we were: D.C., the Philippines, Annapolis. My father would pick up the phone, listen for a moment, and then say simply, "Corfu" or "Irene Dunne" or "the M1 Garand."

I walked into the house one day during the news and stood behind his chair for a moment, watching a report about some outrage or atrocity or tragedy that had unfolded in Deptford, New Jersey.

"Deptford, New Jersey," he muttered, mostly to himself. "There's a Deptford in England, too. That's where Christopher Marlowe was killed."

"Why do you know these things?!" I cried.

But I knew the answer. Like Milton in his day, my father read everything there was to read at the time. He started with fiction and poetry, of course, and I still have his yellowed copies of Hardy and Houseman, some with his inscriptions on the flyleaf of where he was at the time. "W.M. Hamalainen, HM1 USN, U.S.S. Albemarle, AV-5, Norfolk, VA, 12/15/58."

But he lived through the Depression and was 19 years old on VE and VJ Days, so fiction soon lost its luster for him in favor of the history he was living through as well as the history he didn't yet know, and so he moved on to non-fiction and never looked back. With history comes geography, and when he learned that my mother-in-law had grown up in Stromness, he already knew that this was where the German Fleet was scuttled at Scapa Flow in June of 1919. He knew things. He knew for the sheer joy of knowing.

From 1955 to 1958 there was a general knowledge game show on CBS called "The $64,000 Question," a precursor to "Jeopardy." ($64,000.00 was real money back in 1955, when the median household income was around $5,000.00.)

I was only a baby, but I've heard this story many times from members of my family who were there. We were all gathered at my grandparents' house in Pasadena, Maryland. The men were across the road at my aunt and uncle's, watching a ball game, while the women and children cooked and chatted in my grandmother's kitchen and parlor.

With sports came drinking, at least among the men in my family, and my father was well into his cups by the time the guys decided to head back across the road for dinner. Unable to walk straight, my father was supported on either side by my Uncle Johnny and my Uncle Frankie as they bobbed and weaved across Ritchie Highway. The ladies and various children were gathered around the television, leaning in for the climax, and didn't notice the three reprobates behind them lurching in through the back door.

From the TV came the host's dulcet tones, "For $64,000, who said, 'To err is human, to forgive divine?'"

Propped between my uncles and swaying in the doorway, my father blearily burped, "Alexander Pope!"

My Aunt Cassie looked over her shoulder at them and said, "God-dammit, Bill, if it's Alexander Pope I'm going to kill you."

The nervous contestant hesitated, eyes widening, then croaked, "Lord Byron?"

"Oh, I'm so sorry!," the moderator shook his head sadly, as the audience groaned, "The correct answer is: Alexander Pope."

"Goddammit, Bill!" my aunt cried, "why don't you go on one of these shows and win some damn money!?"

But he would have been a terrible game show contestant, slow on the button. He wasn't quick, wasn't facile. He was thoughtful, pensive, contemplative. Knowledge wasn't a party trick, it was a part of his character.

In later years, starting way back when it was hosted by Art Fleming ("Thank you Don Pardo, thank you friends! Let's play 'Jeopardy!'"), my parents watched the show faithfully. At the commercial break prior to Final Jeopardy, my father would always announce, "I'll wager everything!"

My mother would smile and shake her head. "It's easy to wager everything when you have nothing."

My father's brother Vinnie had married his pregnant girlfriend and started a family, and Vinnie and Bob were both 4-F, so their admiration for my father only grew over the years as they watched him head off to WWII, then Korea, then Vietnam. He was 19 years old on his way to the Invasion of Japan when Harry Truman dropped the bombs, and ended the war. Our actions on Hiroshima and Nagasaki remain controversial, but estimates peg casualties from those bombings at around a quarter of a million, while casualty estimates for the Invasion of Japan range from five million upwards. And then there would have been the ongoing casualties on both sides from a war that had already gone on for four years against a determined, brutal, and fanatical enemy.

Still, if the Invasion of Japan had proceeded as planned, this book you hold in your hand might not exist. And Mr. Boyd might still be alive.

Either nothing matters or everything matters. It's almost paralyzing when you realize that every single thing you do has rippling consequences that perhaps only a quantum physicist could unravel. Or perhaps Christopher Nolan.

Every time we walk out the door, pause to pick up something we dropped on the floor, decide to swing by the post office today instead of tomorrow. Every time we choose the slow line at the grocery store (which is every time, isn't it?), or leave a little early today, or forget our phones in the office and have to go back. Every time we stop to chat with the lady walking the cute dog, run back inside to make sure we turned the stove burner off, make just one more trip to the bathroom. Every time we're here instead of there, do this instead of that, leave now instead of then, we're changing something. And when we change something, even just one little thing, we change everything.

There is a poem by the English poet William Earnest Henley (1849-1903) entitled "Invictus," meaning "unconquerable" or "undefeated."

Out of the night that covers me,
Black as the pit from pole to pole,
I thank whatever gods may be
For my unconquerable soul.

In the fell clutch of circumstance
I have not winced nor cried aloud.
Under the bludgeonings of chance
My head is bloody, but unbowed.

Beyond this place of wrath and tears
Looms but the Horror of the shade.
And yet the menace of the years
Finds and shall find me unafraid.

It matters not how strait the gate,
How charged with punishments the scroll,
I am the master of my fate,
I am the captain of my soul.

This poem should be posted on the walls of Travis County PreTrial Services. But it isn't. Probably because it is meaningful and muscular enough to offend, and giving offense must be avoided above all else, especially in public places.

Instead, there are a few platitudinous, feel-good, "motivational" posters about how we can all do this together. You bet we can. But do what?

PreTrial Services is located on a leafy street in the west of Austin, in an area heavy with impressive and imposing PWA Moderne buildings built during the Depression years by the Public Works Administration, scattered law offices in what were once lovely private homes, and dispiriting government bureaucratic office buildings designed to suck out your soul like Harry Potter's Dementors.

Andrea checked in here weekly with her Pretrial Case Manager, Mark Agnosto. I met him briefly only once, and he impressed me as stern, but kind, like the assistant principal of a suburban middle school.

Andrea had two ankle monitors. The smaller one was about the size of a pack of cigarettes, on a thick plastic strap, and it monitored her skin for alcohol consumption. The resulting data had to be downloaded daily to Recapture Healthcare, the contractor and provider, through a dedicated landline we had installed in our house. The strap had to be fairly tight so that it would make contact with the skin. And Andrea did extensive research on soaps, body washes, shampoos, and conditioners that did not contain alcohol. You would be amazed at how many beauty and hygiene products contain some form of alcohol. Go ahead. Go read some labels on your own grooming products right now. I'll wait.

Basically, just off the top of my head, there's alcohol denat, behenyl alcohol, cetearyl alcohol, cetyl alcohol, ethanol, isopropyl alcohol (isopropanol), lanolin, lauryl alcohol, methanol, myristyl alcohol, oleyl alcohol, and stearyl alcohol. It's in everything. If you don't have a valid ID and can't get some guy to buy you a six-pack on a Friday night, you can always go home and chug some NyQuil, mouthwash, or shampoo.

The folks at Recapture Healthcare told Andrea that she could wrap her ankle in plastic while she was showering, but over time that would have made for a pretty dirty ankle, in addition to a hairy ankle, as shaving beneath the strap was impossible. They advised simply rinsing thoroughly.

On the other ankle was a larger, clunkier monitor with a box the size of a fist, and a thicker plastic strap. This was a GPS monitor that tracked her comings and goings, because she was restricted to house arrest, allowed only to go to work, home, and to pre-scheduled doctors' appointments. This monitor had to be on fairly tight as well, to stymie one's ability to slip it over the ankle and past the foot. This monitor made a buzzing noise every half hour and had to be recharged every night for an hour and a half, or the battery would die and Andrea would be out of compliance. Most people charge them at night, while they're sleeping.

So Andrea slept for six months with these two ankle monitors buzzing every half hour, and a cord plugging her into the wall. If guilt, remorse, and anguish don't keep you up all night, this should do the trick.

Any deviations from Andrea's schedule had to be approved by Mark in advance, and she met with him weekly to review her previous week, and to go over her work schedule for the following week.

Andrea has always taken after my mother-in-law, who could be counted on to suddenly run upstairs to change her shoes just as everyone else in the family was ready at the door, making us reliably 10 minutes late, wherever we were going. Similarly, Andrea worked about a 12-minute drive from the house, so could be counted on to be almost ready exactly – or roughly – 11 minutes before she had to be there. Mark had already shaken his head sadly at Andrea's chronic tardiness. But punctuality is a gene, and my daughter doesn't have it.

Andrea's father had been taking her to PreTrial every week, but summer was here, school was out, and now it was my turn. I elected to wait outside in the car, reasoning that it would take her only a few minutes. The wait turned out to be a bit longer, but I was able to observe the area and its denizens. The people on the street were primarily men in suits and women in business attire.

But there was the occasional outlier like the man who plunked himself down on the grass verge under a shade tree next to my car to have a cell phone conversation that sounded something like this, "Goddam you

fucking stupid cunt bitch! What the fuck!? Why do you have to be such
a fucking bitch!? I didn't...! I don't...! That isn't what...! Why do you
always...?! You're such a cunt! You're such a fucking cunt! What do you
mean?! I didn't fucking say that?! You're a piece a' shit, you know that?! A
fucking, bitching, cunting piece a' shit!"

With that he stood up, having taken in enough cooling shade, and
sauntered off down the street, still raving into his phone.

So, the following week, I went inside to Pre-Trial Services with Andrea.

In the lobby, there is a bank of square lockers on the left, manned by a
very nice police officer who takes your bag, asks you if you have left your
phone in the bag, and if it is turned off. They don't want your phone
buzzing and ringing at them the entire time you are upstairs. Then there
is another very nice officer who waves you toward him through the metal
detector.

The metal detector invariably goes off, because of the ankle monitors,
which Andrea then displays by lifting her bellbottoms a few inches to
reveal the monitors to the officer. Andrea had cornered the market on
retro, 60s, paisley-printed bellbottoms in order to camouflage the ankle
monitors.

Most of the time we proceeded through security unremarked. But one
day, one poor police officer who must have been new, or covering for the
regular guy, could not hide his astonishment. "Wow! Two monitors?! I've
never seen that before!"

The poor fellow. When he saw Andrea's crestfallen face, he was so apolo-
getic. He hadn't meant to cause her distress.

She had told me that most of the defendants assigned GPS monitors
and house arrest were suspected sex offenders. Hers was probably more a
question of whether or not she would be a flight risk, with her living in
Texas and her parents in New Jersey. Still, with the obvious justification for
the alcohol monitor, combined with the GPS, she now found herself more
heavily monitored than potential sex offenders. Meanwhile, when he was

in jail, Jeffrey Epstein was allowed to leave every day for work and return in the evening, just like any suburban dad.

Beyond the metal detectors is the elevator bank, and Milan can usually be found somewhere between there and the 4th floor. Milan is a middle-aged black man who keeps the building scrupulously clean. Or, at least, as clean as a municipal building can be. No one can ever really eradicate that dark grunge that builds up in the crack between the baseboards and the linoleum. What the hell is that gunk?

Then it's up in the elevator to the 4th floor. I have no idea what is on floors 2 and 3, or if they even exist.

At this point, PreTrial Services becomes positively Orwellian. Or Kafkaesque. The waiting room on the 4th floor is a large linoleum rectangle fitted with buzzing overhead fluorescent lights, and seven rows of plastic chairs connected in cords of five across, to keep them from being moved around. There is a rack of brochures in one corner, advising on how and where to obtain un abogado.

Upon entering, defendants check in at the plexiglass windows to the right, then take a seat somewhere in the bank of chairs. Most of those who shuffle in are people who have taken a wrong turn in life, made a bad decision – like Andrea – made questionable life choices, or simply run out of luck. Most of the women look like cleaning ladies, who have had to leave children and probably grandchildren at home while they check in at PreTrial. A lot of the men look like the guys who demolish that bathroom you're remodeling, or blow the leaves out of your driveway. These are people who started off at a disadvantage, and it's been downhill ever since.

Andrea, by contrast, is asked a question by a newcomer at least once on every visit, indicating that the questioner has assumed that she works here. She looks as though she doesn't belong here. But she does. She does now.

Some of the denizens of the 4th floor, however, positively reek of malevolence. One fellow with a sparse Mephistophelian beard and mustache stared at her nakedly and hungrily – who could stop him? – with drool practically dripping from his pendulous lower lip. I could tell that he was saving her image in his memory bank so that he could beat off to her later at home.

Everyone watches the screen at the front of the room. And watches. And watches. And waits. And watches. And then, suddenly, a name appears "Andrea S." next to the name of the Case Manager, and it's time to move upstairs to the 5th floor. So, back out to the elevator bank.

The 5th floor waiting room is considerably smaller, like a waiting room at the dentist office, but without magazines, and is ringed with plastic bucket chairs. On the right wall is a glass case, like the ones you see in high school hallways full of football and baseball trophies. But this case is full of empty felt-lined shelves, with no indication of what was ever displayed in there. There are printout signs on the glass and on the remaining three walls admonishing readers to "Check in on the 4th floor" before sitting here.

So we sit here. Here is where we find some of those tepid motivational posters, tacked up as an afterthought. My favorite is: "The Future Belongs to Those Who Believe in the Power of Their Dreams." Is that meant to be uplifting, because it comes across as taunting, frankly. I look around the room and see only people who have long since given up on the power of their dreams, if indeed they ever had any. In fact, "The Future Belongs to Those Who Are Not in This Room."

In those waiting rooms, waiting for Andrea, I met some good people who had made bad mistakes. There appears to be an unspoken rule that no one asks, "Hey, what are you in here for?" And no one would answer, even if you did ask, because all outcomes are pending, so it's generally best not to admit to anything. All we really know about each other is that we're all human, and we're all suffering right now, here, together, believing in the power of our dreams.

I chatted with a young black guy one day. He was worried about being able to take care of his little girl, who had just turned four. He had moved back in with his mother, and wasn't working. He asked me if Andrea had a job and, when I said yes, and that I thought the job was helping her, he shook his head in admiration. "Good for her," he said. "I wouldn't be able to work with all this other stuff going on."

I think about him often, and I hope that all of his "other stuff" turned out okay.

One day, my husband Philip and our friend Ben took Andrea to Pre-Trial services. As one of the few white people in the 4th floor waiting room, she always drew a lot of attention, and this day was no exception. The denizens of Pre-Trial Services filtered in slowly, checked in at the window, subtly sized each other up, and sat down to wait for their names to appear on the screen.

Two huge black men walked in together, looking like a defensive line, muscles gleaming like polished onyx. One nodded at Ben, who is also a big guy, and they shared a moment of acknowledgement that they could probably take on anyone in the room. Andrea's name appeared on the screen and she, Philip, and Ben headed upstairs for the next chapter in the Kafkaesque saga.

After Mark had come to claim Andrea for their meeting, Philip and Ben sat alone in the 5th floor waiting room, until they were joined again by the nodding black guy and his wing man. He started to chat them up, learning that Ben was a lawyer and Philip was Andrea's father. Ben then used his professional license to breech etiquette and ask what had brought the guy to this sorry pass. "Oh, I broke up a domestic altercation for my sister," was the reply, which was probably not all there was to the story. It never is.

Just then, the inner door opened, and Ben and Philip's new friend was ushered inside.

When Andrea emerged from the back offices and the three of them headed home, she filled them in on the part of the story they had missed.

She had been sitting in Mark's office, going over her comings and goings of the previous week, her schedule for the week upcoming. The door to the office was open, and Andrea was sitting just inside, with her back to the door, as various clients walked by on their way to and from their own meetings.

Suddenly, our large black friend ducked inside the doorway and reached over Andrea's shoulder to hand her a small, folded piece of paper. Somewhat taken aback, she looked up, took the paper proffered, and said politely and reflexively, "Thank you." Her suitor smiled and nodded, then walked away down the hall. Unfolding it, she found this message:

Invictus: (512) 555-4478

Mark, on his side of the desk, tilted his head and looked at her quizzically. Andrea turned the paper around and held it up for him to read. His eyes widened and his forehead creased as his eyebrows went up. "That has never happened before," he said. Then he indicated the trash can in the corner of his room. "You can get rid of that, if you want."

"Oh, no," Andrea smiled and shook her head, knowing a good story when she sees one. "I am keeping this forever."

In the fell clutch of circumstance
I have not winced nor cried aloud.
Under the bludgeonings of chance
My head is bloody, but unbowed.

PLAINTIFF'S FIRST SET OF REQUESTS
FOR PRODUCTION OF DOCUMENTS
TO CIVIL SUIT DEFENDANT ANDREA SCOTT

You are requested to produce, within thirty (30) days of service of this request, the following information.

Any and all photographs or other electronic images that contain images of the underlying facts or that Defendant intends to offer into evidence at trial.

A copy of any contract of employment that would govern Defendant's relationship with any other entity or bear on the issue of "course and scope of employment" for which she was employed at the time of the Incident in Question.

Any and all statements made by the Defendant regarding the Collision in Question to her insurance company, its employees, agents, independent contractors, adjusters, or representatives, not including statements made to Defendant's attorney. [Attorney's note: "Objection – we will plead the 5th."]

Any and all drawings, surveys, plats, maps, or sketches of the scene of the Collision in Question.

The entire claim and investigation file, including but not limited to, statements, reports, videotapes, drawings, memoranda, photographs, and documents regarding the Collision in Question generated or obtained by Defendant, Defendant's agents, or Defendant's insurers before Plaintiff filed Plaintiff's Original Petition with the Court. [Attorney note: "Legal question for us."]

Please produce any and all correspondence, communications, letters, notes of oral conversations, and all other documents or writings sent to or received from or exchanged by and between you and your insurance carrier concerning the subject matter of this lawsuit, including, but not limited to, any damage to you, the vehicle in which you were riding, damage to any personal property, and any personal injuries. [Attorney note: "Legal question for us."]

All documents, correspondence, memoranda, notes, or e-mails regarding communications between your insurance company and Thomas Boyd's insurance company or companies regarding the Collision in Question and/or Thomas Boyd. [Attorney note: "Legal question for us."]

A copy of each primary, umbrella, and excess insurance policy or agreement, including the declarations page, which was in effect at the time of the Collision in Question. [Attorney note: "Legal question for us."]

Any documents, reports, photographs, or other written records pertaining to any investigation of the Collision in Question. [Attorney note: "Legal question for us."]

Copies of any document or statement that any witness of Defendant will use or you anticipate may use to refresh his or her memory, either for deposition or trial. [Attorney note: "Legal question for us."]

All documents regarding Thomas Boyd's employment history, status, performance, or compensation obtained by Defendant. [Attorney note: "Legal question for us."]

All documents regarding Thomas Boyd's medical status, treatment, or history obtained by Defendant. [Attorney note: "Legal question for us."]

All documents regarding Thomas Boyd's financial status, earnings history, and tax payment history obtained by Defendant. [Attorney note: "Legal question for us."]

All documents regarding Thomas Boyd's claims history obtained by Defendant. [Attorney note: "Legal question for us."]

All documents, records, reports, notations, or memoranda regarding Thomas Boyd from persons or entities that compile claim information, to include but not limited to, insurance claims, unemployment claims, social security claims, and worker's compensation claims. [Attorney note: "Legal question for us."]

All statements or documents that show the identity of any witness to the Collision in Question, or any person with knowledge of relevant facts concerning the Collision in Question, the events leading up to it, or any damage sustained by Plaintiff and/or Thomas Boyd. [Attorney note: "Legal question for us."]

All documents and tangible things which support your contention that: [Attorney note: "Legal question for us."]

Any act or omission on the part of Thomas Boyd caused or contributed to the Collision in Question;

Any factor other than above, contributed to or was the sole cause of the Collision in Question, including but not limited to, acts or omissions of negligence of any other party or parties, or potential third-party Defendant, sudden emergency, unavoidable collision, mechanical defect, or act of God;

Any factor caused or contributed to the Plaintiff's damages, including but not limited to, pre-existing or subsequently existing physical or medical condition or conditions of Thomas Boyd;

Any or all of the medical expenses or funeral incurred by Plaintiff for treatment of injuries allegedly resulting from the Collision in Question where not reasonable and/or necessary;

Thomas Boyd's injuries were not the result of or caused by the Collision in Question.

Any records or documentation (medical or non-medical) which would indicate that you had alcohol and/or drugs (including prescription or non-prescription, legal or illegal) in your bloodstream or urine at the time or immediately following the Collision in Question. [Attorney's note: "Objection – we will plead the 5th."]

Any records or documentation (medical or non-medical) which would indicate that you were a regular user of marijuana within five (5) years preceding the Collision in Question.

Cell phone records within thirty (30) minutes before and after the accident for any cell phone used or issued to ANDREA SCOTT at the time of the subject collision.

Copies of any and all Vehicle registrations and titles, state permits, purchase orders, and specifications for the Vehicle in Question.

Copies of any and all collision reports for collisions in which the Vehicle was involved including the Collision in Question. [Attorney's note: "Irrelevant."]

Credit and/or debit card statements that would show a record of pur-

chases of alcohol, ATM withdrawals at establishments which serve alcohol for the days of February 18 and February 19, 2018 (sic). [Attorney's note: "Objection – we will plead the 5th."]

Copies of any and all repair orders, damage estimates, appraisals, and maintenance records for the Vehicle for the six-months preceding the Collision in Question through three months after the Collision in Question.

Copies of the front and back of your current and past driver's licenses for the past five (5) years.

Any receipt, money order payment stub, check, cancelled check, or other document indicating payment of fines stemming from any traffic violation or citation received by ANDREA SCOTT prior to or relating to Collision in Question. [Attorney's note: "Irrelevant. Objections – we will plead the 5th."]

~Seven~

In the interest of full disclosure, I should say here that my daughter is not the first person in our family to have killed someone. In her case, it was an accident secondary to a terrible decision on her part. In the earlier instance, it was planned, scheduled. An appointment was made and kept.

On January 20, 1984, when I was 29 years old, I had an abortion at a Planned Parenthood Clinic in Manhattan, just a little over a mile south of the hospital where I would give birth to my daughter a little more than 12 years later.

Now, before you get your panties in a bunch because you're all "pro-life" or "pro-choice" and pro women's "health" and like to go on and on about abortion "care," see if you can overcome your snowflakiness and read something with which you might not agree. You really should try it some time. It can be bracing. And if you are really confident in your argument, anything I have to say should just be what it is: my opinion. It won't hurt you. I promise.

I'm just telling you the truth. Or "my truth," as people insist upon saying nowadays.

I graduated from high school just seven months before the Supreme Court handed down their still controversial decision in Roe vs. Wade, so I have straddled this very divisive issue with my own life. In my senior year in high school, one of my classmates was hugely pregnant, and the subject of much whispering and titillation. Roe vs. Wade came down during my freshman year of college, and it is not an exaggeration to say that it represented a seismic shift in the cultural life of the country.

My first brush with abortion came when I was a junior in college, in 1974. One of my dearest friends at school was Inez, a dorm mate from Ecuador. Her new boyfriend Carlos was from Guatemala, and none of us trusted him. Our friend Raquel was from Puerto Rico, street smart, and said she knew a player when she saw one. When Inez turned up pregnant, Carlos drove her, Raquel, and me to a clinic in Queens. When Inez was taken into the back, the three of us sat in the dimly lit waiting room and played dominoes for hours.

Inez finally emerged, looking ashen. Raquel and I each took an arm and we walked her out to the car.

She recovered within a week, but by that time Carlos had disappeared, gone back to Guatemala, Inez said. He was coming back, she said. He really loved her. A month passed, and then she got a Guatemalan postcard from Carlos, saying that he would be back soon. A couple of weeks later, another postcard, then another. After three months, the postcards dried up, and Inez never heard from him again. It took Raquel to point out to her that the cards were postmarked in the Bronx.

My first job out of college, in 1975, I worked for a publishing house. In the course of some conversation or other, my editor, Joe, told me that his girlfriend Casey had had three abortions. I don't know why this topic came up, but this was in a work setting. Joe and I didn't socialize; we didn't go out for drinks or hang out after work. He humble-bragged that they had "very athletic sex," and seemed to feel that these pregnancies were not tragic accidents, but rather reflections on his insurmountable virility and genius in the sack. Joe was rather spindly and nerdy, more a reader than a lover, it seemed to me. So perhaps he felt the need to slip evidence of his procreative prowess into casual water cooler conversation.

Then I remember that he arranged his features into an appropriately sad and wistful aspect when he said, "We're going to get married one day, of course. Sometimes I wonder and worry that perhaps those were our three healthy children."

I think about Joe and Casey from time to time, and I wonder if they did eventually get married and have children, and I wonder if they ever saw their first three children's faces in the faces of the ones they named.

I had a very dear friend from my work at Circle Repertory Company. Some years later she told me that she had had, as I recall, two abortions. One was by an old boyfriend with whom she had been in love, and one was by the man she eventually married, and with whom she went on to have two daughters. My friend became a midwife, delivering babies at mothers' homes (first in Brooklyn, then in China, and then back in Brooklyn), and we have lost touch in recent years. But I wonder if midwifery was her way of helping to bring lives into being, to make up for the lives she cut short.

I would also like to ask her if having an abortion by a man she ultimately married and with whom she went on to have children is different from the way she feels about an abortion she had as a result of a relationship that ultimately failed.

Because here is the next shoe to drop, courtesy of Jane Eyre: "Reader, I married him."

CIVIL LAWSUIT

PLAINTIFF'S AMENDED RESPONSES TO ALL DEFENDANTS' REQUEST FOR DISCLOSURE

KENMARE AND BOWERY, LLC, d/b/a HighHeel Bar & Grill (here-inafter referred to as the "Defendant HighHeel Bar & Grill) is a Texas corporation.

Defendant HighHeel Bar & Grill violated the Dram Shop Act codified in Alcohol Beverage Code 2.02. Defendant HighHeel Bar & Grill was negligent as providers under the Act as they served, sold, and/or provided alcoholic beverages to a person who was obviously intoxicated to the extent that she presented a clear danger to herself and others. This conduct by Defendant HighHeel Bar & Grill. (sic) The bartenders, wait staff and employees who served alcohol to Defendant Andrea, and the managers who permitted the other employees to serve her, were all acting in the course and scope of their employment with HighHeel Bar & Grill. Said conduct was a proximate cause of death of the Deceased and Plaintiff's injuries and damages.

The amount and any method of calculating economic damages:

RESPONSE:
Funeral Expenses:
Heart of Texas Cremation & Burial Service: $1,100.00
Expenses to Address Deceased's Funeral Arrangement:
Delta Airlines $384.00
Enterprise Car Rental $249.22
Total $1,733.22

RESPONSE:

Defendant HighHeel Bar & Grill served alcohol to Defendant Andrea Scott the night of the incident in question.

C.Q., witness to the wreck, she called 9-1-1 to report the accident in question.

Those listed as Investigators were at the scene of the incident in question and have knowledge of the scene of the incident. Dr. P. examined the Deceased's body and performed an autopsy on same. Dr. H. conducted toxicology studies regarding the deceased.

Dr. E. pronounced the death of the Deceased. J.S. and E.P. provided medical care to the Deceased at the scene of the wreck.

Those listed as Officers arrived at the scene of the accident, investigated the accident, and will testify about the scene of the accident and statements made by Defendant Andrea Scott, witnesses, and the results of their investigative efforts.

Those listed as members of the Austin Fire Department responded to the scene of the accident and have knowledge of the attempts to revive the Deceased and how the accident scene looked after the accident.

Those listed as Assistant District Attorneys are involved in the prosecution of Defendant Andrea Scott for the Death of the Deceased and have knowledge of the fact (sic) leading up to the wreck in question, the death of the Deceased, and the actions of Defendant Andrea Scott after the wreck in question.

The funeral home responsible for final disposition of the Deceased's body. Custodian of records will prove up the records maintained by this entity, and as to the costs of their services.

M.H., friend of the Deceased with knowledge of his medical condition before he died, and background regarding the Deceased's character. A.B. friend of the Deceased who has background knowledge regarding the Deceased's character.

Doctors, staff, technicians, employees, agents, who treated the Deceased for his pre-accident arterio-venous malformation in his brain, accompanied by epilepsy, and prescribed medications for his medical condition.

Manager, Human Resources Director, and staff of hotel with knowledge of Defendant Andrea Scott's work schedule and hours work (sic) the night of the wreck.

Kevin Lawford, attorney representing Defendant Andrea Scott for the criminal charges stemming from the wreck in question and with knowledge of the events leading up to the wreck.

Claims adjusters, Supervisors, Corporate Representatives, and Custodian of Records for insurance carrier for Defendants; knowledge of the facts surrounding the accident in question, the policy limits, and the damages sustained to the Deceased.

RESPONSE:

Each medical expert will testify to the causation, origin, extent, and duration of the Deceased's injuries. They will also testify regarding whether his injuries were caused by the accident made the basis for this action and/or any prior accident/incident/condition in which the Deceased may have been involved; and the impact, nature, extent, and severity of the injuries he sus-

tained; and regarding the issues of causation, sole cause and/or contribution. Each medical expert will also testify to the necessity of medical expenses and as to the Plaintiff's (sic) condition immediately after the accident, and the pain level and mental anguish he likely suffered from before his death.

Each accident investigation/reconstructionist expert will testify about how the accident in question occurred, including but not limited to how the accident could have been avoided, as well as the rules of the road for driving (including the transportation code's applicability to this accident), and proper driving skills.

RESPONSE:

Generally, all medical experts are expected to testify in accordance with the facts known as stated in their respective notes and reports and the reports and notes of the other medical providers which they reviewed, and each medical expert is expected to testify in accordance with the opinions and mental impressions set forth in each of their respective notes and reports. They are also generally expected to testify regarding the nature and extent of the Deceased's fatal injuries sustained as a result of the incident made the basis of this present lawsuit. The facts known to all medical experts are those facts set forth in the full body of the Deceased's medical records as provided to Defendants and as obtained by the Defendants. Such opinions are further based upon each healthcare provider's knowledge gleaned from their respective years of studies and from their respective years in healthcare practice, including the treating (sic) patients with similar injuries. Also, each medical expert is generally expected to testify regarding whether the medical records concerning the Deceased which have been produced in the present lawsuit are produced and kept in the ordinary course of business.

The accident reconstruction experts will provide testimony regarding their investigation of how the accident occurred, including their investigation at the accident scene, discussions with the parties and witnesses present at the scene of the accident, evidence they inspected and reviewed, and their opinions and mental impressions set forth in each of their respective notes and reports. They are generally expected to testify regarding their opinion as to how the accident occurred.

DEFENDANTS' RESPONSE TO REQUEST FOR DISCLOSURE

To: Wade Boyd, by and through his attorneys of record

Defendants: HighHeel Bar & Grill, serve the attached Responses to Requests for Disclosure.

RESPONSE:

Defendant asserts a general denial to all of the Plaintiff's claims and causes of action.

For further answer, Defendant asserts the transaction in question and any damages sustained by Plaintiff were the proximate result of Decedent Thomas Boyd's failure to exercise ordinary care and such failure constitutes negligence of at least fifty-one (51%) percent. Under the provisions of the Texas Civil Practice and Remedies Code, Plaintiff is barred from recovery, or in the alternative, Plaintiff's recovery, if any, should be diminished in proportion to the percentage of negligence attributable to Decedent Thomas Boyd. More specifically, that he was operating a motor vehicle against his physician's orders.

Pleading additionally, or in the alternative, without waiver of the foregoing, Defendant asserts that the incident at issue was caused, in whole, and in part, by the acts of third parties beyond the control of Defendant or over whom the Defendant had no control or any right of control, specifically the acts of Co-Defendant Andrea Scott.

Defendant also asserts as an affirmative defense the applicability of the safe harbor provision of the Texas Dram Shop Act, as its employees were properly trained and certified. Defendant denies that either Defendant or its employees directly or indirectly encourages its employees to violate the law and did not knowingly order or reward its employees for violations of the law.

Defendant contends that it did not serve alcohol to Ms. Scott in an already intoxicated state.

RESPONSE:

At the present time, Defendant is not seeking economic damages. However, Defendant has incurred reasonable attorney's fees and expenses in the defense of this matter. Additionally, Defendant does not stipulate that Plaintiff has suffered economic damages. Plaintiff is required to prove his damages related to and caused by this incident in question. Defendant reserves the right to challenge causation and the calculation of such damages, at the trial of this cause.

"Remember that creating a successful marriage is like farming: you have to start over again every morning."

H. Jackson Brown, Jr

Yes, my husband was the father of what would have been my first child. We were not married at the time. Our relationship was not a year old, and what a year it had been. Philip was engaged when I met him, to a woman back in the United Kingdom, with whom he had gone to drama school. So I suppose I qualify as a homewrecker, but their relationship was on rocky footing already when I entered the picture.

Philip was an American, so couldn't work in the U.K., where agents had seen his work in drama school and wanted to represent him. But he had to return to the U.S., pending the wedding. After they were married, thanks to his fiancée's citizenship, he would be able to work there.

So, instead of being signed by an enthusiastic U.K. talent agent, Philip was just like all the hundreds of unemployed actors who arrive at Newark Airport and Penn Station and Port Authority Bus Terminal every week with nothing but a song in their hearts and their dicks in their hands.

So instead of starring on "Masterpiece Theatre," Philip became a bus boy in the restaurant at the Hotel Intercontinental. Wait staff. That's where the actors are. Leave a nice tip the next time you're out; that guy setting down your Vegetable Bibimbap could be the next George Clooney.

I remember during the inception of the AIDS crisis in the early 1980s when there was still a lot of misinformation flying around about methods of transmission, such as "poppers," and the idea was seriously floated that all gay waiters should be fired. In response, the playwright Christopher Durang exclaimed, "Can you imagine if they fired all the gay waiters in New York? They'd have to call out the National Guard to take your drink order!"

Philip and I met in the basement of the Madison Avenue Presbyterian Church, one of those low-ceilinged gathering rooms with a lot of folding chairs, those rooms that always smell of coffee (and used to have nicotine stained walls) because that's where they hold the AA meetings.

My friend Sally Ross had directed two productions running in repertory: the World War I drama "Journey's End" by R.C. Sherriff and its counterpoint, the Vietnam play "DEROS on the Funny Farm" by Michael J. Shannon. The First World War is my "favorite" war, for its elements of almost perfect Shakespearean tragedy, and I had read a great deal about it, so Sally asked me to write the program notes. For the Vietnam War, I had my father as a resource ("Dad, what's an 'RPG?'" I would ask. "'Rocket-propelled grenade,'" he answered drily.)

I wanted to see the shows, I really did. After all, I had written the program notes. But it was February in New York City, butt-crackin' cold, my apartment was on West End Avenue at 106th Street, and the church was on Madison Avenue at 73rd. The only way to get to and from those two points conveniently and comfortably is by helicopter. Especially in February. I sometimes paid for the Sunday New York Times with a subway token when both were 75 cents; I certainly couldn't afford a cab.

It was warm in my apartment, toasty warm, sitting up reading in my loft bed, snuggling with the two cats, listening to the lullaby of the city sirens. But I don't like to disappoint people, so I pulled myself together and went to the frigid crosstown bus stop, like the good soldier I am.

I knew instantly, as soon as I laid eyes on him, just as my mother had with my father. He came to center stage facing downstage, saluted to one of the other actors, and said, "We're ready for them now, sir!"

Then when I was in a cab with my friend Allison on my way home she said, "Philip is such a great guy. Too bad, once you find out he's engaged." Maybe she was trying to warn me off. Was it that obvious already? But all I could think was: "Engaged? Then someone has made a terrible mistake."

We hit it off. We got along. We started spending a lot of time together.

Meanwhile, back in the U.K., Sophie was busily planning the wedding for three months hence, and had already landed her first job in the West

End, in a production of "Animal Farm." Her career and her life were both on an upward trajectory.

Philip's life, on the other hand, was at a low ebb. Bussing tables, having trouble finding an agent, and moving in and out of a succession of sublets. One apartment he leased from a pair of lesbians in Washington Heights came with strict instructions from them about the "dish sponge" vs. the "countertop sponge." This was because, first thing in the morning when he turned on the light in the kitchen, dozens of cockroaches milling about on the counter would suddenly scatter like... well, like cockroaches. Leaving little brown rectangles of cockroach egg sacks in their wake. The dish sponge preserved the relative sterility of the dishes, while the countertop sponge was for cockroach patrol. After a while, he forgot which sponge was which and reasoned, "Before they come home, I'll just buy them new sponges."

Not long after we met, Philip called Sophie and suggested that they postpone the wedding, just postpone it. He was starting to get some professional traction, being seen for stronger projects. He barely lost out to Matthew Modine for a movie role. He just wanted a little extra time to see where things led, so that he could join her in London for their wedding feeling on an equal footing. If she had a footprint in the U.K. and he had one in the States, and they could both work on either side of the Atlantic, they could become an acting couple force, like Emily Blunt and John Krasinski, or Jamie Lee Curtis and Christopher Guest. Or Elsa Lanchester and Charles Laughton. Or Rhea Perlman and Danny DeVito.

Sophie reacted the way any impending bride would. Remember The Rancor in "Return of the Jedi?"

Yeah. Like that.

So the wedding was off. And Philip and I embarked on that beautiful summer of 1983 as a newly minted couple. We trained together for the upcoming New York City Marathon to be held in November. I was running seven miles a day along Riverside Drive, running to "She's a Maniac" from

"Flashdance." I sunbathed in the park, lost a lot of weight, got into great shape. I was happy.

But then: September. Suddenly, Philip came to me and said that he had to go over to the U.K. to see Sophie, that he didn't feel right the way things had ended, over the phone. "When we're together, she and I, we get along so well. Things have only gone south when we've been apart. I have to see her again, if only to break it off in person. I owe her that. I owe myself that. I even owe you that."

His mother tried to talk him out of it. It was cruel, she said, to keep everyone hanging, to drag things on. The break had been relatively clean; it was best to leave it that way. But he was determined. And so he went over to the U.K. to find closure, and I waited here. It was like having your hair on fire for nine days.

I went back home to visit my parents, to see my high school friends. I tried not to think. But it was no use. I was there, but not there.

By Day Nine, I was back in New York, and Philip's plane was due in at about 2:45 in the morning. I didn't nap, didn't sleep. I was awake. A couple of hours before the flight was due in, I headed to JFK on the Train to the Plane. There was an MTA cop in the subway car who chatted me up about what I was doing on the subway at that ungodly hour, so we got to talking. And because he was a stranger I would never see again, and he had asked, I told him the whole story. In the course of my narrative it came out that Sophie was younger than Philip and that I was almost five years older.

"Gee," my travel companion volunteered gormlessly, "that's something you don't see every day, a younger guy with an older woman. I mean, if he could find somebody younger, what would be the point of hanging out with an older woman?"

Now, mind you, this older woman was 29 fucking years old at the time.

"Because," I drawled witheringly, "an 'older woman' will come and meet your ass at the airport at three o'clock in the morning."

I waited on a balcony overlooking the Arrivals exit and watched for the doors to burst open. When people started streaming through, heading for ground transportation, I scanned the crowd frantically for Philip. I spotted him easily, I could spot him in ten thousand. It's the gait. Even tired, he has a bold, almost cocky walk. Chest out, shoulders back, a slight side-to-side rock, taking on the world. I dashed down the steps and appeared in front of him suddenly, magically. He stopped and blinked, as though having trouble recognizing me, seeing me here, out of context. He didn't smile, wasn't overjoyed, and I felt that first frisson of fear.

"Oh, Mary Kay," he said. Then he reached into his bag and pulled out a bottle of Pimm's, a vile gin-based fruity drink. "Here," he said, proffering it, "I got this for you."

We turned then, and headed for the Train Back from the Plane. We found seats, and he launched right into it. They had gotten back together, of course. The wedding was back on. I think he told me about a trip they had taken to some bed and breakfast somewhere in the lovely, rolling English countryside. I don't remember exactly. I'm not sure I heard him. What I did hear was the blood whooshing through my veins, my heart pounding, indicating that I was still alive, which was strange, because it didn't feel that way.

That train ride seemed longer than nine days.

I went back to my apartment, unplugged my phone, and went to bed.

It didn't last, their rapprochement. Of course it didn't. They were apart again, and I was right there, and I would never have let it happen.

Don't judge me.

At the end of "The Graduate," Dustin Hoffman doesn't just shrug and say, "Well, I lost out on Katharine Ross, but maybe Ali MacGraw is available." Romeo doesn't say, "There's got to be some hot chick in this town whose name is not Capulet." Jane Eyre doesn't say, "Whew, got out of there just in time. That jerk literally had a madwoman in the attic. Mary Poppins never had to put up with this shit!" "Pride and Prejudice" doesn't end with: "Bitch!" "Bastard!"

If it came to it, I was prepared to fly over to the U.K. for the wedding and go all Benjamin Braddock on everyone's ass, pounding on the glass and yelling, "Elaine! Elaine!"

Yeah, I know. They end up in the back of the bus, in more sobering moments, as reality begins to dawn, and they start to ponder – as all sane people would – the consequences of their actions and the unknowability of all that lies ahead. The inevitability of joy and hope and wonder, and also of pain and loss and anguish.

But if I was going to be sitting in the back of the bus, being gawked at by all the other passengers, and staring into the devouring maw of the future, I knew I wanted it to be with Philip.

We moved in together in December 1983, into a 3rd floor loft in an old wood frame building on 4th Avenue and 20th Street in Brooklyn, surrounded by warehouses and industrial buildings. There was a methadone clinic on the first floor and a chicken slaughterhouse across the street. It was a large raw space, just four walls, a ceiling, and a floor. There was no delineated kitchen and no appliances, so we were excited about designing the space ourselves.

I knew something was wrong in December. I was so fatigued, no energy for painting and carrying furniture. I just wanted to lie down, curl up, and sleep. One day I lay down on the roof of the building for just a few minutes to "rest my eyes" and woke up an hour later, shivering in the cold.

We were so busy at work and working on the apartment that it wasn't until early January that I finally felt that first stab of panic. How long had it been? I didn't remember having my period in December. I made an appointment at the Planned Parenthood clinic in downtown Manhattan. I was embarrassed to be there, so gave my name as "Hamilton." They didn't ask for identification.

After the test, I sat in the waiting room until I was ushered into a tiny office, barely a closet, with a grey filing cabinet in the corner, two chairs, and a desk. I had to move my chair to the left slightly in order to close the door. Behind the desk sat a large black woman whose name and title I didn't catch. She was friendly, gentle. What would I want to do, she wanted to know, if the test turned out to be positive?

I hadn't thought about it. I didn't think that anyone who showed up at Planned Parenthood was actually ready to be a parent. Wouldn't I go to a real doctor for that? Wouldn't I be happy, or at least hopeful? I wouldn't be sitting here with my kneecaps pressed up against the front of a metal desk. I think I said something stark like, "I guess I would want to get rid of it."

She looked down at the file on her desk blotter, then looked back up at me and said, "It's positive."

Ah ha. So it was a trick question. But it makes sense. They want you to think about what you would want to do before you have to make that decision.

So I made an appointment for a couple of days hence and headed for the subway to Brooklyn to tell Philip.

I remember that I cried when I told him, but I also remember wondering at the time why I was crying. I didn't want to have any children, so I didn't really spend a moment wrestling with my decision. I think I cried because I was self-dramatizing. Poor me. Look what happened to poor me. Like a character on a soap opera. I had noticed on soap operas that, back when abortion was illegal (or at least individualized by state), all of the pregnant characters yearned for that prohibited procedure. But as soon as abortion was legalized, all of the pregnant characters suddenly wanted to keep their babies. That's drama.

Can anyone imagine Jennifer Aniston's Rachel Green on "Friends" electing to have an abortion? Me neither. She could get one. It was available. It would certainly have simplified her life. It wouldn't even have taken up an entire episode. Where's the drama (or comedy) in that?

Some "progressive" shows like to tout their "realistic" handling of the abortion issue, but I wonder who will do the longitudinal study to find out how these characters (and their IRL counterparts) feel about their decisions twenty, thirty, forty years down the line.

My friend Inez, dumped by her shitty Guatemalan boyfriend. Did she go on to have children later? And if she didn't, does she ever wake up in the middle of the night thinking about that child and the life they could have had together? And if she did become a mother, does she ever see that first child's face in the faces of her other children?

There is an entire, beloved, classic movie that might as well be about the abortion question. It's called "It's a Wonderful Life" and it stars Jimmy Stewart and Donna Reed. Stewart plays George Bailey, a man who comes to feel that he has given up most of his life on behalf of others. He saves his brother Harry from drowning. He intercedes in time to prevent his grieving, drunk pharmacist employer from accidentally killing a patient with poison. He gives up his dream of college when his father dies in order to keep the family business going for his community. He befriends the local town hotsy-totsy and steers her onto the right track. He marries Donna Reed. He lives in a crumbling old house with his wife and entirely too many children. When he faces ruin and prison at the conniving hands of his evil rival, Mr. Potter, George contemplates suicide.

Clarence, an angel trying to earn his wings, is tasked with showing George Bailey what the world would have looked like if he had never been born. Not if he had died at 12 or 27 or 35. If he had never been born. It's a bleak place.

Clarence says to George, "Strange, isn't it? Each man's life touches so many other lives. When he isn't around he leaves an awful hole, doesn't he?"

If I had given birth to that first child, then the best thing that ever happened to me would have sprung from the best thing I ever did in my life, just deciding to keep that child. But I wasn't brave enough, or wise enough, or good enough. And so, instead, twelve years later, the best thing that ever happened to me would spring from the worst thing I ever did in my life.

If I had it to do over again...?

I write this in the wake of the so-called Dodd decision by the Supreme Court to overturn the 1973 Roe vs. Wade ruling which found a right to abortion somewhere in the Constitution. (Wow, turns out those old, white, dead slaveholders actually did not have advanced views on family planning after all. Who knew?)

So, knowing what I know now, and believing what I believe now, would I make the same decision? I think about this from time to time, and I don't honestly know. It's hard to imagine life without the child I have now. But if I had given birth to that earlier child, I almost certainly would not have given birth to the child I have now. But I do know that I would have loved that child as much as I love this one. And perhaps he would have been my happy child. This one is not. Maybe he would have been the child who responded to my texts the same day they were sent. This one does not. He might have become a police officer or a fire fighter, a beloved husband and father, coach of the girls' soccer team. Or he might have become a sad loner doomed to die of an accidental fentanyl overdose in his 30s. We'll never know.

And when I think of the lives Mr. Boyd's life touched, and the lives his life will never touch because it was cut off too soon, it's difficult not to then imagine all the lives left untouched by my first child, starting with my own, and with his father's.

My parents would have had a grandchild for 12 and 14 years, respectively. My in-laws would have seen their grandchild grow to the age of 24 and 27. Instead, my father never knew his grand-daughter, and my mother only knew her for a scant two years. And what of all those other lives untouched? As I write this, my first child would have been 39 years old.

Who would have been his best friend in high school, his wife, his children, their friends and children?

The problem with abortion enthusiasts is multi-faceted. First of all, they talk of all the wonderful opportunities and achievements that will be ripped from their grasp if they stop right now to have a child. But let's manage our expectations here. You're not going to win an Academy award or discover a cure for cancer. Your brilliant career is going to wither into a disappointing job to which you will shuffle back and forth until you are mercifully able to take retirement and spend the rest of your life binge-watching Netflix and waiting to die. You're not that special.

In the meantime, you will have cut off the life of the one person who might have stuck by you once you became old and embarrassing, or worse: invisible. Construction workers no longer wolf whistle as you walk by. Your romantic prospects dwindled from the hot guy who knocked you up in the first place, to the guy in his late 30s still living in a house with four roommates, to your married boss, to the guy sitting on a milk carton on the corner with no teeth and a "Soliciting Donations for Wine Research" sign scribbled on a piece of torn cardboard.

There might have been one person left who was still happy to see you. But you took "care" of that.

Abortion enthusiasts refer to abortion "care" because they won't speak plainly about what it is they actually want, the objection they really have to this new life for which they do not wish to be responsible. It's just not convenient. I just don't feel like it. I just don't wanna.

That sounds selfish, because it is selfish. But if they would just embrace the selfishness, I could at least respect them for their honesty. Yes, objectively, this is a human life. Like the sheet of cookie dough dollops I just put in the oven that, if I leave them alone, will become cookies, so too will this person become completely baked, emerging from the womb with (it is to be hoped) ten fingers, ten toes, and a fully formed personality.

But I am terminating this pregnancy and killing this person because this just doesn't work for me right now. I would pencil this in, but my calendar is fully booked with pilates, and that trip to Turks and Caicos, and a Botox injection for those fine lines in my forehead, and a bridal shower for Shannon in an Escape Room, and a pumpkin latté with my name on it, so I just don't have room for this in my fabulous life. I just don't wanna. It's not convenient for me at this time. No, thank you.

This, at least, would be honesty, and not all this bullshit about "care" and "women's health." Hell, more than half the people we're killing in abortion clinics are potential women. What about their health? She will never know the joy of 20.5 thousand Tiktok followers or the schadenfreude of seeing her arch enemy gain the Freshman 15.

We're told to "follow the science." Well, I saw some science once. I watched a documentary years ago that featured open heart surgery on a baby in utero. This had apparently never been attempted. The surgeons were fearful that if they breached the uterus, contractions would begin, and the baby was not yet viable outside the womb. But the parents and doctors decided to go for it, and when the surgeon made his incision, a little arm attached to a tiny hand flopped out of the slit, as if to say, "Hi!" I gasped. There it was. The surgeon was able to go through the baby's back, operate on the heart, and close the mom up with no complications. It really was a miracle.

It is in those moments that the "Science" intersects with the Divine.

So exercise your right to choose, as I once did. I hope you never have cause to regret it, I really do.

If I had it to do over again...? Hmm.

~Eight~

"And since the day I left Milwaukee,
Lynchburg, Bordeaux, France
Been making the bars
Lots of big money,
And helping white people dance.
I got you in trouble in high school
And college, now that was a ball.
You had some of the best times
You'll never remember with me,
Alcohol..."

Brad Paisley, "Alcohol"

My own relationship with alcohol has been long, on and off, amicable, and troubled.

When I was a kid, my cousins and I all loved to be offered by my folks, my aunts and uncles, just a sip of an ice cold beer on a hot, humid Washington D.C. or Carteret, New Jersey day. There was nothing like it. That ice cold can, beaded with condensation. The little triangle punched into the top of the can with a smaller triangle punched into the other side, to release the vacuum, because this was in the pre-tab opening era. Just that tiny sip of

Ballantine or Hamm's was not only a welcome frisson of refreshment, but came with that tantalizing and forbidden taste of adulthood. Bear in mind that this was back when children aspired to be adults, rather than the other way around.

I didn't drink in high school. My friends and I were so wholesome. No alcohol, no drugs. It was the early to mid-70s, a more innocent time than now, incredibly, coming as it did at the end of the swinging sixties. At least that's how I remember it. We weren't shooting up or rifling through our parents' medicine cabinets. My friends and I mostly hung out at Mr. Donut on West Street in Annapolis, talking until closing, pumped up on sugar and caffeine, and on being 18 years old, and believing that everything would always be exactly the way it was right then, right now, forever.

When I went away to college I started drinking socially, and this quickly escalated. I never kept booze in my dorm room, but we all went out a lot. It was Long Island in 1973, back when Billy Joel was still singing, and before he started driving into people's living rooms at least once a year.

One night in particular I remember being hammered in the backseat when my friends stopped at a Chinese restaurant in Hempstead. I was too drunk to be hungry and certainly too drunk to go into the restaurant for carry out. While they were inside, I opened the car door, leaned out, and vomited extravagantly into the parking lot. A car pulled into the space next to us and I heard a concerned woman's voice ask, "Are you all right?" I wiped my mouth with my sleeve, tried to lift my head to smile at her, and politely said, "Yes, thanks," and closed the car door. She must have had a strong stomach if she continued into the restaurant after that spectacle. Wasn't she worried that this was the aftermath of General Tso's chicken?

I remember having a hangover so bad one day it felt as though I had an ax embedded in my forehead, as though the top of my head was actually open to the sun. Can you think of one other thing we continue to do even though it makes us feel that bad?

I met my college boyfriend junior year, and he didn't drink, so I didn't drink. But then we broke up after I graduated.

By that time, I was working at Endo Pharmaceuticals, manufacturing narcotics at night, which sounds illegal but wasn't. Endo had just come out with an analgesic called Nubain and they wanted to flood the market before a competitor came out with a similar product. This meant putting on a p.m. shift in manufacturing, 4:00 p.m. to midnight. Because we would also be working with Schedule 1 narcotics like Narcan and Narcan Neonatal, Endo didn't want to just hire people off the street, so they turned to their current employees for referrals. Everyone on the evening shift was related to someone on the day shift, so our loved ones were basically held hostage so that we would all behave. My aunt Alice got me the gig, and I will be forever grateful. To this very day, it remains the best job I've ever had.

The people I worked with were the most fun, greatest cross section of humanity I have ever seen. This was before the days of engineered "diversity," and we were organically young, old, black, white, college-educated, blue-collar. There was one guy with a young family, and they were Baha'i, which made him fascinating and exotic. I was in the parenteral department, which means everything other than by mouth. We wore thin plastic spacesuits, gloves, and hairnets and we operated funky, highly specific machinery, filling ampules with injectable solutions and wrapping suppositories in foil, and we alternated duties throughout each night, to help keep us alert and fresh. There were no windows on the factory floor, so it was like working in a Vegas casino, where they want you to lose all awareness of light and dark so that you just keep doing what you're doing without noticing the passage of time.

The best gig was Manual Inspection. About a dozen of us sat around the perimeter of a dark room, about 10x12', backs to one another, facing individual backstops at each station with a black half on one side and a white half on the other, starkly illuminated from above by individual fluorescents. To one side of each of us was a shoebox filled with uninspected ampules, which looked like little glass bowling pins, and on the other side was an empty box into which inspected ampules would be placed.

The idea was to pick up about a half dozen ampules by the top, liquid side down, and shake them in front of the black screen, looking for white particulate matter swirling around, and then hold them up in front of the white screen, looking for black particulate matter. Clear ampules graduated to the box on the right, while contaminated ampules were thrown into a disposal can.

In the Filling Room, the ampules jiggled around upright on a circular table like little soldiers, funneling into a narrow track where a metal needle was lowered into each one for filling. The ampules then waddled further along on the table, where they were sealed by flame at the top. Sometimes the metal needle would make an imprecise insertion into the ampule, nicking the ampule top and chipping tiny shards of glass into the liquid. And even though we filled in a clean room, after entering through an oxygen shower, machines require lubrication and maintenance, so sometimes flecks of oil or dirt from the machines would find their way into the ampules. Hence the search for black flecks or glass particles. None of these particles of glass or dirt were small enough to fit through the needle of a syringe, so our work was more for aesthetics than safety. You just don't want doctors seeing stuff floating around in the injectibles. It's off-putting.

While our eyes and a part of our brains were occupied during inspection, our mouths and vast swathes of our brains were still free. And so we talked. And we listened. And we laughed.

Debbie Wachowski had the softest heart, so when we were inspecting Narcan Neonatal, used to treat babies born drug-addicted, she would cry the whole time, having to wipe tears away in order to see through the glass.

One day, someone suggested that we try to name all 50 states. My father could do it geographically, but all the squarish ones out west look the same to me, so I try to do it more alphabetically, in all those clusters of As and Ms. When I came up with Montana, Shirley exclaimed, "Montana! What the hell's Montana?" After we had named all 50, Shirley said that we weren't done and then, nodding knowingly, she asked, "What about Canada?"

Yeah. We did forget about Canada.

Sometimes we talked about sex, and Shirley reported that once, when her husband Robert tried something different on her, she challenged him, shouting, "Robert! What the hell are you doin'? Have you been readin' a book?!"

We worked 4:00 p.m. to midnight and got paid in cash at the end of every week, which seems shady in retrospect. Most of us were single, so we hit Friday night at midnight with plenty of time to party and more money burning holes in our pockets than any of us had ever made before. We went out drinking and bowling, sometimes just drinking, never just bowling.

One night, we must have had a better time than I will ever remember, because I woke up the next morning kneeling on the floor of my bathroom, next to the toilet, my upper torso draped over the side of the tub, the top of my head pointed toward the drain. I don't remember how I got home. When I pulled myself into an upright position, I hurt in places where I previously didn't even know I had places. There's an old Russian proverb that says: "If you wake up in the morning and you're not in pain, you know you're dead." Well, I was very much alive.

When I pulled myself haltingly to my feet and looked in the medicine cabinet mirror I found that the whites of my eyes were completely blood red, all of the blood vessels in the whites broken, hemorrhaged. I don't know how long I was upside down, unconscious. Hours, probably. It's a wonder I didn't die of a stroke. Imagine my parents getting that phone call when my neighbors began to detect a smell.

But I was young and resilient, 25 years old, so I pulled myself together and went to work that afternoon. Everyone there was horrified by my appearance, but glad to see me alive.

I seem to have been something of a chameleon when it came to drinking, blending in with the scenery. At Circle Rep I dated an actor who didn't drink alcohol. Fresh squeezed orange juice from the Korean markets around Sheridan Square, that was his vice. I didn't drink at all during that period.

When I met my husband, he drank some, so I drank some. And when our old Buick, a hand-me-down from my father-in-law, was stolen from out in front of our Brooklyn apartment building, the issue of drinking and driving became moot for years.

I didn't drink at all when I was pregnant. After Andrea was born, we moved out to the New Jersey exurbs, and I stayed sober for the most part, with a small child in the house. When I went back to graduate school, when Andrea was in 2nd grade, the drinking increased. Grad school was harder than I expected, and alcohol took the edge off the stress.

Christopher Hitchens said that martinis are like a woman's breasts. "One is not enough. And three are entirely too many." Well, my pours started gradually increasing. At first I scrupulously measured to the top of a shot glass. But eventually I would hold the jigger over my glass and let some slop over the top as I measured out the Tanqueray. Soon, tee martoonis had inched their way up to two and a half, maybe three tits. Maybe more.

At the time, I was in the habit of picking Philip up after work from the bus stop in downtown Tenafly, and he says he worried about me every evening. I had started winding down well before he was home from work, so I felt pretty relaxed as I wheeled around Washington Street. Once, I was making a left turn, and a woman was walking in the crosswalk in that blind spot where the car frame separates the windshield from the driver side window. I saw her and braked just in time, but I would not have passed that breathalyzer.

I went with fellow parents to a school meeting in Jersey City one evening, and my friends and I stopped off for drinks beforehand. It was a school meeting, after all. The martinis were delicious, ice cold, fancy flavors like jalapeño, a generous pour. I was feeling no pain when we arrived at the event, and I was an affectionate drunk. I kept hugging everyone and telling them how much I loved and admired them. I really did love and admire them. "Is she drunk?" I heard one of the mothers stage-whisper to her husband. Oh, yes, I was. Toward the end of the meeting I tried to make a discreet exit, but I stubbed my foot, painlessly of course, into the leg of a chair in the back row and made an awful clatter. When everyone turned around to look, I put my finger to my lips and raspberried, "Shhhhh," but there was no secret to keep.

I took Andrea down to Weehawken one evening for a playdate with friends, and I had a playdate with their parents. The parents at Andrea's school were reliably, relentlessly progressive, slightly to the left of Trotsky in his Bronx days. As a conservative libertarian (or libertarian conservative: limited government, free markets, free minds), I was an oddity, and they were fascinated by my views on some topics, as though I had just landed from Neptune. Or Idaho.

We were sitting around a picnic table in the backyard, surrounded by strings of fairy lights, feeling the humid New Jersey evening descend on us, growing darker and cooler, as we drank and talked and laughed comfortably, watching the fireflies begin to glow and blink.

The conversation turned to "A Woman's Right to Choose" and all eyes turned toward me, as the resident oddball. Could there possibly be any other take on the topic, other than the "correct" one? (Jordan Peterson says that if you know what most people think about one thing, you know what they think about everything, and that's not good.)

Before I realized what was coming out of my mouth, in that hyper-precise articulation and high-falutin' syntax of the drunk who does not want to be found out, I found myself saying something like, "It may surprise you to know that I actually had an abortion, back in 1984. I also had a daughter in 1996, and I can tell you now that it's impossible to pretend that there is a distinction between those two..." At this point I began blubbering like an idiot, and the party began to break up quickly. They were embarrassed for me, and I was embarrassed for them, and for myself. People stood, throats were cleared, chairs scraped, eyes averted, and the next thing I knew I was driving home with Andrea in the backseat.

No one tried to stop me, and they wouldn't have been able to if they had tried. We always want to deputize others ("Friends don't let friends drive drunk."), but friends might also find themselves with their teeth knocked down their throats if they attempted to intervene. I don't blame them. I blame me. I drove home drunk with my daughter in the car, not for the first or the last time. And we got home okay. But not because I'm a better driver than my daughter, or even a better drunk driver. We got home okay – and everyone else got home okay – because I was lucky. That's it.

I knew that I was becoming too dependent on alcohol for stress management, so I tried little fixes. I stopped drinking during the week, only drinking on Friday and Saturday nights. But then I expanded "the weekend" to include Sundays (it was part of the weekend, dammit!), and I was still looking forward entirely too much to that first sip on Friday evening. On Monday, all I could think about was, "four more days...," on Tuesday, "three more days...," on Wednesday, "two more days..." I thought about drinking more when I wasn't drinking than I did when I was drinking.

I read once that you know you have a drinking problem when you don't know when is the right time to start drinking, and then you don't know when the right time is to stop drinking. This was what happened to my parents. During the work week, they began drinking as soon as they got off work. But on weekends, they began drinking immediately after breakfast. Because they could. They were affable drunks, like me, smiling with a vague gaze, a little blurry around the edges.

In my last year of graduate school, our culminating academic event was the Comprehensive Exam – "The Comps." This was an all-day assessment of skills you couldn't really study for, because it was comprised of every single thing you had or hadn't learned in those three years. We, my classmates and I, sat in a dank, dim classroom at Montclair State University in early November with a cold, driving rain pelting the windows, and we filled blue composition book after composition book with what we hoped would be enough accurate ravings about communication sciences and disorders to allow us to pass through the portals of the university as licensed speech-language pathologists.

We were supposed to get the results by mail within a month. But December and January turned into February and March with no word. We were all emailing one another frantically. Had anyone heard? What was the holdup? All that time, all that work. I was 53 years old, a "non-traditional student" as they say, and I was tired.

The three of us – Philip, Andrea, and I – went out one evening to a restaurant in Westwood called The Melting Pot. It was a fondue place everyone raved about. As usual, Philip and I held up the bar for a while before being seated for dinner, Andrea in tow. I was trying to be in the moment with my family, but I couldn't stop ruminating on the Comps, the results, when would they come? By the time we were seated for dinner, I couldn't focus on anything else.

At The Melting Pot, there is what amounts to a stove or a hot plate or a pit of hot oil in the middle of the table in which the customers apparently have to cook their own food. This is supposed to be fun, I assume. Or, as David Foster Wallace would say, "a supposedly fun thing I'll never do again."

When our waitress brought our order, she rattled off a list of instructions about which food should go into the cooker in what order and how long before we were expected to fish it out. My head felt compressed at the temples, and her directions sounded like the protocol for installing and programming the air traffic control system based on code for the UK NAS and the E3D AWACS.

I lost it. In a fit of pique, I picked up all of the food and threw it into the pot, got up from the table, and lurched out of the restaurant. I can only imagine Philip and Andrea's disappointment and embarrassment (and hunger) as they paid the check and left to find me waiting outside sobbing.

Andrea was just shy of 11 years old. This was the example I set for her.

We all drove home hungry and in silence. I kept my face turned away, pressed against the passenger window, my tears trapped against the glass. I was so ashamed of myself.

As long as I live, I will never be able to make it up to my family for that evening. I had reached what looked and felt like rock bottom.

But, even so, I still didn't stop drinking altogether for another two years.

".... Strife.... demands union, and abhors separation.... however much of blood and treasure the separation might have cost."

Abraham Lincoln

During the primary season leading up to the 2020 presidential election, some mild attention was directed to candidate Robert Francis "Beto" O'Rourke's 1998 DUI, when he was 26 years old, which included some allegations of attempting to flee the scene. O'Rourke had reportedly made no attempt to hide this incident, and had expressed regret and remorse, while continuing to deny the accusation that he had attempted to avoid responsibility.

The September 27, 1998 police report of the incident reads as follows:

"On September 27, 1998, I was dispatched to I-10 East Mile Marker 2, reference to a motor vehicle accident. I met with the reporter and driver of American Medical Ambulance. The reporter said that while he and his partner were traveling East bound on I-10 they observed a green in color Volvo pass them at a high rate of speed. The vehicle then lost control moments later and struck a truck traveling the same direction. After the driver/defendant struck the truck it sent the defendant's vehicle across the center median and to a complete stop facing east bound. The defendant/ driver then attempted to leave the scene, the reporter then turned on his overhead lights to warn oncoming traffic and to try to get the defendant to stop. When I made contact with the driver I asked him if he was hurt and that if (sic) he needed medical attention. Defendant was unable to be understood due to slurred speech. Defendant also had glossy eyes and breath smelled of an alcohol beverage, I then asked the defendant/driver to step out of the vehicle, upon doing so the defendant almost fell to the floor. I asked the defendant if he had consumed any alcohol beverages that morning and he answered yes. I then decided to conduct the one leg stand and the walk and turn tests. I fully instructed the driver/defendant on how to complete both tests. The defendant/driver could

not count in a paced manner on the walk and turn and on the one leg stand the subject attempted several times and failed by totally losing his balance. At this time I placed the defendant behind my patrol unit. Sgt.____ arrived at the scene at this time and advised me that he would handle the motor vehicle accident. I transported the defendant to the El Paso Police West Side Sub Station where he was read the Police Officer Statutory Warning and agreed to take the breath test. Defendant blew a .136 and a .134, he was later transported to Judge _____ for Magistrates Warning and Bond Setting and later booked into the county jail."

The time of the incident is variously reported as 01:00 and 03:00, and the Volvo is described once as "green" and once as "black." The witness is not identified and it is not clear what actions taken by O'Rourke led the officer to believe that O'Rourke was trying to flee the scene in his car.

O'Rourke said that he had been celebrating his birthday the evening before, drinking Jameson whiskey in El Paso with his father – a former county judge of El Paso county – and that he had later had "two beers" with a friend. At the time of the accident, he was driving his girlfriend back home to Las Cruces, New Mexico, about an hour's drive.

An accident report filed with the Texas Department of Public Safety that would have included a sketch of the scene as well as identification of and an affidavit by the lone witness was missing from the physical file and could not be located.

This was evidently O'Rourke's second brush with the law, after a May 1995 incident at the University of Texas at El Paso when he and two friends were accused of trespassing in the yard of a university facilities building, setting off an alarm. O'Rourke referred to this incident as "horsing around," and the charges were later dropped.

Kevin Lawford

Attorney at Law

Below is an itemized list of legal services provided for the dates December 12, 2019 to February 17, 2020.

DATE	SERVICE	TIME
2-13-2020	*DF & KL: Inspect Vehicle at lot, along with Coltrane, all present during this vehicle inspection. Reviewed Scott's vehicle and Mr. Boyd's scooter, took photographs, measurements, and inspected vehicle.*	3.25
1-28-2020	*Review and send Affidavit showing Mr. Boyd did not take a motorcycle safety course. He was therefore required to wear a helmet.*	.07
1-16-2020	*Review Accident Reconstruction Expert's request for data codes and sent email to prosecutor regarding interpretation of codes.*	.17
1-15-2020	*Attempt to view motorcycle and Jeep. Meet with Accident Reconstruction Expert, however Det. Chavez presented incorrect address, as the vehicles had moved from one tow yard to another lot. Det. Chavez was no longer available to meet at new yard on this date. Instead, Coltrane, DF, and KL met at office and reviewed case plus pictures. Determined for the first time that it is possible Mr. Boyd was on the wrong side of the road.*	3.75
1-15-2020	*Prepare Subpoena for Mr. Boyd's registration and inspection records.*	1.75
1-13-2020	*Email plus phone discussions with Coltrane and APD Evidence Custodian Detective Chavez regarding time to meet to review evidence on 1-15-20 in mid-morning.*	2.00
	DF's contracted rate: $300.00 per hour (4.21 hours)	$1,414.00
	KL's contracted rate: $400.00 per hour (2.00 hours)	$800.00
	Contemporaneous Work contracted rate: $650.00 per hour (7.63 hours)	$5,070.00
	Previously billed credit applied	(-$627.50)
	Total Withdrawn from Retainer on Deposit:	$6,656.50

There is a public service announcement I've heard saying that a DUI could cost you $10,000.00 and result in your living in your parents' basement for a time, which will in turn result in your having difficulty on the dating scene. This PSA seems laughably optimistic.

Let me throw ice water in your face.

Should your DUI result in loss of life – someone else's rather than your own – let me rush to assure you: as with the price of a yacht, if you have to ask how much it will cost, you can't afford it. Remember the $90,000.00 to $120,000.00 for the attorneys? Let's start there.

But then, the car you totaled was worth about $20,000.00. All figures will be in second-to-third-decade-of-the-21st-century dollars, so not adjusted for inflation, which is upwards of 9% as I write this. So whatever this ended up costing us, in purely monetary terms, I promise you: it will cost you more.

You may be surprised to find that you're on the hook for everything: court costs, rental of the Intoxi-Lock installed in your car for five years, a year or so of the Portable Alcohol Monitor you breathe into four times a day, the ankle monitor for any period of house arrest during pre-trial, your probation officer's fees and expenses.

The probation officer fee is $85.00 a month, the Intoxi-Lock ignition lock is $50.00 a month, the fellows who monitor and calibrate the Intoxi-Lock (you have to take it to them periodically to be finely adjusted to stay in compliance) get another $50.00 a month, and your new, more expensive auto insurance (because you are clearly in a higher risk category; you killed someone with your car, remember?) is $100.00 a month.

So that's $10,200.00 for the probation over ten years, the ignition interlock is $3,000.00 over five years, the calibration is another $3,000.00 over five years, and the auto insurance is, let's say, $12,000.00 over ten years.

So that's $28,200.00 you might have wanted to spend on something else. But, no. And it doesn't stop there.

When you're in jail or prison, you will have to pay for use of a tablet (if you want to listen to music and talk with your family). You will have to pay phone charges and for items you might want from the commissary, such as Moon Pies, unless you want to subsist entirely on faux cheese made from beans.

So, all in we spent about $200,000.00 on this extravaganza, which will be a lot higher by the time you end up here. Imagine what you could have done with all that money.

Ah, well. Go ahead. Hop in the car. You're feeling okay: relaxed, in control. You're not like us. You're different. Special. Better.

What could possibly go wrong?

"She discovered with great delight that one does not love one's children just because they are one's children but because of the friendship formed while raising them."

Gabriel Garcia Marquez, "Love in the Time of Cholera"

When I was about seven months pregnant, my lady chums at Playwrights Horizons threw a shower for me across the street from the theater at the West Bank Café. After the shower, I made a careful list of the gifts and the givers so that I could send out thank you cards, and after sending out the cards I threw the list away, because I'm a tosser, not a hoarder.

Thus I do not know who gave us our most treasured baby gift, but it's just as well. Instead of identifying the giver, I can choose to think that it came from all of my friends.

It is a doll. But not just any doll. This is a pink and white terrycloth doll, about nine inches long, with a small tuft of blonde yarn hair sticking out from a lace doily fringe that crowns the soft round head. She has blue painted-on eyes and two dark pink lines that make a nose and a mouth. Her feet and hands are soft cloth, and Andrea used to twiddle the doll's hands between her fingers, for comfort, in a lovely little fluttering baby finger gesture. She had a small satin bow affixed to her neck, but I cut it off immediately so that Andrea wouldn't chew it off and swallow it, because I was as paranoid and terrified of everything as any new mother.

Most children have a favorite toy or a blanket to which they cling for comfort. This must be a drive innate to humans, to find that comfort object. I don't remember when it became apparent that this was Andrea's totem, but I do remember how she got her name. My mother-in-law, with her Orcadian accent, christened the doll "Dolly," which she pronounced to rhyme with "roly" and "poly," and "holy moley." Andrea, being just a toddler, wasn't yet pronouncing her "Ls" because "L" is a later developing speech sound in children, much to the chagrin of those mothers and fathers of Laurens and Larrys and Lucys and Lilahs. (Lawrence Luckinbill's parents must have been frustrated for a very long time with little Wawence Wuckinbiw.) So Andrea christened her doll "Dodie" and Dodie she was.

Dodie appears in all of Andrea's early photographs, even the formal ones taken at photography studios or for annual pre-school photos. She is featured prominently in Andrea's early drawings of our family.

I was quickly faced with a familiar dilemma in families: when and how to wash the beloved object. We washed her during Andrea's naps, of course, but those grew less frequent and longer between. I could wash her at night, after Andrea was asleep, but I might fall asleep myself before the wash or dry cycle, and then what would happen when Andrea awakened?

The tag said "Eden Toys," so I found them in New York City and called to inquire where I might buy duplicates. Lord & Taylor, in the Baby Department, I was told, so I secured two more and we rotated them out for years, until I accidently, while Andrea was standing next to me, opened a dresser drawer where the doppelgangers were hidden. I quickly slammed the drawer shut, but my daughter is no fool and her steely voice rang out, "Mommy. Open that drawer," and so the jig was up.

But she took it well, the more the merrier, and then I had to find a time when I could wash all three of them.

I returned to the Baby Department at Lord & Taylor many times to buy shower gifts for friends, and I often wondered if it was wise of me to gift these new families with the moppet equivalent of cocaine. And should I have gifted three of them each time?

We were visiting my friends in Maryland once when I had to ask Philip to FedEx one of the spares down to me because I had mistakenly come away with only one, which was now filthy.

And once we were at some sort of Mommy (and the occasional Daddy) and Me dance class or yoga class or art class or some such thing at the Monroe Center for the Arts in Hoboken, and I noticed a little girl with furrowed brow and trembling lips sitting on her father's lap and glaring at us. The dad leaned over to explain to me that his daughter had the very same doll and that he had persuaded her to leave it in their locker in the hallway. She was now convinced that we had stolen it.

We rode down together in the elevator after the class, all six of us, and the little girl continued to give Andrea, Dodie, and me the stink eye and a very wide berth, even as she clutched her own doll protectively, newly restored to her arms. In retrospect I should have taken the opportunity to whisper to the dad, "Baby Department. Lord & Taylor."

"All his life he tried to be a good person. Many times, however, he failed. For after all, he was only human. He wasn't a dog."

Charles M. Schulz

Simply put: we wouldn't have made it without the dogs. (And, to a somewhat lesser extent, the cats.)

There was only one to start: Giacomo, Andrea's fawn-colored pug. She named him after Danny Kaye's character in "The Court Jester," because pugs are comedic in their antics, the jesters of the canine world. "King of Jesters, and Jester of Kings."

She snuck off to get him in Houston literally in the dead of night, in October of 2016 when her father was away in New Jersey, because she thought that if she asked for permission rather than forgiveness, she would never have a dog. And she was right. She saw his picture on Puppy Find, a cute little tan guy with a multi-folded, pushed-in black face, eight weeks old, three and a half pounds.

The adoption process was sketchy. She met the breeder/owner in a deserted parking lot in downtown Houston at 11 o'clock at night. The puppy was in a cardboard box. Andrea hadn't brought any money with her, because she figured this would prevent her from making an impulsive purchase. The puppy guy was a wiry Hispanic named José who said that this was his favorite pup from the current litter. He pulled back the box flaps to reveal a miniature pug, perfectly formed, who gazed up at Andrea with his liquid brown eyes. Sensing her brief hesitation, the puppy turned his back, presented his butt, and cut his eyes at her sideways over his shoulder as if to say, "Check this out. How could you say no to this ass?" And, yes, that sealed the deal. It was love at first butt.

Andrea went to the closest ATM machine and withdrew $500.00.

Giacomo was hers, and she was his.

He turned out to have giardia, right off the bat, causing diarrhea and dehydration. But he was treated at Austin Urban Vet and turned out to be a strapping young lad, growing up to be large for a pug.

Months after his adoption, Andrea chanced upon a news story about the raid of a criminal pug puppy mill in Houston. Many of the families who adopted dogs from this breeder reported that their puppies were sick from the moment they were brought home, and subsequently died. This was the breeder from whom Andrea had adopted Giacomo, and it's a miracle that he survived the appalling conditions reported.

Giacomo immediately proved himself to be the perfect companion. He rapidly developed the trademark pug neck skin, folds and folds and folds of soft, pliable neck skin, perfect for sinking one's fingers and face into and mushing and massaging around. He set up shop on the back of the sofa, facing the front window, and from there he could bark and yell at all the delivery trucks on the block – FedEx, UPS, USPS. And it worked! As soon as the trucks arrived and stopped in front of the house, or anywhere else he could see from his perch, he would begin a cacophony of outraged barking of sufficient power to lift him up off his front legs into a full-throated bucking position, again and again, until the offending truck decamped. So he created his own positive feedback loop. Trucks arrived, he barked, and – voila! – the trucks left. He had found his calling.

I heard a story once on NPR about a place in South America where people had lived in tribal villages for centuries and where private property was unknown. But there came a time when it became necessary for claims to be staked so that homesteads could be efficiently passed down from one generation to another. But how to determine where one family's property line ended and another's began? The surveyors hit upon an ingenious solution. They would walk along the dirt roads from one house to another, and when they heard a dog barking from the neighboring homestead, they would know that this was where the family dog considered his territory to begin, and so this was where each property was staked and, gradually, homesteads were delineated and demarcated. It turned out to be a perfect system.

Giacomo knew that those trucks out front were getting dangerously close to intruding upon his family's territory.

In quiet evenings Giacomo sat curled up next to Andrea on the sofa, content to bask in her warmth. In exchange for all of his canine gratitude, loyalty, and affection, all he asked was to be fed and loved. Why can't we all be so simple and undemanding, so close to what it means to be alive and joyful in every moment?

The night of the incident, all Andrea wanted was to go home tired from work and sit with her dog. But a friend was in pain, so she relented and went out to drink. The moral of the story is: if you have a choice between going out drinking or spending a quiet evening with your dog...

While the police questioned her on the front porch, Giacomo barked frantically from behind the front door, behind the front window. Something was happening, something bad, or had already happened, and his angel heart could sense it. He wanted to help, to protect, to comfort. But Andrea was past all that now. His role would be changed now, and forever. He would not be there simply to charm, to delight, to soothe, not any longer. His role would now be one of healing, binding the wounds, trying as hard as he could to put Andrea back together.

His muzzle went grey over the months following the incident and Andrea's return home. She would forever blame herself, convinced that it had happened overnight, and that she had been the cause. But photographs from that time indicate that the process was actually quite slow, occurring over a period of months or even a year or more, so it's unclear whether or not the incident itself was the precipitating event of Giacomo's apparent aging. But watching her sitting outside for hours – being questioned by the police, finally leaving in the squad car – must have been stressful for him.

So, she would always blame herself for this, as she would for everything else.

When Giacomo was three years old, a year after the incident, Andrea started idly scanning Puppy Find once again, the way many mothers of three-year olds start to get that itch for another newborn. One day, she found a cute little black pug in Waco wearing a yellow rain slicker and yellow rain hat, his lower jaw and teeth somewhat askew in a jaunty, unselfconscious monster mouth.

Andrea had installed a Nanny-Cam in the house so that she could monitor Giacomo's movements throughout the day while she was at work, and noticed that he spent most of it either sleeping or discouraging neighborhood deliveries. "He's lonely!" she lamented. "He needs a puppy."

"You can get a puppy for yourself," I said, "or for the family. But you can't get a puppy for your dog." I told her to ask her father, and he was surprisingly onboard with the idea.

So a puppy for our dog was exactly what we got.

Bonsai came from a breeder in Waco who also bred quarter horses, and he looked as though he had been kicked in the jaw by one of these "step brothers." He turned out to be a crazy little guy, prone to sudden inexplicable spells of some sort of canine complex partial seizure: wild eyes, growling, spinning around in circles trying to find his butt, then moving in slow motion like a Japanese horror movie dog, an inability to cross thresholds. His eyes had the look of Bradley Cooper's in "Silver Linings Playbook." An agonized gaze that said, "Please help me there's something weird going on with me over which I have no control and I don't know where it came from or how to stop it!"

Giacomo is the Feeler and Bonsai is the Thinker. Giacomo's eyebrows shift back and forth and up and down, as though he's trying to understand the internal and external emotional terrain in which he finds himself. Bonsai's eyes shift back and forth, and he can hold eye contact for an uncomfortable amount of time. Friedrich Nietzsche said that "when you look into an abyss, the abyss also looks into you," and he could have been speaking about Bonsai. His gaze is unrelenting. You will blink before he does.

He's animatronic in his movements. While Giacomo trots along at a pug-like rocking, rolling gate, Bonsai's movements are all straight and rapid, a constant tik-tik-tik-tik-tik, dashing here and there and ricocheting like a pinball.

They both love their pack and are happiest when the pack is together, but Giacomo also loves the privacy of his crate on occasion and is "his own pug," as Philip says. Bonsai, on the other hand, hates being alone and must always be lying alongside someone for warmth and comfort.

If you don't have a dog during a painful and pivotal period in your life, I recommend that you go right out this minute and get one. You won't be sorry.

While all this was going on, during the first two post-incident years, Philip and Andrea were down in Austin while I remained in New Jersey with our two elderly amber tabbies, Betty and Wilma.

Wilma was my lap cat, and she would curl up with me on Saturday and Sunday mornings while I read in bed. Whenever I picked her up onto my shoulder, she would wrap one paw around my neck and hold on, like a hug. And when she gazed up at me from my lap she looked at me the way no one ever has and no one ever will again, with such pure and concentrated love that it felt like a physical force.

I was down in Austin visiting Andrea for the summer in 2018 when Philip had to take her in for her final visit to the vet. She was 18 years old.

So when I returned to New Jersey in the fall for the start of school, it was just me and Betty against the world.

We had always assumed that Wilma was the cuddly one and that Betty was a bit more aloof. Affectionate, to be sure, but more independent. But it turns out that she may have simply been deferential to Wilma all that time, for as soon as Wilma was gone, Betty picked up the slack. It was then she who curled up in my lap on Saturday and Sunday mornings while I read in bed. She may have sensed that loss in me, as pets do, and attempted to fill it. And she was quite successful at it.

When I came home from school in the afternoons, I looked forward to hearing her hop down from the sofa as she began to cross the living room floor to once again harangue me for my inexplicable habit of evidently going out to stand in the yard for eight hours every day before coming back inside (as she knew nothing about my commute and my working life). Dogs may have some sense that we've actually gone someplace else, as they occasionally do as well. But most cats, and certainly the ones who only live indoors, must wonder about what we're up to on the other side of that door for hours. Sure, they make the occasional foray to the vet's, but that's just a traumatic hellscape for them that I'm sure they do their best to delete from their memory banks as soon as they return home.

Betty had always been a feisty gal, with a firm personality with which she seemed quite satisfied. I often thought of E.B. White's musing on Fred, his "large and dissolute dachshund," of whom he wrote, "Of all the dogs whom I have served, none has ever understood so much of what I said, or held it in such deep contempt." That was Betty.

She and I made it through 2018 and 2019, through the incident, the loss of Wilma, and then the worldwide SARS-CoV-2 lockdown in March of 2020. By this time, she was in renal failure, and I was administering subcutaneous fluids daily in order to flush out her kidneys.

A couple of months earlier, pre-lockdown, I had taken her to the vet for a routine physical and bloodwork, which had revealed the chronic and progressive organ failure. Dr. Gillen had then hung a bag of saline solution from an IV stand and attached a fresh needle to the end of the descending tube, pinched an inch of neck skin up from behind Betty's head (the thick part that mama cats grab with their teeth and use to carry their kittens around), and punched the needle into the neck skin, parallel with her back. She emitted a tiny 'Eh!" sound, but was otherwise unperturbed. He then opened the pinching valve on the tube and allowed half of the bag of saline to course down the line. When the bag was half empty, he pinched the tube closed and pulled out the needle, then rubbed the back of her neck gently.

He then turned to me and said, "So, you think you can do that every morning?"

Um. Excuse me. What?

I might have been paying closer attention if I had been forewarned that I was going to be the home health aide, but what did I expect, really? I wasn't going to be driving her down to the vet every day or hiring a vet tech to live-in. Still, it was like being invited to sit up in the cockpit with the pilot, chatting casually with him about his family, training, and flying history as he flew and then landed the plane uneventfully, and then having him turn to me and say, "So, you think you can do that every morning?"

Turns out I actually could do that every morning. Deliver the subcutaneous fluids to Betty, I mean, not land an airplane. I took down a picture in the living room and hung the bag on the hook. She was a good girl, stoic, which was not generally her style. The first time I poked her essentially in the back of the neck with a needle and waited while the bag emptied, I was completely drenched in sweat by the time we were finished. But I got better at it, and a little more relaxed. She still made that little "Eh!" sound every time the needle went in, but she put up with all of it, because she must have sensed that this procedure was helping her to feel better.

She stopped eating about a month into the SARS-CoV-2 lock down. We used to close both Betty and Wilma into a separate half of the apartment at night – along with their food, water, and litter box – because Betty would invariably decide at 3 a.m. that this might be a good time to eat, and so she would wake us up.

But toward the end, that last month or so, she was so laid back that I figured I would leave all the doors open so she could come upstairs and join me in bed if she felt like it. But she never did. She was probably just too weak and tired and old by that time. I know the feeling. Still, I wish I had tried the experiment sooner, when she might still have had the energy to make her way up the stairs. I'm sad that I didn't get to spend a few nights with her snuggling behind my knees.

When she didn't eat for a week and had lost a good half of her original body weight, I called Dr. Gillen and told him that I thought it was time. (I have a longstanding theory that in any household of two cats, one of them agrees to be the skinny cat and the other one the fat cat. Betty had been the contractual fat cat, but no longer.)

I wanted to be sure that the time was right. On the one hand, I didn't want to let her go too soon simply because she was the only thing keeping me tethered to New Jersey, away from the rest of my family. But I also didn't want to keep her around longer than I should, simply for my sake. I would never be ready to say goodbye, so I wanted to make sure that our parting would be her idea.

It was about a 20-minute drive down to the vet's and I set her carrier up in the shotgun seat next to me, so I could talk to her and poke my finger through the holes and she would know that I was there. She had always howled most of the way down to the clinic, but this time she was uncharacteristically quiet, subdued, perhaps serene. I think she knew it was time, or perhaps she was trying to reassure me that it was time.

We had just entered lockdown, so I was masked, as was everyone else. But they let me into the examination room and Dr. Gillen explained the procedure, with which I was already, sadly, familiar. He would administer a sedative and then they would leave me alone with her for a few minutes to say goodbye. Then he would come back in with the kill shot.

So he sedated her, and he and the tech stepped out discreetly. Betty just lay there on the towel, on her right side, her eyes wide open. She was so weak and thin by then that the sedative alone probably did the trick. Still, I petted her and talked to her, but only a little bit. She was almost 20 years old, just a few months shy. If she didn't know how much we loved her by then, my pitiful musings at the last minute were not going to get the point across. I looked into her eyes and saw only pupils, and that vast, ancient knowledge that exists in the depths of the eyes of all cats. I'm sure she was already gone.

I went to the door, opened it, and told the vet and the tech that I was ready. They seemed surprised. I'm not sure how much time is customarily spent wailing over cats and dogs, but as I've said, everything that she and I needed to pass between us had happened long before we showed up together on this last day.

The inside of my mask was a petri dish of teary, snotty, disgusting effluvia. The sweet little tech told me that it would be okay with them if I took it off, but it was fine. I didn't need to add my mucous-saturated face to the festivities.

Dr. Gillen began to wrap Betty in the green towel, so I thanked them, turned around and left, and went to the reception desk to pay for the procedure, the cremation, and the wooden box with the gold nameplate.

I took the empty carrier with me and set it back on the passenger seat. The hardest part of the day, harder than saying goodbye, was that all the way home I kept turning to say something to her next to me, to complain about the traffic, to plan the rest of the day and evening.

But she wasn't there.

The next morning I went straight to the local pet rescue shelter and arranged to host a series of temporary foster cats until it was time to move down to Texas.

The need for the new is tribute to the old.

November 25, 2020

Re: Notice of Offer to Other Party

Dear Ms. Scott,

Thank you for your choosing us to provide for your insurance needs. We value you as a customer and appreciate the opportunity to be of service.

As you are aware, we have been investigating and handling the claim(s) made against you as a result of the accident that occurred on February 9, 2018. This letter is to inform you that we have made an offer of settlement of $50,000.00 to Thomas Boyd for the Survival claim filed against you.

We will continue to protect your interest and work toward resolving this matter. In the meantime, please contact us if you receive any kind of paperwork related to this claim.

If you have questions or concerns, call me.

Thank you.
Jared McIntosh
Senior General Claims Adjuster

"Be calm. God awaits you at the door."
                    Gabriel Garcia Marquez, "Love in the Time of Cholera"

In March of 2020, my oldest friends in the world were in a near panic over the coronavirus. They had begun to stockpile water, canned goods, sanitary wipes, ammo, batteries, and gasoline. They were more or less naturally self-quarantining, all being women in their mid- to late-60s, mostly retired, and my only thought was: "But we've had our turn, with precious little to show for it. What about everyone else, those just getting started? What about them?"

If I had met someone back then, at the very beginning, who told me he had tested positive, I would have licked him all over his face. You mean I might not have to feel like this much longer? Sign me up.

By July 31, 2020, Texas had seen more than 100 state prisoners die of SARS-CoV-2, more than any other prison system in the country, and by September 1, 2020, the total number of deaths was rising by 5% a week. Thousands of inmates had been approved for parole but then were stuck in a kind of limbo for months, awaiting release. Reasons given varied from having nowhere to send them, to prisoners not having completed participation in mandatory life skills programs, to fears that prisoner release would flood Texas with possible SARS-CoV-2 carriers.

There are more than 100 state-run jails and prisons in Texas, and only one in four has air conditioning in inmate housing areas, this in a state where the outdoor temperature routinely hits triple digits during the summer months. The relentless heat exacerbated the fevers experienced by many inmates with the disease, and increased water rations were sometimes the only palliative used to prevent dehydration. The misery of poor living conditions and food were compounded by a deadly virus rampaging through a vulnerable prison population.

And inmates were not the only concern. By August 14, 2020, Walterio

Rodriguez, the 67-year old chaplain who had worked with the Texas Department of Criminal Justice, had become the 18th Texas prison employee to die with SARS-CoV-2.

In other U.S. systems, different measures were being taken. Starting in March, the federal system began releasing more than 7,000 medically vulnerable prisoners to home confinement, and the New Jersey legislature took steps toward releasing up to 3,000 inmates close to their scheduled release dates.

By August 2020, Texas had postponed the release of thousands of prisoners, citing CDC guidelines designed to contain the virus. And so many inmates continued to see their periods of incarceration converted to death sentences.

And ye shall hear of wars and rumors of wars: see that ye be not troubled: for all these things must come to pass, but the end is not yet.

Matthew 24:6

It started quietly and far away, from the east, but we were preoccupied with our own internal convulsions. On December 18, 2019, the House of Representatives had approved articles of impeachment against the president, charging him with obstruction of justice and contempt of Congress. On February 5, 2020 he was acquitted by the Senate. For more than three years the country had been preoccupied to the point of obsession with this man.

Americans have always been a self-absorbed, self-obsessed people, little interested in anything that goes on beyond our shores. And so we failed to notice when disquieting rumblings had begun in China as early as November 2019, and perhaps earlier, when almost 10,000 cases had been reported throughout at least 21 countries by the end of January, and when the first case of SARS-CoV-2 was officially diagnosed in the United States in Snohomish County, Washington, on January 19, 2020. We were not interested in the Chinese man in the great northwest, so obsessed were we with the Orange Man in Washington, D.C.

In the early days, even the "experts" told us we had nothing to fear. On January 21, 2020, Dr. Anthony Fauci said, "Obviously, you need to take it seriously and do the kind of things the CDC (Centers for Disease Control and Prevention) and the Department of Homeland Security is doing. But this is not a major threat to the people of the United States and this is not something that the citizens of the United States right now should be worried about."

On February 24, 2020, Speaker of the House Nancy Pelosi visited San Francisco's Chinatown to help support local businesses decimated by fears of SARS-2 saying, "That's what we're trying to do today is to say everything is fine here, come, because precautions have been taken; the city is on top of the situation..."

On February 27, 2020, CDC Director Robert Redfield, when asked at a hearing on Capitol Hill whether healthy people should wear face coverings, had responded simply, "No."

On February 29, 2020, U.S. Surgeon General Jerome Adams begged Americans in a Tweet to "STOP BUYING MASKS!" asserting that masks were "NOT effective in preventing [the] general public from catching coronavirus" and would deplete mask supplies for healthcare providers.

Also on February 29, Vice President Mike Pence in a White House press conference said that the "average American does not need to go out and buy a mask."

In fact, there is evidence to suggest that many of the "experts" thought early on that masks might be effective in preventing community spread, but feared a run on N95 surgical masks which might keep masks out of the hands of first responders, and so sought to downplay the efficacy of mask-wearing. (By 2023, it appeared that the "experts" had been right the first time, and that cloth masks, surgical masks, and basically anything short of N95 masks were almost totally ineffective in preventing infection with or transmission of the virus.) So they were actually inadvertently telling us the truth when they thought they were lying, at least in that single instance. And now they wonder why they've lost the public trust.

On March 2, 2020, Mayor Bill de Blasio urged New York City residents to "Go about your lives, go about your business. This is not, so far, something that you get through casual contact. There has to be some sort of prolonged exposure."

At the elementary school where I worked at the time, there were mutterings of concern and a single staffer was reported to have tested positive. Anxious colleagues scanned the roster of absentees trying to identify our fallen comrade.

My first intimation of looming disaster came in the form of an eccentric colleague, a peculiar woman with a strained, whiny voice who seemed perpetually bent under the weight of living. Agatha was mopey and morose, a human Eeyore, and she had a hypernasal whiny twang that made me wonder if she had taken speech-language courses in order to seek a fix for her own voice, and ended up taking so many classes that she woke up one bright Thursday morning with a degree in the field.

"I spent over a hundred dollars last night ordering things online from Amazon," she whinged to me one early March morning. I thought she was referring to the educational and therapeutic supplies that teachers and clinicians routinely pay for out-of-pocket.

"What were you buying?" I asked her.

"Toilet paper!" she croaked. "There's none on the shelves near me."

Toilet paper? What for?

"I even ordered almond butter!" she asserted, with some resentment. "And I don't even like almond butter!"

Something strange was happening.

There had been a distant drumbeat for a few weeks about a respiratory virus coming out of China, but this was a new level of absurdity. I was proud of my New Jersey neighborhood, where there seemed to be no sense of panic or urgency, and the store shelves, at least as of the evening before, had remained fully stocked.

I thought Agatha was overreacting. I still do. But then came Friday the 13th of March, 2020, and the world collectively lost its mind, panicked, and hid under the bed.

Friday, March 13, 2020 was our last day in school. At the end of that day we were told to take home with us two weeks' worth of work to push out to our children online. Two weeks would be sufficient, it was thought, to "flatten the curve." The virus would still be with us, but we would prevent hospitals and first responders from being overwhelmed with a sudden spike in cases.

Overnight, streets were deserted. There was no morning or afternoon hum of rush hour. Curtains were drawn and blinds were folded shut. March had become a nuclear winter. And two weeks turned into six months, and beyond.

At first I was strangely buoyed, almost elated. It was an odd feeling, and I didn't understand its origin. Everyone was frightened, terrified even, miserable, cowering. Why did I suddenly feel almost euphoric? It made no sense.

And then it did. It wasn't a simple case of "misery loves company." I felt genuine compassion for the people I knew would be dreadfully hurt by this lockdown, even more so than by the pandemic itself. Not the Zoom Class. I knew they would thrive, content to sit in their shirts and ties and pajama bottoms sipping chai lattes and "working from home," wondering why everyone else wasn't as willing as they were to stay home indefinitely to "Stay Safe."

My thoughts ran to those people who actually have to show up for work: hotel housekeepers and valets, landscapers and construction workers, waiters and waitresses, retail clerks, small business owners, maintenance and repair, seasonal migrant workers, hospital workers and other first responders. And not just in this country. All over the world, the hardest hit would be the most vulnerable. Not just those vulnerable to the virus, but those in poverty or just barely out of it, who would now sink back down into that quicksand, never to be able to pull themselves up out of it again. I felt for them, suffered for them, and prayed for them.

So why then did I feel better instead of worse? And then I recognized the origin of this strange buoyancy. I had been miserable for more than two years now, terrified, fearful, sleepless, uncertain. I didn't want other people to feel the way I did, wouldn't wish it on my worst enemy, but for the first time in more than two years, I didn't feel quite so alone.

I was dismayed by the complacency of my closest friends. Most of them retired and receiving their checks in the mail regardless of international catastrophe, they were in favor of an indefinite total worldwide shutdown.

"Just stay home! Stay safe!" was their mantra. "Why doesn't everyone just stay home?!" they wondered myopically. My friends stayed home, snacked on the sofa, watched "Tiger King" on Netflix, and their checks continued to show up in their mailboxes. They put their masks on to tiptoe out in the front yard to retrieve their mail, and left the envelopes sitting in the sun for a few hours before opening, to kill off the virus.

The second anniversary of our incident had come and gone on February 9, 2020. We were still in limbo, but had the good news from Kevin and Daniel that a trial date would probably be set for summer 2020. And so we continued to wait in hope.

Historians will debate for decades over whether the cure was worse than the disease, and everyone had their own experience of the SARS-CoV-2 pandemic. Many were lost to the disease, and many were lost to the reaction to the disease. The true costs are incalculable, and will be felt for generations.

In the earliest days of the SARS-CoV-2 pandemic, I continued going for long walks up the hill near our place in New Jersey, bemused by those driving alone or walking alone, ostentatiously masked, heads down, glancing at me furtively, with fear and suspicion in their eyes, as if I were Typhoid Mary, with my entire naked face exposed for all the world to see. And I remember thinking, "Wow. Wearing a mask while walking alone on a largely deserted suburban street, at least ten yards from another human being. You must really want to live. Please remind me. What does that feel like?"

Years later Philip and I would watch a movie featuring a man trying to kill himself by eating himself to death, only to vomit up his cake and pizza efforts the way many people who try pills do, and my thought was, "You should have known that you couldn't commit suicide like that. If it were that easy, hell, everyone would do it."

For us, SARS-CoV-2 only meant that there would be no trial for us in the summer of 2020.

"Science is the belief in the ignorance of the experts."

Richard Feynman

Meanwhile, Philip and Andrea were locked down in Austin, Andrea having been furloughed from the hotel as the hospitality industry shut down worldwide. I was still in New Jersey, hunkering down with Betty the cat and providing speech-language therapy services to my students online (which doesn't work). You can call it Telehealth, you can call it Telemedicine, you can call it Teletherapy, you can call it "Leroy," if you like, no judgment here. But it doesn't work.

Neither does "remote learning." Children who are easily distracted by a bird outside the window or a pencil rolling on a table are even more distracted when they're in their own homes, their own environments, surrounded by every distraction doting parents can provide: Legos, toys, videogames, television, phones, pets, snacks, siblings, Mom, Dad. One of the kindergarten teachers at my school was tasked with wrangling over a dozen five- and six-year-olds online. At one point during her lesson, one of her charges wandered out of frame. A few minutes later, his mother peered into the camera from the side and asked Kelly, "Where did he go?"

"How the heck should I know?" Kelly asked, exasperated, "He's in your house!"

The kids' defenses were down. Most of them stayed in their pajamas all day, nodding through classes and participating in therapy from bed. One of my 3rd graders happily dug into his nose and chewed gamely on the boogers he recovered, licking his fingertips and smacking his lips. "You know I can see you, don't you?" I asked him.

At first, everyone seemed to enjoy the novelty. There were whole families out walking, skateboarding, biking. I saw one dad on a bike surrounded by three or four blond biking kids weaving merrily along, side to side, like the goddam Von Trapp family singers, and he was calling out to them as they rode, "What's 9 times 7?" and "What's the capital of Kenya?" and "Who wrote the Declaration of Independence?" as though he were auditioning for Father of the Year. "Look at me! I'm biking with my kids and playing Double Jeopardy! How great a dad am I?! Look upon my works, ye mighty, and despair!"

But after the first month or so, the street carnivals disappeared and everyone reverted to their electronic devices indoors, Zoom Class parents to online meetings, their children to playing video games just off camera while pretending to be listening to the teacher. The streets were quiet, except for the lone Peloton truck delivering home gym equipment to shut-ins, rumbling up behind me as I trudged up the lonely hill on my daily walks.

There was a volunteer opportunity assisting nurses in mobile units testing seniors at the Actors Fund Home in Englewood, NJ. This is the place where old troupers can go to live out their last years after retiring from that great big wonderful Business we call "Show." It was a chance to actually do something, rather than cower, and I wasn't afraid of catching SARS-CoV-2, not for a single second, never. If I caught it and lived, I might be protected by antibodies. If I caught it and died, well, at least I wouldn't have to feel like this anymore.

So off I went and held out vials for geriatrics to spit into. When I sealed one tube and shook it vigorously to mix it with the testing medium, one charming, theatrical old Queen exclaimed, "Oh, for God's sake, don't shake it!" Then ruefully he added, "It bruises the gin."

~Nine~

This Full & Final Release of All Claims & Compromise Settlement Agreement is made and entered into on this 18 day of May, 2021.

Wade Boyd, Laura Atlas, and Wallace Boyd as Heirs and Representatives of the Estate of Thomas Boyd, hereinafter referred to as the "Releasing Party" specifically includes Wade Boyd, Laura Atlas, and Wallace Boyd as Heirs and Representatives of the Estate of Thomas Boyd.

The Releasing Party warrants that Thomas Boyd was never married; and, therefore, Thomas Boyd had no surviving spouse. The Releasing Party warrants that Thomas Boyd had no children born to him nor any children adopted by him. The Releasing Party warrants that Thomas Boyd was not survived by any of his parents.

Andrea Scott and Philip Scott hereinafter referred to collectively as the "Released Party" specifically includes each of the above individuals and his or her spouse their employees, agents, servants, legal representatives, heirs, assigns, insurers and attorneys, and any and all other persons, firms, organizations, or corporations in privity with Andrea Scott and Philip Scott, whether named herein or not.

The accident that occurred on or about February 9, 2018 in Travis County, Texas is hereinafter referred to as the "Occurrence."

The Releasing Party acknowledges receipt of good and valuable considera-

tion in the sum of One Hundred Fifty Thousand and 00/100 $(150,000.00) paid to the Releasing Party in hand by Insurance Company.

In Witness Hereof, I have signed this release on the 18 day of May, 2021.

April 1, 2022

Dear Wade & Maureen,

I don't know how to start this letter, so I hope it's okay that I jump in without much build-up.

I want to say that I'm sorry, but in this context, those words seem insulting. "I'm sorry" is something that you say when you forget to reply to an email, or mispronounce a name, or cancel a dinner engagement with short notice. Without serious behavior change, "I'm sorry" is just a sequence of sounds that holds no inherent meaning, so I'm not going to disrespect you or the man I killed by telling you that I'm sorry. Instead, I'm going to demonstrate that I'm sorry, and I'll start by providing the long-overdue explanation you're both owed. To preface, I wish I had a better one.

I was a troubled young woman whose lack of awareness of my own self-centeredness made me dangerous to everyone around me. Had it ever occurred to me that someone else would become the victim of one of my countless ego-driven attempts to self-destruct, I would never have gotten behind the wheel that night. A man had to lose his life for me to realize that the world doesn't revolve around me, and for that, I'm disgusted with myself. If the universe was a fair place, I would have been the one who died that night. Please know that I live with this understanding and all the remorse and self-loathing that comes with it every single day.

Perhaps the ugliest aspect of this for me to have to face is the fact that I left. Why didn't I stop the car? Why didn't I look back? How long was he in pain? How could I have left him there to die like that? These questions haunt my every waking thought. I don't think I'll ever stop trying to answer them. I've read books, done research, talked to therapists, talked to God - I've done everything trying to make sense of this, and I've been largely unsuccessful.

The few details of that night that weren't absorbed completely by the shock were heavily diluted with alcohol, so I don't remember anything with tremendous clarity. What I do remember is knowing that something was wrong, but not understanding what. I remember the flashing lights outside my bedroom window, my dog being scared by the knocks on the door. As I'm sure you're aware, when the officer asked me what I thought "the bump" was, I replied, "roadkill." I remember saying that word, and I want you to know how much I hate that I did. I never, ever thought of him that way. This word was nothing other than a careless, clumsy attempt on my part to explain something that objectively didn't make sense.

My intention in revealing the following things to you is not to tug at your heartstrings or make myself out to be the victim in any way. There was a victim that night, and it was not me. I'm merely opening this window into my life in the hopes that you will be comforted knowing that I didn't walk away from this unscathed – that I haven't been insulated from the consequences of my own actions.

Not a lot of people know this, but my best friend of 8+ years leading up to that night lost her father to a drunk driver when she was four years old. Growing up without her dad shaped her and her brother's lives. She used to passionately scold our friends who drove drunk, sometimes even swiping car keys from purses when she sensed someone was reaching their limit. Knowing all of this, after the news broke, I thought she would never speak to me again. When I got out of jail and saw all the worried, heartfelt texts she'd been sending, relief washed over me. I thought that our bond would prove strong enough to withstand this blow. I was wrong.

Junie wanted so badly to be there for me, and she tried to be. She fought for our friendship so hard – much harder than I deserved – but the battle caused her so much pain that eventually she had to let it go. Losing my best friend this way was excruciating, because not only did I lose the love and companionship of my closest friend and confidante – I also watched her lose me. I watched her face fall and turn to stone in slow motion as the person she had once counted on to be there for her through anything morphed into nothing more than a walking reminder of the father she lost, and of the monster who took him from her. And there was nothing I could do or say to comfort her, because I *wasn't her best friend anymore; I was merely a symbol of everything she'd lost.*

Most of the friendships I've lost in my life were meant to end, but ours wasn't. We would have been in each other's weddings, been "aunts" to each other's kids, and sent each other daily check-in texts with various memes from sitcoms well into our 80s, but I ruined that. I ruined so many things. I watched my parents spend the money they'd set aside for retirement on cleaning up the mess I made, wondering how many of the new lines on their faces would have been there by now anyway and how many were carved by my own hand. I watched my now-5-year-old dog go gray from stress overnight before his second birthday. I've watched all this knowing full well that the only person at fault for it is me.

I would never ask either of you to forgive me for what I did; I have no right to. The only thing I humbly ask is that you steer me in the right direction to honor the memory of your brother and friend as best I can. I took his voice from him, and now I don't know how to use it... or if it would be disrespectful of me to even use it at all. His personhood shouldn't just be erased by my negligence, but I'm afraid that if I try to tell his story, I'm going to get it wrong. There's no roadmap for this situation, and I'm completely lost.

Is there something he would have wanted me to do, a cause for which he would have wanted me to fight? You may have noticed that I've avoided using his name... that's because I don't know how he would have wanted me to refer to him. Would "Mr. Boyd" be too formal? Would "Tom" not be formal enough? Would it have even mattered to him? Please tell me. I want to know as much about him as you're comfortable sharing with me. He deserves better than to be forgotten.

Thank you for taking the time to read this; I'm sure it wasn't easy. I pray that you can derive some benefit from it somehow, though I recognize that this may be unrealistic. I just don't want to take more from you than I already have.

Andrea

"Finally, all of you, be like-minded, be sympathetic, love one another, be compassionate and humble."

1- Peter 3:8

The "mediation," as it was called, was scheduled to take place at the Enduring Peace Lutheran Church in south Austin, which was, according to our GPS, just off a road called Convict Hill, as the Gods of Irony would have it.

The mediator would be there, as would Maureen and Wade. Andrea had been invited to bring someone with her, for support, but had elected to fly solo, presumably so that she wouldn't have to put anyone else through what was bound to be an emotionally wrenching experience.

She was instructed to arrive at 9:30 a.m. on Monday, April 4, 2022, but not a moment before, preferably a few minutes later, so that Maureen and Wade could be settled in and there would not be any awkward meeting beforehand in the parking lot, lobby, or hallway.

Andrea was wearing a short black and white flower print dress under a black blazer, with pink high-heel pumps. She had run the outfit by us earlier because, she said, she felt bloated from stress, and even though the dress was a bit too festively short, it was one of the few in her closet that would fit her. Her hair was darkening at the roots, because she couldn't afford to have the color touched up. Her natural hair color was beautiful, a dark brown with dark red highlights, courtesy of her maternal great grandmother. I loved her natural color, because it complemented her ivory complexion and grey eyes. But Andrea had dyed it platinum a few years before, loved the color, and kept it in a 30s style wave down to her ears, cropped in the back. At almost 26, she looked like a completely different person than the sad, tired, puffy 21-year-old in her mug shots.

Because the car line for the church food pantry snaked through the parking lot and around the front of the building, Philip and I dropped her a few yards away from the front door and watched her make her way into the building. We then moved the car back into the parking lot and sat to watch the pantry line move.

Volunteers from the church moved back through the line, apparently taking orders or requests for items. We calculated that it took about a half hour for a car ten spots back to make it to the front of the line.

There are evidently a lot of hungry obese people in south Austin, Texas. The Lutherans doing the order-taking and the heavy lifting were all old, skinny, and wiry, and we watched as car after car with two fat young people sitting in the front made their way to the front of the line, where they simply popped the trunk and waited while people twice their age and half their weight filled up their cars with boxes and boxes of provisions. We saw no one getting out of their cars to help load. The Lutherans worked tirelessly and patiently; they're better than I am and closer to God. I would have told some of those people to get off their fat asses, out of the car, and help me help you.

Philip and I talked a little, but mostly sat with our phones, as people do nowadays, he reading The Wall Street Journal, me playing a Water Sort Puzzle app calling for me to virtually pour liquid back and forth between brightly colored beakers until I got them all to be monochromatic. We occasionally got out of the car to breathe and stretch our legs.

After two and a half hours, we got a text from Andrea saying that she was done, and we could swing by the front of the church to pick her up, where we got stuck for twenty minutes in the pantry line with the fat young Texans.

Andrea described Maureen as "lovely," and said that Wade was stoic, reminding her of her father, and that he would probably rather have been anywhere else on the planet Earth than sitting there for two and a half hours in a church basement with two crying women. They told Andrea that Mr. Boyd had been sensitive and thoughtful, that he loved the band "Rush," and that she should think of him as "Tom." They gave her a picture of him with two other friends, and asked her to carry it with her every February.

Andrea showed me the picture, and pointed Tom out. He was tall and rangy, bespectacled, slightly stooped at the shoulders, with medium brown hair flopping onto his forehead, and a benign, diffident smile. He looked like an actuary, or the kind of guy who would work in a bookstore. Or maybe an Assistant Professor in the sociology department of a small Midwestern liberal arts college, the kind of non-threatening instructor all the women in the class (and some of the men) would have a crush on.

We drove home. Andrea was taking her plea tomorrow in court, so we needed to be rested and ready.

"Well, I've been afraid of changing
'Cause I've built my life around you.
But time makes you bolder,
Even children get older,
And I'm getting older too.
Oh, I'm getting older too."

Stevie Nicks, "Landslide"

If you don't know how long four years is when your only child is in peril and your hair is on fire every moment of every day, here are just some of the events that transpired between the incident and our day in court. And this is just the highlight reel.

Teenagers began to record and post videos of themselves eating Tide detergent pods.

Seventeen people were slain at the Margery Stoneman Douglas High School in Parkland, Florida.

Evangelical preacher Billy Graham died at 99.

The U.S.A. men won the gold medal in curling at the Seoul Winter Olympics.

It was revealed that Cambridge Analytica had harvested personal information from 50 million Facebook users during the 2016 presidential campaign (when the product is free, you are the product).

Physicist Stephen Hawking died at 76.

In Austin, Texas, 23-year old Mark Anthony Conditt, a serial bomber, killed two and injured five before blowing himself up as a SWAT team closed in.

Jeff Bezos was worth only $112 billion.

An Iowa family of four was found dead in a Quintana Roo vacation condominium, presumably due to inhalation of toxic gasses from a faulty water heater.

Linda Carol Brown died at 76. She was the Kansas girl at the center of the 1954 Supreme Court Brown vs. Board of Education decision that struck down segregation in public schools. Winnie Mandela died of complications related to diabetes at 81.

A "vegan activist" (who knew there was such a thing?) wounded three at YouTube's headquarters in San Bruno, California, before turning the gun on herself.

Fleetwood Mac ousted guitarist Lindsey Buckingham. Probably over "creative differences." So that he could "spend more time with his family."

Former First Lady Barbara Bush died at age 92.

The more-than-half-century Castro Era in Cuba came to a close when Miguel Diaz Canel was elected President of the Council of State.

William and Kate, the Duke and Duchess of Cambridge, welcomed their third child, Prince Louis. Mini-series to follow in 2047.

Seventy-two year old Joseph DeAngelo, the "Golden State Killer," responsible for at least 13 murders, 50 rapes, and over 100 burglaries between 1974 and 1986 was identified and apprehended in Citrus Heights, California.

Hawaii's Kilauea volcano erupted; more than 2,000 people were evacuated from the area.

So, did you hear "Yanny" or "Laurel?" (Hint: it was "Yanny.")

Prince Harry (prince) and Meaghan Markle (actress) tied the knot at Windsor Castle.

Writer Philip Roth ("Portnoy's Complaint") died at 85 from congestive heart failure.

Harvey Weinstein was arrested for rape, as the culmination of the #MeToo Movement that had begun in 2017.

Designer Kate Spade was found dead at 55, an apparent suicide, in her apartment in New York. Anthony Bourdain was found dead at 61, an apparent suicide, in a hotel room in France.

The FCC's 2015 "Net Neutrality" rules were repealed, causing a tizzy in the virtual world.

A boys' soccer team, "The Wild Boars," was trapped in a cave in Thailand and rescued by an international team of divers after an 18-day ordeal, on the eve of monsoon season. A former Thai Navy SEAL, Saman Kunan, perished while supplying oxygen to the trapped boys and their coach.

Joe Jackson, patriarch of the Jackson Five clan, died of pancreatic cancer at age 89.

France won the World Cup.

Singer Demi Lovato was found unresponsive after an apparent drug overdose and was revived with naloxone (which I used to manufacture and inspect; you're welcome).

Iconic singer Aretha Franklin died of cancer at 76. Former Secretary General of the United Nations Kofi Annan died at 80 after a brief illness. Professional bon vivant Robin Leach ("Lifestyles of the Rich and Famous") died of a stroke at 76. Vietnam veteran, war hero, former Senator, and former presidential candidate John McCain died of cancer at 81. Playwright Neil Simon ("The Odd Couple") died of pneumonia at 91.

Christine Blasey Ford accused Supreme Court nominee Brett Kavanaugh of sexually assaulting her at a party when they were both teenagers.

Actor Burt Reynolds ("Smokey and the Bandit") died of a heart attack at 82.

Hurricane Florence hit the Carolinas, killing 53.

Journalist Jamal Khashoggi walked into the Saudi Arabian Consulate in Istanbul and never came out.

A judge dismissed Stormy Daniels' defamation suit against Donald Trump.

Eleven people were killed by a gunman at the Tree of Life synagogue in

Pittsburgh.

Democrats regained control of the House of Representatives. Stacey Abrams was defeated by Brian Kemp in the race for governor of Georgia.

A 27-year old man named Telemachus Orfanos, who had survived the 2017 Las Vegas shooting, was killed along with 11 others (including the gunman) in a bar in Thousand Oaks, California.

Marvel comic creator Stan Lee died at 95 of congestive heart failure.

Hurricane Michael killed at least 43 people when it slammed into the Florida panhandle.

Massive wild fires from July to November killed more than a hundred people and consumed almost two million acres of California.

Stephen Hillenburg, creator of "SpongeBob SquarePants" died at 57 of ALS.

Former president George H.W. Bush died at 94 of vascular Parkinsonism.

The federal government shut down due to stalled budget talks. Aside from the improvement, no one seemed to notice.

After being held in a remote cabin for three months, Jayme Closs escaped from Jake Patterson, who was later convicted of murdering her parents and kidnapping her.

Actress Carol Channing ("Hello, Dolly!") died at 97. Journalist Russell Baker ("Growing Up") died at 93.

"Boardwalk Empire" actor Jussie Smollett claimed that he was the victim of a hate crime in the middle of a frigid Chicago night when two men wearing MAGA hats beat him up, put a noose around his neck, poured bleach on him, and shouted racial epithets.

Mexican drug kingpin Joaquin "El Chapo" Guzman was convicted on 10 federal criminal counts, including money laundering, cocaine and heroin distribution, and firearms charges. Guzman claims to have killed 2,000 to 3,000 people, which comes out to between 35 and 52 a year over the entirety of his lifetime at the time of his arrest, or three to four per month, or about one a week, which sounds exhausting (and messy). So one murder a week. Starting at birth. Somebody call Guinness.

Baseball outfielder and Major League baseball's first black manager Frank Robinson died at 83. Long time Michigan congressman John Dingell died of prostate cancer at 92. Brooklyn Dodgers pitcher Don Newcombe died at 92. Monkee Peter Tork died of adenoid cystic carcinoma at 77. Conductor, composer, pianist, and father-in-law to Woody Allen, Andre Previn died at 89.

A storm system in southwestern Alabama killed 23 people.

Actor Luke Perry ("Beverly Hills, 90210") died of complications from a stroke at 52.

Boeing 737 Max planes were grounded after two crashes within five months killed 346 people.

Fifty-two people, including actresses Felicity Huffman and Lori Loughlin, were accused of fraud, lying, cheating, and bribery in the "College Admissions Scandal." (If you give a university $10,000.00 a year for their "building fund" every year for five years, and your kid gets in, you're a "donor." If you give a university $50,000.00 all at once, and your kid gets in, you're guilty of bribery.)

A gunman killed more than 50 worshippers in two mosques in New Zealand.

Protestors of extradition and supporters of freedom and self-determination took to the streets in Hong Kong.

Three historically black churches in Louisiana were burned to the ground.

The first photograph was published of a black hole weighing as much as 6.5 billion suns (the black hole, not the photograph).

The spire of the 850-year old Notre Dame Cathedral in Paris was consumed by flames.

Special investigator Robert Mueller released his report on Russian interference in the 2016 presidential election.

Basketball player John Havlicek died of Parkinson's disease at 79. Film-maker John Singleton ("Boyz 'n the Hood") died from a stroke at 51. Actor Peter Mayhew, who played Chewbacca in the "Star Wars" franchise from 1977 to 2015, died of a heart attack at 74.

Archie Harrison Mountbatten Windsor was born. Seventh in line to the British throne, he is the son of self-identified commoners Meghan and Harry.

Singer and actress Doris Day ("The Man Who Knew Too Much") died at 97. Grumpy Cat, also known as Tardar Sauce, died of a UTI too soon at age 7. Architect I.M. Pei died at 102. Football legend Bart Starr died from a stroke at 85. Italian director and producer Franco Zeffirelli ("Romeo and Juliet") died at 96. Heiress and fashion designer Gloria Vanderbilt died of stomach cancer at 95. Mohamed Morsi, former president of Egypt, member of the Muslim Brotherhood, and USC alum died of a heart attack at 67 in Cairo's Tora Prison. Developer of the Ford Mustang, Lee Iacocca died from complications of Parkinson's disease at 94.

The U.S. Women's National Soccer team won its fourth World Cup.

Billionaire and former presidential candidate Ross Perot died of leukemia at 89. Baseball player and best-selling author Jim Bouton ("Ball Four") died of a stroke at 80. Former Supreme Court Justice John Paul Stevens died from complications of a stroke at 99. Li Peng, suppressor of the 1989 Tiananmen Square protests, died at 90. Theresa May went out as British Prime Minister, and Boris Johnson came in.

Broadway theater impresario Harold Prince ("Cabaret") died at 91 in Iceland following a brief illness. Iceland. What the hell was a Broadway theater producer doing dying in Iceland?

A gunman killed 22 and injured dozens in a WalMart in El Paso, Texas and 13 hours later, another shooter killed nine in Dayton, Ohio.

Nobel laureate and Pulitzer prize-winning author Toni Morrison ("Beloved") died of pneumonia at 88. Convicted sex offender, accused sex-trafficker, and billionaire Jeffrey Epstein committed suicide in his

Manhattan jail cell. (Or did he?) Actor Peter Fonda ("Easy Rider") died of lung cancer at 79. Actress Valerie Harper ("The Mary Tyler Moore Show") died of cancer at 80. Zimbabwean strongman Robert Mugabe died of cancer at 95.

Hurricane Dorian killed hundreds in the Bahamas.

TV journalist Cokie Roberts died of breast cancer at 75.

Neurodivergent teenager Greta Thunberg scolded her elders at the United Nations Climate Action Summit.

Former president of France, mayor of Paris, Harvard student, and former Howard Johnson's dishwasher (fun fact!) Jacques Chirac died of kidney failure at 86. Opera singer Jessye Norman died of septic shock and organ failure at 74. Groundbreaking black actress Diahann Carroll ("Julia") died of breast cancer at 84. Drummer Ginger Baker died of COPD at 80.

Christina Koch and Jessica Meir made history with the first all-female spacewalk. (No word on whether they wore Jimmy Choo or Manolo Blahnik.)

As U.S. Special Forces stormed his hidey hole in northwestern Syria, Abu Bakr al-Baghdadi detonated a suicide vest, at 48 years too old. Soviet dissident Vladimir Bukovsky died of a heart attack at 76. Long-serving Michigan congressman John Conyers died at 90. Carroll Spinney, puppeteer of Big Bird and Oscar the Grouch died at 85. Former Chairman of the Federal Reserve Paul Volcker died of prostate cancer at 92.

Barnard College freshman Tessa Majors was robbed and stabbed to death by a 13-year old and a 14-year old in Morningside Park in Manhattan.

The House and Senate voted to impeach President Donald J. Trump. Round One.

Spiritual guru Ram Dass died at 88. Radio "shock jock" icon Don Imus died of chronic lung disease at 79.

New York Yankees pitcher Don Larsen, who pitched the only perfect game in World Series history in game five of the 1956 World Series against the Brooklyn Dodgers, died at 90 of esophageal cancer. Iranian General

Qasem Soleimani was killed in a U.S. drone strike at 62.

The World Health Organization announced news about a deadly new coronavirus that had emerged in Wuhan, China.

The CDC announced on January 21, 2020 the first officially documented case of SARS-CoV-2 in the United States.

Terry Jones, of the Monty Python comedy team, died at 77 of dementia.

Michelle Carter, convicted in 2017 of involuntary manslaughter for encouraging her boyfriend to commit suicide, was released from prison for good behavior after serving 11 months.

Basketball star Kobe Bryant died at 41 in a helicopter crash that also took the lives of his 13-year old daughter and seven others.

After years of controversy and struggle, the United Kingdom exited from the European Union.

The Iowa Caucuses melted down into chaos due to reporting errors and utilization of a new, untested app. Donald Trump was acquitted in his first impeachment trial after one month, two weeks, and four days of domestic drama.

Indestructible actor Kirk Douglas ("Spartacus") died of a stroke at age 103.

"Parasite" became the first non-English-language movie to win Best Picture at the Oscars, along with Best Director, Best Screenplay, and Best International Feature Film.

The Boy Scouts of America filed for Chapter 11 bankruptcy.

A black man named Ahmaud Arbery was chased and gunned down by three white men while he was out jogging in a Georgia neighborhood.

Movie producer Harvey Weinstein was found guilty of third degree rape and first degree criminal sexual acts.

NASA mathematician Katherine Johnson died of natural causes at 101, which is a prime number. Hosni Mubarak, military and political leader and fourth president of Egypt, died of kidney failure at 91. Former Chairman and CEO of General Electric Jack Welch died of kidney failure at 84.

Actor and national treasure Tom Hanks and his wife Rita Wilson became the first major celebrities to announce that they had contracted SARS-CoV-2.

The National Basketball Association became the first major sports league to cancel their competitive season due to the SARS- CoV-2 epidemic. The NCAA followed suit, and the Tokyo Olympics were postponed.

A 26-year old EMT named Breonna Taylor was shot to death in her home during a botched raid.

In March 2020, much of the world shut down due to SARS-CoV-2 fears, sending us into a global depression, both fiscally and psychically. Panic over the novel coronavirus resulted in a global financial meltdown, plunging millions back into poverty. The Dow Jones Industrial Average suffered its steepest one-day point drop in history (-2,017.76, or 7.8%).

Country music singer Kenny Rogers ("The Gambler") died of natural causes at 81. Musician Bill Withers ("Lean on Me") died at 81 of heart complications.

In Canada's deadliest mass shooting, Gabriel Wortman killed 22 people in Nova Scotia.

So-called "murder hornets" were spotted in Washington state.

Roy Horn of Siegfried and Roy died of SARS-CoV-2 complications at 75. He had been disabled since October of 2003 as the result of an attack by one of their white tigers during a Las Vegas show at The Mirage. Musician Little Richard (né Richard Wayne Pettiman of "Tutti Frutti") died of bone cancer at age 87. Comedian Jerry Stiller ("Seinfeld"), husband of Anne Meara and father of actor Ben Stiller, died of natural causes at age 92. Former actor and police officer Ken Osmond, who played the incredibly annoying Eddie Haskell on TV's "Leave it to Beaver" in the 1950s and 60s, died of COPD at 76.

A black man named George Floyd died at 46 in Minneapolis, Minnesota when a police officer knelt on his neck for almost nine minutes.

Playwright and AIDS activist Larry Kramer ("The Normal Heart") died of pneumonia at 84.

Elon Musk's SpaceX became the first private company to launch astronauts into space, bringing the possibility of space exploration back to the United States for the first time in nine years.

The Supreme Court halted President Trump's effort to end the Deferred Action for Childhood Arrivals (DACA) program, protecting from deportation hundreds of thousands of immigrants brought to the U.S. as children.

The band formerly known as The Dixie Chicks changed its name to The Chicks in order to distance itself from names associated with the Confederate south. Whatever was known about the word "Dixie" was known in 1989 when the band was founded, but I suppose evolution is a wonderful thing.

Comedy genius Carl Reiner ("The Dick Van Dyke Show") died of natural causes at 98.

Enterprising revisionists began tearing down historic statues across the U.S., including those of Abraham Lincoln, Ulysses S. Grant, Thomas Jefferson, and Frederick Douglass.

Musician Charlie Daniels ("The Devil Went Down to Georgia") died of a stroke at 83. Congressman and civil rights activist John Lewis died of pancreatic cancer at 80. Talk show host Regis Philbin ("Live with Regis and Kathie Lee") died of coronary artery disease at 88. Actress Olivia de Havilland ("Gone with the Wind") died of natural causes at 104.

With the public squares throughout the U.S. and elsewhere largely deserted due to SARS-CoV-2 lockdowns, and amid mounting racial tensions, an epidemic of rioting and looting began across the United States.

A massive explosion at a Beirut airport killed at least 190 people and injured thousands of others.

Musician Trini Lopez ("Lemon Tree") died at 83 from complications related to SARS-CoV-2.

Joe Biden became the presidential nominee of his party on the second night of a "virtual" Democratic National Convention and selected Senator Kamala Harris of California to be his running mate. Twenty-nine year old Jacob Blake was shot by a police officer in Kenosha, Wisconsin and was paralyzed from the waist down. Police had been responding to a 911 call reporting a "domestic incident" made by the woman who had previously filed a criminal complaint accusing Blake of sexual assault, domestic abuse, disorderly conduct, and trespassing.

Forty-three-year old actor Chadwick Boseman ("Black Panther") died of colon cancer. Miracle Mets pitcher Tom Seaver died of Lewy Body dementia at 75.

In September, the number of SARS-CoV-2 deaths in the U.S. passed 200,000, but these figures would later come into question, as many of the deceased died "with" SARS-CoV-2 as opposed to "of" SARS-CoV-2, as hospitals received federal funds for recording pandemic-related cases.

Supreme Court Justice and household saint for millions of white, college-educated, suburban women, Ruth Bader Ginsburg died of pancreatic cancer at age 87. Gale Sayers, who at 34 became the youngest player to enter the Professional Football Hall of Fame, died of Alzheimer's disease at 77. Helen Reddy ("I Am Woman") died at 78 of Addison's disease and dementia.

President Donald Trump and First Lady Melania tested positive for SARS-CoV-2, with quick recoveries for both, much to the chagrin of Democrats.

Eddie Van Halen ("Jump"), guitarist and songwriter for his eponymous band, died at 65 from cancer. Hall of Famer Whitey Ford, New York Yankees pitcher for 16 years, died of Alzheimer's Disease at 91. Joe Morgan, Hall of Fame 2nd baseman for the Cincinnati Reds, died of polyneuropathy at 77.

Judge Amy Coney Barrett was confirmed as an Associate Justice on the Supreme Court, with all Republicans in the Senate but one (Susan Collins of Maine) voting for her and all Democrats voting against.

The Los Angeles Dodgers won the World Series in the first year of the SARS-CoV-2 pandemic.

James Bond "007" Sean Connery died of atrial fibrillation and pneumonia at 90.

Joe Biden became president-elect, with Kamala Harris by his side as vice president-elect. A record number of voters turned out for the election, topping 160 million.

Beloved "Jeopardy" host who died at 80 after a long battle with pancreatic cancer. Who was Alex Trebek? Lucille Bridges, who escorted her 6-year-old daughter Ruby to a newly integrated school in New Orleans in 1960, died of cancer at 86. Former New York City mayor David Dinkins died at 93, just over a month after the death of his wife Joyce.

Many Thanksgiving and Christmas plans with friends and family were cancelled, and for many, the last time they had seen their loved ones would turn out to be the last time indeed.

Actor, bodybuilder, and weightlifter David Prowse, who played Darth Vader in the "Star Wars" franchise, died at 85 of complications related to SARS-CoV-2. Pilot and astronaut Chuck Yeager, who broke the sound barrier, died at 97.

The U.S. Food and Drug Administration issued the first emergency use authorization for an experimental vaccine to prevent SARS-CoV-2 infections.

John Le Carré (né David John Moore Cornwell), British spy novelist and author of "The Spy Who Came in From the Cold," died at the age of 89 after suffering a fall in his home.

In 2021, Trump supporters protesting the certification of the 2020 presidential election stormed the Capitol building in Washington, D.C. One protestor, Ashli Babbitt, died at the scene, while four others, including one Capitol police officer and three other protestors, died in the days following the uprising.

Filmmaker Michael Apted ("Coal Miner's Daughter," the "Up" series of British documentaries) died at 79. Vietnam war correspondent Neil Sheehan who, in 1971, received thousands of pages of classified documents from the Kennedy and Johnson administration (dubbed "The Pentagon Papers") died at 84 of Parkinson's disease. Long-time Dodger manager Tommy Lasorda died of a heart attack at 93. Siegfried Fischbacher of Siegfried and Roy died of pancreatic cancer at 81, eight months after the passing of his partner Roy Horn.

Joe Biden was sworn in as the 46th president of the United States. Hall of Fame right fielder Hank Aaron died at 86. Television and radio host Larry King died of sepsis at 87. Actor Christopher Plummer ("The Sound of Music") died at 91, two-and-a-half weeks after a fall that resulted in a blow to the head. Boxer Leon Spinks died of prostate cancer at 67. Former holder of four different U.S. Cabinet-level posts, George P. Schultz died at age 100. Singer Mary Wilson, founding member of The Supremes ("Where Did Our Love Go?") died at 76 of cardiovascular disease. Jazz musician Chick Corea ("Spain") died of cancer at 79. Publisher and pornographer Larry Flynt died of congestive heart failure at 78.

Almost four weeks after leaving office, Donald Trump became the first president to be acquitted twice on impeachment charges. Round Two.

A freak winter ice storm caused weeklong power outages in Texas, where 200 people died as a result.

Conservative political commentator Rush Limbaugh died at 70 from lung cancer.

The NASA rover Perseverance persevered for 300 million miles to land on Mars.

A gunman in Atlanta killed eight people, including six Asian women, in several Atlanta-area "spas." The incident was cited as a hate crime against Asians, but the gunman claimed that he killed to avoid sexual temptation.

Novelist Larry McMurtry ("The Last Picture Show," "Terms of Endearment") died at 84. Watergate conspirator G. Gordon Liddy died at 90 from Parkinson's disease. Children's book author Beverly Cleary (the

"Ramona" series) died at age 104. Prince Philip, Duke of Edinburgh, husband of Queen Elizabeth II, died at 99. Former U.S. Attorney General Ramsey Clark died at age 93. Former vice president Walter Mondale died at 93.

Former police officer Derek Chauvin was convicted of the murder of George Floyd.

Apollo 11 command module astronaut Michael Collins died of cancer at 90.

Hackers shut down the Colonial Gas Pipeline in a ransomware attack, leading to massive gas shortages.

Children's book author and illustrator Eric Carle ("The Very Hungry Caterpillar") died at 91 of kidney failure. Former Senator, Secretary of the Navy, and 6th husband of actress Elizabeth Taylor, John Warner died at 94. Singer B.J. Thomas ("Raindrops Keep Fallin' on My Head") died at 78 of lung cancer.

The Delta variant of SARS-CoV-2 arrived in the U.S., sparking a summer surge in deaths which then peaked in early September 2021.

Criminal defense attorney F. Lee Bailey died at 87. Actor Ned Beatty ("Deliverance") died at age 83.

A beachside condominium tower in Surfside, Florida, suffered a partial collapse, killing 98 people. More than 80 rescue units responded and search, rescue, and recovery operations continued for weeks.

Former Secretary of Defense Donald Rumsfeld died at age 88 of multiple myeloma. Filmmaker Richard Donner ("Lethal Weapon") died of atherosclerosis at 91. Organized labor boss Richard Trumka died of a heart attack at age 72.

After enjoying a year and a half of worship by "Cuomosexuals" who tuned in breathlessly every day for his SARS-CoV-2 briefings, New York governor Andrew Cuomo resigned amid sexual misconduct allegations.

Don Everly, of rock duo The Everly Brothers ("Bye Bye Love"), died at 84. Rolling Stones drummer Charlie Watts ("Get Off My Cloud") died at age 80. Actor Ed Asner (Lou Grant on "The Mary Tyler Moore Show") died at age 91.

The United States precipitously withdrew all troops from Afghanistan, leaving behind hundreds of U.S. citizens, countless Afghanis, aides and interpreters who had assisted in efforts to stabilize the region, and hundreds of millions of dollars worth of military hardware. The Taliban quickly assumed control of the country. A war that had cost the lives of more than 2,000 U.S. service members and over 20,000 wounded was over.

In Texas, a controversial "fetal heartbeat bill" outlawed abortion once the baby's heartbeat could be detected, as early as six weeks' gestation, before most women know they are pregnant.

Weatherman and clown Willard Scott ("Ronald McDonald") died after a brief illness at 87. Comedian's comedian Norm MacDonald died of cancer at 61. Filmmaker Melvin Van Peebles ("Sweet Sweetback's Baadasssss Song") died at age 89. Former Secretary of State Colin Powell died at 84 from a rare blood cancer exacerbated by SARS-CoV-2.

Actor and producer Alec Baldwin accidentally shot and killed cinematographer Halyna Hutchins and wounded director Joel Souza on the New Mexico set of the movie "Rust."

At the Astroworld Music Festival in Houston, ten people died and hundreds were injured in a surging crowd. Performers, unaware of what was happening, continued playing for a half hour while people were crushed and asphyxiated in the scrum.

Kyle Rittenhouse was acquitted of all charges stemming from the Kenosha, Wisconsin shooting that had taken place on August 25, 2020.

Three Georgia men were convicted of murdering Ahmaud Arbery, the black jogger they chased down and killed on February 23, 2020.

Composer and lyricist Stephen Sondheim ("Sunday in the Park with George") died of stomach cancer at 91. Lee Elder who in 1975 became the first black American to compete in the Masters golf tournament died at age 87. Former Kansas senator Bob Dole died of lung cancer at 98. Musician

Michael Nesmith of The Monkees ("Different Drum") died at age 78 of heart failure.

A late-season tornado outbreak tore 250 miles across Arkansas, Missouri, Illinois, Tennessee, and Kentucky, killing at least 90, injuring over 100, and causing over $20 billion dollars in damage.

Writer Anne Rice ("Interview with the Vampire") died of a stroke at age 80. Writer Joan Didion ("Slouching Towards Bethlehem") died of Parkinson's disease at 87.

Minnesota Police Officer Kim Potter was convicted on two counts of manslaughter for shooting motorist Daunte Wright back on April 11, 2021.

Anglican bishop and anti-apartheid activist Desmond Tutu died of cancer at 90. Football coach and sports commentator John Madden died at 85. Former Nevada Senator Harry Reid died of pancreatic cancer at 82.

Ghislaine Maxwell was convicted of sex trafficking dozens of young girls during her decades-long relationship with dead sex offender Jeffrey Epstein.

America's Sweetheart Betty White ("Golden Girls") died of a stroke at 99.

In 2022, The United Nations declared 2022 as the International Year of Artisanal Fisheries and Aquaculture, International Year of Basic Sciences for Sustainable Development, International Year of Sustainable Mountain Development, and the International Year of Glass, which seems like a lot for a year to live up to. "Sustainable Mountain Development?"

Joan Copeland, soap opera actress and sister of playwright Arthur Miller, died in her sleep at 99. Actor Sidney Poitier, the first black man to win a Best Actor Oscar in 1959 for "The Defiant Ones," died of prostate cancer at 94. Filmmaker Peter Bogdanovich ("The Last Picture Show") died at 82 of Parkinson's disease.

The number of "official" worldwide SARS-CoV-2 cases exceeded 300 million.

Comedian Bob Saget ("Full House") died in a hotel room at age 65 after accidentally hitting his head.

The first successful heart transplant from a pig to a human was reported.

Novak Djokovic, the world's number one men's tennis player, was deported from Australia for failing to meet that country's draconian vaccination demands, thus preempting his bid for a 21st grand slam title.

Actor Peter Robbins, the voice of Charlie Brown in the animated "Peanuts" specials, died a suicide at 65. Singer and actor Meat Loaf (Michael Lee Aday, "Paradise by the Dashboard Light") died at 74 of complications related to SARS-CoV-2. Fashion and fragrance designer Thierry Mugler ("Angel" cologne) died at 73.

The number of SARS-CoV-2 vaccinations administered worldwide surpassed 10 billion. As of this writing, there are approximately 7.8 billion people in the world.

Ash Barty became the first Australian woman since Chris O'Neil in January 1979 to win the Australian Open women's singles championship.

Filmmaker and television director Ivan Reitman ("Ghostbusters") died at 75. Libertarian political satirist P.J. O'Rourke ("Parliament of Whores") died of lung cancer at 74.

The average price of a gallon of regular gasoline in the U.S. hit $4.33, which – who knows? – may seem like a bargain by the time you read this.

The first woman Secretary of State, Madeleine Albright, died of cancer at age 84.

Judge Ketanji Brown Jackson, inexplicably unable to define the word "woman," was nominated to the Supreme Court to replace the retiring Stephen Breyer, thus becoming the first black woman (whatever that is) on the Supreme Court.

The U.S. inflation rate hit 8.5%, the highest in 40 years.

During a live broadcast of the 94th Academy Awards, Will Smith marched up on stage to slap presenter Chris Rock after Rock made a joke about Jada Pinkett Smith's short hair. "The Slap Heard 'Round the

World" caused such a stir that Smith was subsequently barred from Academy events for a decade when what should have happened (if the Awards show producers had any sense at all) is that Smith and Rock should have immediately been signed to co-host the 95th Annual Academy Awards broadcast.

Do the Academy and the network want ratings, or not?

"To love at all is to be vulnerable. Love anything and your heart will be wrung and possibly broken. If you want to make sure of keeping it intact you must give it to no one, not even an animal. Wrap it carefully round with hobbies and little luxuries; avoid all entanglements. Lock it up safe in the casket or coffin of your selfishness. But in that casket, safe, dark, motionless, airless, it will change. It will not be broken; it will become unbreakable, impenetrable, irredeemable. To love is to be vulnerable."

C.S. Lewis, "The Four Loves"

Before our plea time, we met at Kevin and Daniel's offices for a briefing. They ran us through what would happen. Judge Wise would ask if Andrea understood what she was doing, if everything had been explained to her. We looked over the details and particulars of the plea. Mr. Boyd's family and friends would be invited to make a Victims' Impact statement. Andrea would sign some papers, Judge Wise would sign some papers, and it would be over.

Fifteen minutes before we were due, Kevin drove us over to the court-house, which was within walking distance, but I suppose the brief drive leant a touch of formality to the proceedings that would have been missed by the short trek on foot.

Something happened to the architecture and interior design of churches and courthouses somewhere along the line, and I wonder if the blandifica-tion of both started at roughly the same time, perhaps for the same reasons.

When the Cathedral of Notre Dame was built in Paris in 1163, more than 800 years ago, the design and detail must have seemed overwhelm-ing. The design and detail remain overwhelming today. Without modern machinery and building methods, it took some serious dedication, blood, sweat, and tears to erect such an ornate and intricate structure, an appeal to God reaching 211 feet toward heaven. Whole generations were born, toiled, married, parented, lived, sickened, and died while early cathedrals were being built. Today's churches often look as though they were thrown up in a single afternoon based on design plans adapted from those of the local Denny's.

Similarly, courthouses were once built to inspire awe, wonder, and humility. The stark, gothic Victoria County Courthouse in Texas, built in 1892, looks like a more imposing Bates Motel, and the Dallas County Courthouse, with its multiple turrets, would be at home in the Scottish Highlands or at Disneyworld.

Both churches and courthouses have traditionally been situated in the center of town squares, befitting buildings housing institutions at the core of American public life. But the trajectory of church and courthouse design seems counterintuitive. As modern building techniques, abilities, and capacities have evolved, capable of more refinement and ambition, design has devolved, simplified, flattened, homogenized.

My former church in Englewood, New Jersey was built in 1870 in the Victorian Gothic style. A fire destroyed the sanctuary in March of 2016 and it has yet to be rebuilt as of this writing. I expect that the exterior, which is mostly intact, will be restored to comport with the rest of the building, but I have seen plans for the interior and they are a crushing disappointment, at least to me. It's all blond wood and straight, clean lines, a church designed and built by Ikea and just as inspiring. Windows will be clean and simple, not the ornately detailed stained glass bible scenes of older churches. Older churches were heavenly; modern churches are earthly.

The same is true of modern courthouses. Upon entering, you would think you were walking into the Department of Health and Human Services or the Department of the Interior. There is a TSA-like conveyor belt and metal detector just inside the revolving doors, and a black marble floor leading to the elevators. There is no majesty. No awe. No indication of the life-altering gravity of the issues dealt with in this building day in and day out. No one enters this building and then leaves it exactly the same, ever, but you would never know this from the innocuous interiors. This is not the banality of evil; it's the banality of banality.

We took the elevator up to courtroom 299 and took our seats in the third row of the gallery.

Frankly, Judge Wise deserves a better courtroom. Philip and Andrea sat there monthly for check-ins prior to the SARS-CoV-2 lockdowns, and had come to appreciate her greatly. They report that she is no nonsense, but fair, and occasionally hilarious, because working in criminal justice relies on graveyard humor, or the people who spend all day every day laboring in these particular coal mines will lose their minds. It's like working in a hospital. If you can't joke about the patients with your colleagues every once in a while, the weight of what you're doing and what you're seeing and what you're hearing will crush your soul.

The courtroom was lined with blonde paneling, and there was a picture, a painting, of a white-haired eminence grise, smiling sagely, hanging in the center of the far wall. A shallow gallery of seats was lined up facing the raised judge's bench. The court officer paced by a door to our left, from which currently incarcerated defendants would emerge. To our right was a gallery of large overstuffed leather chairs lined up perpendicular to the viewing gallery; this was clearly seating for any potential jury. A court reporter sat in her station between the judge and the witness stand. The setting was serious and serviceable, if not awe-inspiring.

Tom's best friend Maureen was tall, voluptuous, and dramatic, wearing black pants and a powder blue diaphanous blouse with diamond cut-outs at the shoulders. She may be bi-racial, because she is a creamy caramel color all over: eyes, hair, lips, skin. She has a smooth, high forehead with her hairline set back, like Queen Elizabeth I. Her nose is long and strong, and she seems always to be leaning toward whomever is speaking, her energy reaching outward. Maureen is very present.

Wade was a stark contrast. Also tall, but beanpole thin, he sat stooped throughout the proceedings, elbows resting on his knees, hands dangling, occasionally hanging his head. He wore a soft red plaid shirt and dark blue jeans. He was bald on top, with shoulder length white shocked hair, like Benjamin Franklin. When I approached him after the sentencing to tell him how sorry I was, he seemed to smile ruefully as he conceded that the entire affair was "a tragedy for everyone involved" and I immediately felt guilty because I could see that he was trying to help me to feel better about the terrible wrong my family had done to his, the way that hospital patients are obliged to rally in order to lift the spirits of their visitors.

They sat two rows in front of us: Stacy the family liaison on the left, Maureen in the middle, Wade on the right. Aside from attorneys, the judge, the court reporter, and the court officer, they were the only other people in the courtroom, but still Philip leaned over to me and gestured toward them with his head and a questioning look, "Who are they?" "That's them," I mouthed back. "Oh."

Two cases went before us. The first was a bail hearing for a Mr. Lopez. He was short, bald, and thickset, wearing a grey and white jumpsuit. He could have been anywhere from 35 to 65 years old, because we could only see the back of his head. He was waiting in jail on a domestic abuse charge lodged by his girlfriend. The first witness called was his estranged wife, who offered to put up $4,000.00 bail for his release so that he could live with her and "help out" with their 14-year old son. She allowed that their relationship had been abusive as well, but that this had all changed now that they had been apart. She worked long hours, she said, and could really use his help at home.

Next, a woman named Valerie from Victims' Services testified on behalf of Danielle, who was apparently the current victim of Mr. Lopez's domestic improprieties. Valerie outlined the use of something called the Jackie Campbell Danger Assessment, created by a nurse named Jacquelyn Campbell. Victims respond to the twenty questions and fill in a calendar of abusive incidents so that they can see for themselves what their risk levels are.

Danielle's risk score was evidently highly elevated, and so bail was denied and Mr. Lopez was shuffled offstage by the court officer.

Andrea had had a bit of a crush on the judge's court officer for the past four years. He looked like a slightly darker Mark Wahlberg, muscular and tightly packed in his uniform and bullet-proof vest. He now sported a black beard, and maintained the same purposeful, vigilant attention to his surroundings, no matter the dull repetitiveness of some of the sad cases that meandered through the courtroom.

The next case featured a fellow in a bright orange jumpsuit who had been in jail awaiting trial for almost four years. His charge was child sexual abuse, and it wasn't a first offense.

Throughout these preliminary proceedings, Maureen had been paying rapt attention, often leaning over to her left and whispering to Stacy, or over to her right to put a reassuring hand on Wade's back. She fidgeted in her seat and shook her head often in incomprehension at the folly and evil of man.

The accused had recently agreed to take a plea of eight years in prison, but had since decided instead to reject the offer, much to the consternation of his court-appointed attorney. He now wanted to go to trial. Judge Wise did her very best to make sure that the accused understood the risk involved. "The plea would be for eight years, with credit for time served, almost four years. If you go to trial, Mr. Jackson, with a prior, your minimum sentence upon conviction would be 15 years, and probably much more. But if you're feeling lucky…"

The accused, despite all evidence to the contrary, was apparently indeed feeling lucky, as he continued to insist upon a trial, and so Judge Wise set jury selection for the following Monday. Maureen bounced in her seat a couple of times as though she wanted to leap to her feet and cry out, "Don't be an idiot! Take the plea! I haven't even heard the evidence yet, and I'm ready to send you away for life!"

Perhaps Mr. Jackson simply liked his chances better in prison than on the outside, and so he was shuffled offstage to await a jury of his peers.

And then, suddenly, after more than four years of waiting, it was our turn.

How much had we all changed over those four years, Andrea, Philip, and I? How much had the country changed? The world?

Right after the accident, I would go for long walks up the east hill of Englewood, New Jersey, rehearsing the speech I would make to the judge and the jury before sentencing, if we were allowed to speak. I would explain who Andrea is, who she is to me, who she has been to us and to her friends, to the people who love her, that she's not a monster who would leave someone to die in the street. Sometimes I just walked and cried and thought, "Forty years, forty years; she'll be over 60 when she comes out of prison, a whole life wasted." I tortured myself with fears of what might happen to her in prison. Some homely inmate would be jealous of her beauty and would slash her face with a sharpened spoon. She would grow old and fat and pasty from the prison food pyramid of starch, starch, and starch. I would die while she was in prison. Her father would die. The pugs would die.

Four years of waiting. And I thought about Mr. Boyd every single day of those years, and for a good part of every day. And I often thought, "I'll bet that Mr. Boyd's brother Wade and his friend Maureen haven't thought about him every single day of these four years." There must have been a day, even if just one, when they didn't think of their lost brother, their lost friend, so caught up were they in the other contours and mundane dramas of their own lives. But the incident was the dominant contour of our lives – of my life – every single day.

Denial, anger, bargaining, depression, acceptance: Elisabeth Kübler-Ross's five stages of grief.

The Denial was the initial shock, the sheer unbelievability of it all. It simply could not have happened. It was a nightmare. I would wake up.

Anger was the questioning of what Mr. Boyd could possibly have been doing out there on a moped at three o'clock in the morning in the first place. And why hadn't Andrea simply taken an Uber? Austin had finally allowed Ubers, after some early resistance from taxi drivers. Why hadn't Mr. Boyd had the bike inspected, why wasn't he wearing a helmet, why didn't he go to the grocery store during the day, like a normal person? Why did all those horrible people feel the need to voice their opinions on line regarding people and an incident they knew nothing about? Oh, plenty of Anger. Gobs and gobs. Anger I haven't even used yet.

I wanted to trade places with Mr. Boyd. That was the Bargaining phase of my grief. I would rather have been dead and have him alive and her free of this, no question, in a heartbeat.

Depression settled in for months, then years. This book represents the Acceptance.

CONDITIONS OF COMMUNITY SUPERVISION

In accordance with the authority of the Community Supervision Law of the State of Texas, you have been placed on community supervision this date April 5, 2022, for a period of Ten (10) years. It is the order of the Court that you shall comply with the following conditions of community supervision:

Commit no offense against the laws of this or any State or of the United States.

Avoid injurious or vicious habits.

Avoid the use of all narcotics, habit forming drugs, alcoholic beverages, and controlled substances.

Avoid persons or places of disreputable or harmful character.

Report to the supervision officer as directed by the judge or the supervision officer or by mail if deported and obey all orders of the Court and the rules and regulations of the Community Supervision and Corrections Department.

Refrain from disorderly conduct, abusive language, or disturbing the peace while present at the office of the Department.

Permit the Supervision Officer to visit you at your home or elsewhere. Work faithfully at suitable employment as far as possible.

Do not change residence without permission and report changes of employment to Supervision Officer as directed.

Remain within Travis County [or another county] or State of Texas unless given permission to depart by the Supervision Officer.

While on community supervision, you must have on your person at all times a current, valid Texas Department of Public Safety photo identification within thirty (30) days of the date of your community supervision.

Support your dependents.

Submit a urine or breath specimen at the direction of the Supervision Officer and pay all costs if required.

Pay to and through the Community Supervision and Corrections Department of Travis County, Texas, in one lump sum or in installments, as set forth in the collection schedule, the following:

Court Costs: $ To be determined Fine: $0.00

Attorney Fees: $0.00

Supervision Monthly Reimbursement Fee of $60.00 per month

Restitution: $ To be determined to Crime Victim's Compensation Program

Crime Stopper Fee of $30.00

Family Violence Center Fine $100.00

Do not operate a motor vehicle without a valid Texas Driver's License and proof of automobile liability insurance.

Surrender your Driver's License for a term of 1 Year.

Participate in, and comply with the rules of the following program(s): Ignition Interlock and follow Ignition Interlock Additional Conditions of Community Supervision.

Other Device: PAM for sixty (60) months; can be removed after one (1) year if no violations.

Complete 300 hours of Community Service Restitution at a place approved and designated by the Community Supervision and Corrections Department.

Report to, cooperate with, and participate in all programs (until successfully discharged), and pay all costs for any classes as determined by the Supervising Officer.

Report to the supervision office for an evaluation for the following program or services and follow the recommendation and pay costs incurred while in the program:

Counseling/Treatment designated by the Supervision Officer Aftercare, as directed by treatment provider

Entered this 5th day of April, 2022, Kate Wise, Judge Presiding

ADDITIONAL CONDITIONS OF COMMUNITY SUPERVISION

Serve 180 days in the Travis County Jail, on or before 10/02/2022; straight Drunk Driving Panel (MADD)

Do not refuse blood or breath tests requested by any law enforcement officers.

Show proof of completion of IOP (Intensive Outpatient treatment) to supervision officer.

Continue with Mental Health services and provide proof to supervising officer.

You are hereby advised that under the law of this State, the Court shall determine the terms and conditions of your community supervision, and may at any time during the period of community supervision, alter or modify the conditions of your community supervision. The Court also has the authority at any time during the period of your community supervision to revoke your community supervision for violation of any of the conditions set out above.

IGNITION INTERLOCK ADDITIONAL CONDITIONS
OF COMMUNITY SUPERVISION

You are ordered to install an ignition interlock system on your personal motor vehicle before the 30th day (05/05/22) after the sentencing date. You will participate in this program for 60 months as a condition of Community Supervision.

Effective immediately, unless otherwise specified by the Court, you may only operate a vehicle equipped with an ignition interlock system. The only exception to this is when a defendant operates a vehicle for their employer and the employer is notified in writing of the defendant's requirement to have an ignition interlock device on their personal vehicle. Article 42.12 of the Texas Code of Criminal Procedure provides that "...if a defendant is required to operate a motor vehicle in the course and scope of the defendant's employment and if the vehicle is owned by the employer, the defendant may operate that vehicle without installation of an approved ignition interlock device if the employer has been notified of that driving privilege restriction and if proof of that notification is with the vehicle. This employment exemption does not apply, however, if the business entity that owns the vehicle is owned or controlled by the defendant whose driving privilege has been restricted." (YOU MUST PROVIDE A COPY OF THE NOTIFICATION YOUR EMPLOYER PLACES IN THE VEHICLE TO YOUR PROBATION OFFICER.)

Do not attempt to adjust, tamper with, alter, or circumvent the ignition interlock system installed, the electrical wiring to the unit, or the ignition system.

Do not remove, or attempt to remove the ignition interlock system from the vehicle.

Do not allow any other individual to access the ignition interlock system. Exceptions must be approved by the Supervision Officer.

Calibration and maintenance of the ignition interlock system must be performed in accordance with each agency's conditions.

Abide by all rules of the agency providing the ignition interlock system. Ignition Interlock System must include the camera component.

If not driving, install a Portable Alcohol Monitor (PAM) and abide by all rules of the agency providing the PAM.

WRITTEN ADMONITIONS ON INELIGIBILITY TO POSSESS FIREARM OR AMMUNITION AND INSTRUCTIONS ON INELIGIBILITY TO VOTE IN STATE OF TEXAS

FIREARMS
NOTE: THIS ADMONITION ONLY APPLIES TO PERSONS CONVICTED OF FELONIES, AND CERTAIN VIOLENT MISDEMEANORS, ON THIS CASE OR ON A PREVIOUS CASE.

You are, by entry of order or judgment, ineligible under Texas law to possess a firearm or ammunition.

Beginning now, if you possess a firearm or ammunition this could lead to charges against you. If you have questions about how long you will be ineligible to possess a firearm or ammunition, you should consult an attorney.

Under Texas Penal Code 46.01(3): a "Firearm" means any device designed, made, or adapted to expel a projectile through a barrel by using the energy generated by an explosion or burning substance or any device readily convertible to that use. "Firearm" does not include a firearm that may have, as an integral part, a folding knife blade or other characteristics of weapons made illegal by Penal Code Chapter 46 and that is (1) an antique or curio firearm manufactured before 1899 or (2) a replica of an antique or curio firearm manufactured before 1899 but only if the replica does not use rim fire or center fire ammunition.

VOTING
WRITTEN INSTRUCTION ON INELIGIBILITY TO VOTE
IN THE STATE OF TEXAS

If you are convicted of a felony, you will not be eligible to register to vote in this State. To regain eligibility to vote after conviction of a felony, you must fully discharge your sentence (including any term of incarceration, parole, or supervision), complete the period of probation ordered by any court, or be pardoned or otherwise released from the disability to vote.

~Ten~

"Jesus promised his disciples three things—that they would be completely fearless, absurdly happy, and in constant trouble."

G.K. Chesterton

July 1, 2022

Dear Travis County Assistant District Attorney,

In case the answer is just going to be "no" regardless of what I do or do not divulge in this letter, I'll save you some time: on pages 5-6, I'm going to ask that the jail portion of my sentence be substituted with 900 additional CSR hours and $15,000.00 in charitable donations. Before that, though, I'd like to explain how I became the person who killed Thomas Boyd that February night back in 2018, who that version of me was, and how I've since become the version of myself who's writing you this letter now. I'm sure that keeping myself out of jail is going to seem like my primary motive, but my reasons for writing this go far beyond that. Simply put, I'm doing this to confront more honestly than I ever have before the role I played in an innocent man's death, in my own undoing, and in the ongoing suffering of everyone I've ever loved. Whether or not you choose to accept the alternative sentence I propose, I know *that I will get something out of writing this letter, and I hope that you will get something out of reading it.*

I can't offer you an excuse for what I did that night, because there isn't one, but what I can offer you is an explanation. To say that I killed a man because I loathed myself would be a colossal oversimplification of the narrative and make little to no sense out of context, but it's a place to start. Seeing as how most happy, well-adjusted people who value their own lives typically don't make a habit of drinking until they can't feel and hopping in their Jeeps without a second thought, my dysfunction was hardly invisible, but it wasn't until recently that I figured out exactly how I'd sunken so low as to turn myself into a full-fledged villain, and I'd like to share that story with you. Since this would be hundreds of pages long if I told the story in full, I'll spare you most of the details, but I'll keep the parts that are relevant (even if they don't appear to be at first).

The things I've done to myself are shameful to admit and agonizing to confront, but I'm through with this business of keeping up appearances, because time and experience have taught me that it's unsustainable. Life is a marathon, not a sprint, and no one finishes a marathon without sweating through their clothes.

Maybe that's why I was always more of a sprinter. Distance running was never my strong suit; I was so harrowed by discomfort of any kind that I insisted it only ever come in short, intense bursts (and with minimal consequent dishevelment), so I started sprinting. I sprinted as fast as I could to myriad imaginary finish lines, away from everything and everyone that mattered in the process. From feeling, trauma, reality, responsibility, myself – anything and everything intense enough to make me crave escape. For years, I was fast enough that I started to think I was unstoppable... until 2018, when I finally encountered something faster than me. Sprinting had once freed me from the burden of having to find out whether or not I had what it took to go the distance. Not only that, it spared me the discomfort of having to see the destruction I left in my wake, having to watch everyone else clean up my messes for me. The silly little 100-meters I ran let me delude myself into believing I was a track star, when in reality I was little more than a clown with a baton. Thomas Boyd's death was hardly the first disaster I caused; it was just the first one I wasn't the victim of, and the first one from which I couldn't get away. Sure, I may have been able to flee the scene in the moment, but I watched every second of the aftermath play out in excruciating detail. Perhaps the most painful part of it for me to witness was when the person I'd turned myself into finally drove away the best friend I've ever had.

An important thing to know about my best friend: her father was killed by a drunk driver when she was four years old. Junie never knew him; whatever memories she had of him were cobbled together from blurry childhood freeze-frames intertwined with secondhand recollections of family members whose lives overlapped with his longer than hers could. She didn't get to grow up with him, be raised by him, have a relationship with him – that chance was taken from her by her father's own best friend, who'd been the one driving the car that night. For eight years, I knew this. For eight years, I comforted her when she cried for the man he might've been. For eight years, I tried and failed to help her answer the questions she would never be able to ask him.

I had shared her outrage when she told me that her boyfriend had tried to talk her into the passenger seat after he'd had a few too many, joined her in admonishing our friends who drove under the influence. I was even in the backseat the day she got into her first accident. I watched her run from the car and crumple immediately into a ball on the sidewalk, knowing that her tears were about far more than a dented fender... and I bet you'll never guess what I did next. We all know that I drank my weight in Long Island iced teas, got behind the wheel of my car, killed an innocent man, left his lifeless body in the middle of the street, and took out my neighbor's fence in one fell swoop. That's not up for debate. What most people don't know is that the carnage didn't end there, because I still had my best friend's heart to pulverize. And Tom's death, while gruesome and senseless, was at least quick... but Junie? No. I took my time with her.

Shortly after being released from jail, I found out she'd been trying to reach me. I never would have imagined that she would want anything to do with me again after what I did, but she'd called and texted dozens of times; she even reached out to a former classmate of ours who lived in the area to see if he could get in to see me. Seeing her name on my phone moved me to tears, filled my heart with hope that maybe our friendship could withstand what I'd put it through. Then, being who I was at the time, I proceeded to punish her mercilessly for being there for me. Two and a half weeks after the wreck, the night my boyfriend walked out my front door for good, she was studying for the MCAT, and I pulled her away to talk me off the ledge. I made her put down her own future to listen to me weep over yet another man who was barely worth a second thought, and then I had the audacity to apologize to her for the death I'd caused. I wish I could say it was because I was sorry, but I had no idea yet at that point how sorry I would be. My apology that night was a shameful ploy for some fanciful idea of absolution, a pardon she had no obligation to provide me, and I'm so glad that she didn't. I could feel how badly she wanted to. Few things in this world will bring you to your knees faster than realizing you're proud of someone for leaving you.

She asked me for help proofreading her medical school admissions essays, and I missed the deadline. I hadn't even bothered to ask when it was. Time and time again, she put her life on hold to be there for me; time and time again, I failed to show up for her in return. Shortly after the wreck, she asked me if I knew anything about the man who died. My response? Knowing won't bring him back. What kind of soulless, pathetic excuse for a human being would say such a thing? I already knew his name; I was just too much of a coward to use it. Even then, she tried to protect me from the downfall I'd brought upon myself, but within a few months, it all became too much for her. Quietly, she pulled away. In January 2020, after a year and a half of radio silence, I reached out to her to clear the air, and she said something I'll never forget: "I don't know if you remember, but my dad passed away because of a drunk driver."

Who had I become that the person I loved most in the world thought for a moment that I could have forgotten how her father died? Who had I become that I could have brushed off her question about Tom like it was nothing, like he was nothing, while I sprinted at full speed away from the guilt I was too hollow to feel? Who had I become that my best friend, the one person outside of my immediate family who'd never turned her back on me for even a second, couldn't bear to look at me anymore?

Most of the people I've spoken with about that night have said the same thing: That could've happened to me. They've excused my mistake without much hesitation – waved it off as nothing more than a wrong-place, wrong-time kind of deal. Just an accident, nothing more. At one point, I agreed with them, but Junie made me see that there was nothing accidental about my being the one behind the wheel that night. I was a deadly combination of self-absorbed and self-destructive, careening towards ruin at 100 miles per hour with my eyes squeezed shut, and I don't know that I would ever have opened them if it hadn't been for her. She showed me that the pain I'd put myself through had turned me into a monster.

Numerous people have told me in the years since that the events of that night don't have to define me. I strongly disagree. The consequences of the choices I made that night aren't the kind that can exist in a vacuum, so I think that having killed a man should necessarily define me, but I also *think that I have the agency to choose the way in which it does. Mediocrity is a luxury I won't allow myself again in this lifetime, so I strive every day to be a slightly less disappointing version of myself than I was the day before, and I'm grateful to report that most days I achieve that goal. Over these last four years, I've learned how to ask for and accept help before my need for it becomes someone else's emergency. I've attended weekly sessions with an EMDR therapist, I've worked with a psychiatric nurse to find the right combination of medications to stabilize me, and I've found friends who support and encourage my sobriety. I've even made professional connections, and they've helped me secure employment with the first company that's ever paid me enough to be able to support myself.*

As a college dropout and convicted felon, I'm under no illusions as to the limitations of my earning potential. In spite of these obstacles, I've managed to work my way up in my field rapidly – so rapidly that I've been the youngest person in the room at nearly every meeting or leadership seminar I've attended, and I've already been able to begin digging myself out of debt. I've built a support system here, I've found more success than I ever would have thought I deserved, and I couldn't possibly be more grateful. Going to jail for six months would mean losing this job, having to move back in with my parents once I'm released, and leaving behind the support system and vital therapeutic relationships I've built in Austin. These things all threaten to sabotage the momentum I've built, and I'm petrified that the stability I've fought for will be compromised; I don't want these patterns of behavior I've worked so hard to break to come back again.

More importantly, if I go away, the crime that I am solely responsible for having committed will yet again be everyone else's problem to solve on my behalf. My parents, who have already poured a hefty portion of their retirement savings into helping me crawl my way out of this hell I created for myself, will be left behind to pay my probation fees and other debts; my colleagues, one of whom has already stuck her neck out for me to get me the job I have now, will have to find someone else to complete the work I signed on to do; the people of Travis County, whom I have already harmed and endangered with my negligence, will have to pay for my stay in the Department of Corrections. Meanwhile, I will be sitting in a cell, adding no value in the community, and living parasitically off the hard work of countless other people. Going to jail now feels like leaving Tom's body in the street again. Going to jail now feels like sprinting.

I don't want to sprint anymore. I want to run this marathon, slow and steady, as I wasn't brave enough to do before.

Now for the specifics of my alternative sentence suggestion: firstly, I would like to increase my mandatory CSR hours from 300 to 1,200.

Considering that I took a man's life away from him and from all those who loved him, this feels like a miniscule price to pay, and it ensures that I'll be able to complete at least the 300 to which I was initially sentenced right here in Travis County. Further, it guarantees that making amends will be a consistent part of my life over the course of the next decade – not just another sprint. Secondly: my understanding is that, in 2012, it cost an average of $59.00 a day to house an inmate in the Travis County Department of Corrections. If we account for inflation, that brings the number to $76.14, but I'm sure there are many other factors at play as well and that my stay would likely be more expensive, so I suspect that $83.34 would be a more accurate estimate. This means that it would cost the county roughly $15,000.00 to incarcerate me for 180 days. With this in mind, for the second part of my alternative sentence suggestion, I would like to make a symbolic donation of my own money (not my parents' money or anyone else's) totaling $15,000.00, $5,000.00 each, to three charities by the end of my probation term. To demonstrate my commitment to this, my intention is to donate the *first $5,000.00 (split three ways at $1,667.00 each) by the end of 2025, and to provide proof of these donations to the court once they have been made. The following organizations will be the recipients: the Austin chapter of Mothers Against Drunk Driving, the Health Alliance for Austin Musicians, and the SIMS Foundation.*

My reasons for choosing MADD need no explanation, but allow me to shed some light on the other two. I selected HAAM because Tom was a longtime guitar player and Austin resident who had an arteriovenous malformation, which is why he was on his way to the grocery store at 3 o'clock in the morning that February. He was prone to sunlight-induced seizures, and wasn't able to go out during the day. I'd like to donate to an organization whose mission is to help other Austin musicians like him who are battling significant health issues that interfere with their daily activities and quality of life. I chose SIMS because I'm a professionally trained singer who's struggled with mental illness and substance abuse issues since my teen years, and I would like to help people like me get the help they need before they end up spinning themselves into a web too large and complex to unravel. All three of these causes are profoundly meaningful to me, and I believe they would have been meaningful to Tom, as well.

If I were still the person I was when this happened, if I were still a danger to myself and others, it would make perfect sense to spend upwards of $15K keeping me behind bars, but I laid that person to rest a long time ago. Since then, inexplicably, I've become someone upon whom others depend. My friends and colleagues often come to me for advice, which is frankly disorienting, knowing what a serial screw-up I once was. I'm even starting to be able to rely on myself. I don't see the value in allowing me to continue draining resources when I have become someone who has the means to create them.

As of this writing, I've begun taking steps to finally extricate my family from this situation. I elected not to fight for an occupational license because the price tag associated with doing so was too high for me to afford on my own, and I didn't want to pass yet another legal cost along to my parents. What I can easily afford, however, is a local bus pass. Now I take the bus to and from work, my parents are no longer paying for my insurance, and I've given my car back to my father. My lawyer Kevin also told me he could work on getting the IOP portion of my sentence waived if I could provide proof of my consistent participation in private mental health treatment over the last several years, but I elected not to have him do that, either. I chose to enroll myself in IOP because I thought it was the conscientious thing to do. I paid for it out of my own pocket, and had perfect attendance in the program. On the 18th I began aftercare, for which I have already paid, and I also intend to pay whatever legal fees are associated with presenting this letter (which my attorneys had no idea I was writing until it arrived in their inboxes) to the court. The last thing my representation offered to do was have my PAM testing requirement changed from four times a day to three (as it was during pretrial), but I decided not to fight for this accommodation, either. Having to take my tests at regular intervals throughout the day keeps me in a rhythm, and as someone who struggles to create structure for myself, I've actually found it more helpful than inconvenient. The PAM payments have also been coming out of my own pocket – but this isn't about money. It never has been.

What this is about is responsibility. The fact of the matter is that there is nothing I will ever be able to do to undo the damage I've done. I'm painfully aware of that. I will never be able to give Wade the opportunity to give his brother the guitar he bought him for his birthday – the one that now hangs in Wade's house, waiting for the day it'll finally be played. I will never be able to give Maureen the chance to hear the songs that Tom wrote for her, or Tom the opportunity to play them. I will never be able to unsay the inexcusable things I said to Junie, or give her the chance to spend one more day together that isn't overshadowed by my failure to be the friend she deserved. I will never be able to make this okay… but what I can do is this. I want to do this, and I intend to one way or another. I hope I've made it clear that I'm not asking to be freed from accountability for my actions – what I'm asking for is your oversight while I hold myself solely and personally accountable for said actions, for all the harm those actions caused, and for righting my own wrongs as best I can over time, through long-term sustained effort. Living under a microscope these past few years has been taxing, but I believe that it's helped me to grow, and I want to leverage the force of that pressure to make sure I stay grown and keep growing.

For the first two decades of my life, I sought refuge in bunkers of submission and dependence. That asylum came at the expense of my agency and self-respect, turning me into a person I loathed. For the next decade and beyond, I wish to play an active, participatory role in my own redemption, because sitting idly by while it's done unto me feels like taking the easy way out. Truth be told, the mere thought of seeing all of these commitments through – the job, the counseling and treatment, the CSR hours, the donations – absolutely exhausts me, but that's how I know it's exactly what I should do. I felt the same way about writing this letter, mainly because most days I want nothing more than to astral project out of my body and punch myself in the face as hard as I possibly can. I'm still furious with myself for the things I've done and for the person I've allowed myself to be, more so than I will ever be able to articulate to you. Knowing that I've been the lone architect of my own misfortune since Day One makes it difficult to root for myself, but I am in my own corner now because so many other people stood here first, and my days of punishing people for believing in me are over.

No one ever needed me to be a track star. What people needed from me (and what I needed from myself) was to be reliable, to be steadfast, to follow through on my commitments and carry my own weight at my own sustainable pace. As complicated and stormy as my relationship with myself may be, I know now that the only way I can be someone worth fighting for is by taking care of and respecting my own needs, rather than viewing them as demons to outrun. By refusing to put my own mask on before assisting others, I'm forcing them to perform life-saving measures that wouldn't have been necessary if I'd had the wherewithal to first make sure I could keep breathing on my own. I am not invincible, I never have been, and I never will be. So now, this is me putting my mask on, years later than I should have, praying that air might still flow.

Before the mediation, I was told, "if the parties reach a positive under-standing and wish to use the outcome for the benefit of the parties, the specific terms of the plea agreement can be revisited." This vaguely suggested some sort of negotiation, but I never for a moment entertained the idea of hijacking the mediation – something meant to heal and restore – for use as a vehicle of self-advocacy. A genuine apology has no agenda. As the people who were most hurt by what I did, I'm thankful Wade and Maureen sat down with me at all, and to have asked them to show me more clemency than they already had at that point would have been a gross misuse of my opportunity to speak with them. It's not their job to feel for me, to forgive me, to help me, just as it wasn't Junie's job to absolve me. Those things are my responsibility. I was also told before the mediation that "the final determination to change any terms of the plea agreement on the part of the State would rest with the District Attorney's Office, and not with the participants in the mediation process," which is why I'm directing this missive to you.

Please know that I recognize that this is not how the system works. I under-stand that people can't just write lengthy letters, pepper them with SAT vocab words, and send them to the District Attorney's office with the expectation that doing so will magically free them from the shackles they placed upon their own feet. Rest assured that I have no such expectation. I also recognize that the plea deal I accepted was practically unheard of for an offense as severe as mine, so I hope that you won't interpret my decision to ask this of you now as a sign that I'm not immensely appreciative of the mercy I've already been shown, because nothing could be further from the truth. I'm asking this of you now because, through this process, I have turned my life around to the point where I have finally found enough self-respect to be able to show up for myself. Not a lot of people could have made it through all of this self-inflicted suffering without giving up on themselves, but I did, and that counts for something. I'm not going to add being too intimidated to write and send this letter to the list of things for which I must forgive myself.

Lastly, irrespective of the outcome, I would like to take this opportunity to say thank you. Not just for taking the time to read this, but for the kindness and professionalism I've been extended throughout this process by every member of the criminal justice system. Lord knows I haven't always respected myself, but I've been treated with nothing but decency and compassion by this system, and that's something for which I will always be grateful. No matter what happens next, I will be out here moving heaven and earth every day for the rest of my life to make sure that no one has to see, read, hear, say, or even think my name in a court of law ever again.

That is a promise.

With gratitude,
Andrea Scott

"Do something every day for no other reason than you would rather not do it, so that when the hour of dire need draws nigh, it may find you not unnerved and untrained to stand the test."

William James

But the letter to the ADA fell on deaf ears, if letters can fall on ears. On deaf eyes? On blind eyes? Whatever. As with most signposts in life – birth, school, court, marriage, kids, illness, and death – what constitutes a seismic event for you, to most others may be just another Tuesday morning between 9:55 and 10:20 a.m. The upshot was six months in jail, which was a helluva lot better than the 40 years in prison maximum we had been looking at four years and eight months earlier.

However, when it came time for Andrea to surrender for her six-month jail sentence, no one seemed to know where she should go to do that. Our lawyer thought that perhaps she should go directly to the county jail in Del Valle, which didn't seem quite right.

So I started calling around.

I called one number for the jail and got no answer. When I called another, the line was reported to be out of service. I finally reached someone, a very nice young woman, who transferred me to a very nice young man, but neither of them seemed to know where we should go either.

I was referred to Jail and Warrant Information. I spoke to another very nice woman who tried to help, but then interrupted herself to ask what the charge was. When I said, "Intoxication Manslaughter," she apologized and said, "Oh, I'm sorry. We're Misdemeanors. You want Felonies."

"We're Misdemeanors." Now there's a sentence I bet she never thought she'd say, back when she was dressing up as a princess and stumbling around in mom's heels, dreaming of being a Kardashian one day.

Well, I don't really want felonies, but I think you might be on the right track in this instance.

It was suggested that I try "Bonding," which sounded kinky, then

"Booking," then the Court Clerk, and I began to wonder, "Hasn't anyone ever done this before?"

At last, there seemed to be a consensus surrounding Central Booking, at either 500 West 10th Street or 509 West 11th Street. So that I wouldn't break out in a cold sweat on the 2nd of October, 2022, I made a dry run on the 1st. This was the same building that housed the courtroom where Andrea had entered her plea six months before. So do you turn yourself in at the courthouse? On a Sunday? That didn't seem quite right.

There was a bell to ring on the façade of the building, so I pressed it, and as I peered into the darkened foyer, an officer in uniform began to emerge from the murky depths of the lobby. He opened the door, leaned out, and asked if he could help me. He seemed strong and competent, no nonsense, like Ed Harris in "Apollo 13."

"My daughter is supposed to surrender tomorrow for a six-month jail sentence. Does she come here?"

"Yes," he said, nodding and with no hesitation, then closed the door. And I believed him. Because he was the first person I had spoken to in 24 hours who seemed certain in his knowledge.

Day 1: October 2, 2022, 0.57% of the way through her sentence

Andrea kissed the dogs goodbye and cried. I managed to hold it together, because she once told me how much it hurts her to see me cry. But I cried all the way home in the car. If drivers in other cars glanced to the side, they must have wondered what was going on: an old lady in a brown Kia Sportage wailing and sniffling.

The nice officer, a different one from the day before, had come to the door when we buzzed, and asked me to wait in the car, that Andrea could phone me within a few minutes if she was indeed being booked. But we figured she wouldn't be able to bring her phone, so we had left it in the car. All she had with her were the clothes on her back, a piece of paper with some phone numbers scrawled on it (because nobody knows phone numbers by heart anymore, since they're stored in our phones), and a bag with two empty bottles of prescription medications, in the hope that the pharmacy at the jail would keep her adequately stocked.

Because we were without a phone, the officer asked me to wait outside on a bench while he took Andrea inside to make sure that she should indeed surrender herself to begin her six-month sentence. (He should have consulted with yesterday's guy.) Andrea and I hugged, which is unusual for us. Then she glanced over her shoulder briefly as she went inside and we smiled ruefully at one another.

I paced for a few minutes, too agitated to sit down, and then the officer came to the door, poked his head out, and said, "We're gonna keep her. You have a nice day." I thanked him and wished him the same, and he ducked back inside.

"We're gonna keep her." That was it.

Then I burst into tears and went back to Andrea's apartment to pick up the dogs.

Thus began six months of "This is a prepaid call from – Andrea Scott – an inmate at the Travis County Correctional Complex. To accept this call, press zero..."

This is a letter to myself from today to the Me of February 9, 2018.

Dear Mary Kay,

Right now your world as you knew it, is over; it truly is. It will be a long time, if ever, before you are able to look back on happy memories – Christmas, beach vacations, school assemblies, youth theater performances, baby pictures – and feel anything other than loss.

To have a child is to lose a child, because that child will grow into an adult, and the child they were at every stage of their lives will be lost to you forever. You see her in photographs and in your mind's eye, but you will never see that infant, that toddler, that child, that adolescent, that young adult ever again. You will never again pick her up under the armpits and hoist her onto your hip in the crook of your arm. And The Occurrence overlays another kind of death onto those lost memories and feelings, that you will never feel the same way about anything ever again.

Right now you're alone in New Jersey, while those you love are down in Texas handling the early stages of this tragedy. You try to stay busy working with your students at school, but The Occurrence and the fear are never far from your mind. This is the first thing you think about every morning when your eyelids flutter open and it's the last thing you think about before you mercifully lose consciousness at night, and it will be this way forever. It will. That will never change.

You go for long walks, and torture yourself with the uncertainties. The maximum prison sentence for these crimes is 40 years. Andrea will grow old in prison. Her dogs will die, her cats will die, her father will die, you will die before she walks free again. She is responsible for the death of another human being, a moral injury from which she – and you – will never recover.

But I am telling you, from a little over four years out, that there is more mercy in the world than you think. Yes, the moral injury is there, and always will be, the guilt, the ruminating on what could have been, what might have been. But there is no time machine. And, as you've often told others who obsess about the past, long before you had to take this advice yourself: Don't look back. We're not going that way.

God is good and Fate is kind. There is forgiveness. There is compassion. You will meet people you would never have met otherwise, and these people will become as important and as vital to your life as anyone you have ever known. You will meet people at First Presbyterian Church of Englewood, New Jersey, then at Trinity Presbyterian in Flower Mound, Texas, and then at St. Peter Lutheran in Northlake, Texas. Police officers and corrections officers and lawyers and judges will be kind. Even Tom's family and friends will be kind, and even forgiving. Friends and family will rally. Prayers will be answered.

Andrea will not go to prison for 40 years, but to county jail for six months, followed by ten years of probation. There will be restrictions and expenses, but nothing insurmountable. There will be daily reminders of the enormity of the event, but you wouldn't need those daily reminders anyway, as The Occurrence is never far from your thoughts and never will be. That prediction, at least, will come true.

But even that very first day, when you told the very first person the beginning of the story that would redefine the rest of your life, because you had to tell her so that you could explain why you had to leave work abruptly and fly down to Texas for at least a week, that person reached out to you like the hand of God and said, "You know, I read this article in the New Yorker magazine a few months ago about this organization that offers peer support to people who have unintentionally taken a life…"

And so even in those first moments, you were shown the way, the only way, the only way out: through. And you met the people of what was then Accidental Impacts, now The Hyacinth Fellowship, a brave group of people who struggle with their own humanity every day and who understand your struggles the way no one else can.

And you will find a way to invest what happened with meaning and with purpose. Because you have no other choice. This is your life.

Be not afraid. Onward.

~Eleven~

"I'm going down
Follow if you want, I won't just hang around
Like you'll show me where to go
I'm already out of foolproof ideas, so don't ask me how
To get started, it's all uncharted..."

"Uncharted" by Sara Bareilles

Day 2: October 3, 2022, 1.14% of the way through Andrea's sentence

Thanks to Philip, my husband and IT guy, we spent most of that first afternoon online and on the phone trying to fund a commissary account and a communication tablet for Andrea to use in jail. We had to have the funds sent to her jail account through Western Union, and had our credit cards declined several times because when you try to send money to someone in jail, the credit card companies, understandably, suspect fraud.

We also went 'round and 'round with the tablet-funding people because there were two separate entities that were connected, but don't do the same thing, and the links on the Sheriff's website took us there anyway. When I say "we," I mean Philip, because I wasn't even comfortable with the technology in the 20th century, much less the 21st. If he dies before I do, I will be instantly thrown back into the stone age. What was the matter, really, with snail mail and outdoor privies?

I am reminded of the priceless, hilarious David Sedaris and his husband Hugh. Hugh handles all technology for the household and Sedaris has said that if Hugh dies first and the refrigerator stops working, he wouldn't know what to do and so would have to turn it into an armoire. That's me. If anything happens to Philip, I might as well throw all the electronics out the window (which I would like to do anyway) because I can't navigate any of them. I just don't think the way the crazy people who designed and built these things think. Every time I'm asked for my password, I break out in a cold sweat. Hackers can get into all my accounts, pimply teenage boys in their parents' basements can get into all my accounts. Know who can't get into all my accounts? Me.

Day 3: October 4, 2022, 1.7% of the way through
To: Caroline, NYC
Missy Caroline! I think you can send just notes and letters and cards, drawings, if you want, anything in regular mail. There are some restrictions on books. I think she just wants to hear from people.

It's dreadful, I must say. I just keep looking at the clock and thinking, what is she doing now...? And now...? And now...? And now...? And now...?

And she wasn't allowed to bring her prescription meds in with her, of course, just the scrips from the doctor, so I hope those can be filled quickly. They have a pretty extensive on-site pharmacy with a pharmacist, two pharmacy assistants, and the Texas corrections system apparently fills 7,500 prescriptions a week. Sheesh again.

We have the pugs, and the cats' noses are out of joint because they're relegated to one half of the house. Catborough vs. Dogville. My money is on the cats. The dogs are all bark...

Day 8: October 9, 2022, 4.54%

To: Pastor Jonah

I appreciate the observation on our isolation, especially in the wake of SARS-CoV-2. I heard a while back -- and I think this was even before SARS-CoV-2 -- that bottled water sales had surpassed beer sales for the first time, and someone observed that this was a bad sign because beer is a beverage generally enjoyed with others, while bottled water is usually consumed alone while on the treadmill or out jogging. Alone. Ah, but aren't we all? Alone, that is. Vance Packard's "A Nation of Strangers" was published in 1974, so this has been going on for a long time.

And I particularly worry about it, working with middle schoolers, because many are suffering from what I can only describe as social PTSD in the wake of the pandemic.

Some time back, I heard about a community outside Austin that had been established for the homeless by the man who owned the land. He built tiny houses for residents with front porches, because he said that they don't need just roofs; they need communities. So residents have to work, they have to participate in therapy and recovery, if needed. And they are encouraged to sit outside on their porches and know one another, reach out to one another, establish community and accountability. Not just so that they won't do the bad things, but so that they will do the good things.

Day 9: October 10, 2022, 5.11%

To: Doris

Downstairs D! Philip has spoken with Andrea and said she sounded pretty good. She can call us but, of course, we can't call her. No phones in cells, apparently.

Philip is heading down there today to do some Uber driving in Austin, where it's easier and more lucrative than DFW because everything is closer together. Up here it's tough to make money because everything is 45 minutes away from everything else. DFW is like L.A. in its spread as well as the amount of traffic. So Philip wants you to know that his earnings are all offset by miles driven and associated depreciation of the vehicle. Down there he can get to the airport in 15 minutes, back into town to drop someone off and pick someone else up, back to the airport, maybe three or four fares an hour.

Day 11: October 12, 2022, 6.25%

We received a yellow carbon copy sheet in the mail from Andrea. This was titled "Return to Sender Contraband Mail" and listed all the many items that inmates cannot receive. We had attempted to send her a blank journal from Fine Keepsakes in El Paso, but it was returned with the odd notation "Not from a book store. Could not locate." Could not locate? Wasn't the book right there in your hand? What was it you couldn't locate? The bookstore? It's in El Paso.

The sheet went on to detail what constitutes "contraband" at the Travis County Correctional Complex. Andrea's notes to us are in brackets [X].

*"The following list of items are considered **contraband**. The **marked** items were received, rejected and **all contents** of the letter/package are being returned.*

[For future reference, this is the fascist list of things I can't have mailed to me. I can buy a sketchbook through the commissary, when available, or get a composition book through a program (and then stop attending). I can also get a legal pad through the commissary, when available.]

Money: *negotiable instr #$ (cash, check, or money order). Money orders or cashier's checks only must be sent to: Inmate Trust Fund.*

Stationary *(sic),* ***Games, Documents, Etc.:*** *postage stamps, metered/stamped envelopes; blank paper; blank or addressed envelopes; address labels, sticky notes, stickers, tape, lamination,* ***no adhesives;*** *art supplies including writing instruments, water colors/paint, glitter, glue, felt, ribbon, color pencils, beads, magnets, etc.; blank/unsigned greeting cards or postcards; greeting cards with musical devices or attachments/over 8x10/glitter;*

hard plastic items or cardboard items; credit cards, phone cards, driver's license, photo ID's; games or playing/flash cards, CDs, DVDs, audio or video tapes; original documents, birth certificates, marriage certificates, social security cards, car titles, etc., items over 8x10/posters.

Photographs, Drawings & Letters: *photographs over 8x10; polaroid photos, framed photos or albums; slides or negatives – no lamination; photos/drawings depicting gang related signs (includes any hand signs), symbols or tattoos, altered or blacked out photos; photographs, photocopies or drawings depicting partial/nude persons (including baby photos), excessive violence, abusive/unlawful activity, obscene gestures, sexual content, gun, racial material, hankerchief (sic) drawings.*

Hazards: *perfume/cologne, body secretions, lipstick, saliva or **unknown substances** on paper/letters/literature; substances such as drugs, tobacco products, medication; food, clothing, shoes, jewelry, hygiene items, napkins; hair, feathers, flowers, plants, etc.; sharp or metal objects including staples, paper clips, etc.*

Letters, Literature, Books: *books, magazines, or newspapers not (sic) accepted must be sent in directly from U.S. publisher, publication supplier, or bookstore; return address must have a store hand stamp, no storefronts, no individuals; torn out pages from any books or magazines; more than 25 pages of internet copies or prints; hardback books, oversize books, spiral binding; maps, calendars, mail order catalogs, coded books, sketch books, blank writing journals, posters, diagrams; literature depicting violence, abusive/unlawful activity, gang related, obscene sexual contents, weapons, or racial materials, nudity, drugs, Wicca, Santa Muerte; damaged/discolored/soiled used books/magazines; correspondence enclosed/inscribed-no writing; excessive books/literature, allowed only **2 books** and **2 magazines** in a shipment.*

Safety and Security: *contains material regarding safety and security of correctional facilities, law enforcement, criminal activity or drug related material; information does not belong to the inmate currently incarcerated – 3rd party mail; threatening or harassing language.*

Travis County does not have any control over the time it takes the Post Office
to return the mail back to the senders."

My biggest takeaways were... Bodily secretions? Wicca? %-)

Day 13: October 14, 2022, 7.39%
To: Dan Paterson
Andrea seems to be doing okay. She has three roommates (she's in a top
bunk at 5'3" and no ladder %-) and says she's "making friends." Ultimately,
we're hoping that this will be a positive learning and eye-opening experience for her. She will be able to see a side of life and some of the struggles
others face that most of her peers will never know.

Day 16: October 17, 2022, 9.09%
DD! The in-person visit was good, but weird. Visits are only 20 minutes,
and you have to do that iconic "Law & Order" thing where you both pick
up phone receivers on either side of a plexiglass divider. We both had to
stand, because her cord was too short for her to sit down, and my back
was to a window, so when I sat down, because of the reflection, I couldn't
see her. So we both stood there for 20 minutes, like the losers we are.
The website where you make the appointment to visit is at pains to say
that phones and phone stations are sanitized between visitors, but sista
puh-lease.

She actually seems pretty good. She looks good. She was wearing a baggy
maroon top, like a tee shirt, and baggy grey and white horizontal striped
pants. "New outfit?" I asked.

She has three roommates, and when I asked her where she goes to the
bathroom, she said, "In front of three other women." So the toilet and sink
are right smack dab in the cell. I asked if she likes her cellmates and she said
yes. I asked if they like her and she said, "Everybody likes me."

And when she met with the counselor last week, the first thing the woman said was, "You don't belong here." When Andrea perked right up at that, the counselor hastened to assure her, "Oh, don't get me wrong. You have to stay here. But you don't belong here."

I'm sure she makes life easier for her cellmates and for the staff at the jail. Imagine what they've seen. All of it. To have at least one person under their supervision who is just going to follow the rules and eat the lousy hospital-grade food must be such a relief to everyone.

Day 20: October 21, 2022, 11.36%
Dear Anna Louise,

I asked Joanne early on if she had filled you in on Andrea's situation, and she said yes, so I felt comfortable talking about it when we all got together. I don't like to just spring it on people, assuming that they know, because it can be very shocking, of course, and then it takes a long time to tell the whole story. And there are also people who have been personally affected by drunk driving, so you never know if someone is going to be "triggered."

There is a small "outdoor space" at the jail, but the walls around it are high. I asked if she can at least see the sky and she said yes, but there is a net over the opening. (So she's sort of like Jesse Pinkman near the end of "Breaking Bad" when he's kept in the hole outside and Ricky Hitler lowers stuff to him in a metal bucket.) No real opportunities for exercise.

She says, "Don't get me wrong; it's not fun," but I think it's turning out to be a more positive experience than she might have feared. It's all a learning curve, and she's very empathetic, so I'm sure she's a good person for the other inmates to talk to. She really "gets" people.

Day 25: October 26, 2022, 14.2%
Dear Alan,

Andrea has been writing on the backs of blank medical forms, but she was able to purchase loose lined paper from the commissary, so I'm not sure why blank journals are not allowed. I get the whole spiral thing, because

I suppose you could unwind it and use it to hang yourself or garrote someone else. But blank paper?

A loophole: apparently there exist journals with prompts, like Christian journals asking for your responses to particular Bible passages, and you can evidently send those, and then inmates can write whatever they want in them, not just responses to the prompts.

She wouldn't mind hearing about France at all. I have to say this about my kid: she has never begrudged anyone else's good time, even when her times have sometimes been shitty. She really doesn't have that comparison/envy gene. She says, "comparison is the thief of joy," or something like that. She genuinely celebrates everyone else's wins, and doesn't compare them to her losses. And she seems sincerely grateful for her wins.

She doesn't like unfairness. That's where she seems to draw the line. And she understands how unfair life is, so she gets it. She's in a place now where she knows how much more fortunate she is than most of the people she's in there with. They haven't had the advantages she's had going in, and they won't have the advantages she will have coming out. Most of them never had a chance from the get-go. I think she's more determined than ever to address some of those disparities when she's back. I'm proud of her.

Frankly, I think she's better off in there than we are here on the outside. People are being pushed onto subway tracks. Meanwhile, she and her cellmates were laughing and joking last evening while she was on the call with me.

The funny thing is: they put these people together under these circumstances on the inside, they bond, and then it's a condition of their probation/parole that they're not supposed to hang around with people like them. Whaddaya gonna do? %-)

Day 31: November 1, 2022, 17.61%
Dear Ben,
She sounded okay the last time we spoke. The mattress is about three

inches thick and lumpy, so she and her cellmates tend to put their scratchy wool blankets under the mattress for a little extra padding between them and the metal frame. There is no pillow, so she bunches up a sweatshirt and uses that.

We blended the pugs and the cats last weekend, and it went surprisingly well. I think when you eliminate the mystery of what's on the other side of the door, they just think that the "other" smells funny, and they tend to give one another a wide berth. We won't leave them alone together, though; they only get supervised visitation. %-)

Day 32: November 2, 2022, 18.18%
Dear Alan,

Back at the old house in Austin, where Andrea was living when the incident occurred, we had a neighbor across the street who it turns out had also killed someone with his car. He was sober, it was night, and he came up over a blind hill and ran over a woman who was standing in the middle of the road facing him. The woman was deeply troubled, as it turns out, and suffered from crippling depression and other mental issues. Another neighbor of ours assured our friend that the circumstances sound as though she was waiting for him, that she was essentially committing suicide by car, and that he was the unlucky instrument of her will.

Day 37: November 7, 2022, 21.02%
To: Kevin Lawford

I have a few items I would like to run by you, per Andrea:

We turned in the PAM device when she entered TCCC on October 2, and they cheerily informed us that they have a brand new model available when she comes out of jail in late March 2023. (A new model. Yippee!) At one point you had mentioned that we might be able to get the court to waive the PAM when she comes out of jail because she will have been on it for six months prior to incarceration (as well as back in 2018) and then in jail for six months, so that would be the year, and then some. Are we still looking at that scenario, getting the reintroduction of the PAM waived?

In the same vein, her driver's license was suspended for a year starting April 5, 2022, when the case was resolved. Will she need an Occupational License to look for/go to a job at the end of March, or will her license be reinstated by that time? If the former, is that a process we can start getting in motion now, so she can be up and running with a valid license of some sort by the end of March?

At one point, you had mentioned perhaps petitioning for a brief furlough from jail for the holidays. We consulted Andrea, and she does not want to do that. When she comes out of jail, she wants it to be for good, as it would be very difficult, emotionally and psychologically, for her to come out for a brief period and then have to go back in again, so she would rather serve the sentence in one go.

Along those lines, we are wondering about early release to house arrest with an ankle monitor. Andrea has apparently heard through one of the post officers that TCCC is suffering from over-crowding, understaffing, and the resultant poor conditions. Some inmates have reportedly been moved to other counties, and some awaiting trial have been sent home with ankle monitors on house arrest. And now the CDC is warning about a resurgence of respiratory illness, SARS-CoV-2, and a bad flu season this fall and winter, especially in crowded institutions.

Is there any possibility that we could petition the Court, the D.A., the family to have Andrea released to our custody on house arrest for the remainder of her sentence? If not now, then perhaps starting during the holidays, for the last half of her sentence?

She initially appeared to us to be doing well, but we have recently noticed some struggles with recurring depression, anxiety, a reemergence of her eating disorder. And her meds are all over the place. The inmates are given nothing productive to do: no KP duty, no laundry detail, no indoor or outdoor exercise. They just sit there.

For the four and a half years awaiting trial, she was active, productive, kept her nose clean, and moved up in her career. This seems unnecessarily cruel and pointless, in my opinion. Punishment, yes. But to what end, really?

I get it. Jail is jail. And we were extremely lucky to get the deal we got, thanks to you and Daniel. But we're also seeing what's going on outside, violent criminals with lengthy records being released without bail every single day to reoffend, and we're asking ourselves if society is safer with Andrea Scott on the inside.

Someone reading this email might charge me with trying to exercise "white privilege." Okay, guilty as charged. (After all, what the hell good is "white privilege" if you don't use it? If I'm supposed to feel guilty about an immutable characteristic, I might as well reap the alleged attendant benefits.) Most of the TCCC inmates are white and they, along with their peers of color, are all experiencing the same pointless detention. Perhaps Travis County should rethink the design and content of its detention programs. I'm not sure I see the "correctional" aspect of this program, so much as the pointlessly punitive.

We are still attempting to navigate the vagaries of contraband (e.g., no blank journals, for some unknown reason), but if you would like to send her a note, a card, a letter…

Please let us know if you can help out with any of the items above.

Day 38: November 8, 2022, 21.59%
To: Kevin Lawford
Andrea asked me to correct one thing on a previous email. She's now been told that they're only supposed to have three hours per week outside of the cell (not three hours per day). But it hardly matters, because they're not getting that either.

We're concerned about her mental health, which she says has "taken a nose dive" over the past several weeks, and she began to cry on the phone with us, which is not like her. Philip submitted an Online Inmate Mental Health Form through tcsheriff.org, and I'm going to give them a call on their 24/7 line as soon as I finish this email.

Please let us know how your consultation goes with your colleague who has jail expertise. If there is a way that she could qualify for house arrest under our care, she would be able to see her regular therapist, and we could take care of any physical health issues she might be presenting with as well.

Day 39: November 9, 2022, 22.16%
To: Alan

I think it is possible to send reading material from Amazon, but not too much, as they have the word "excessive" in there. That's pretty subjective. She was struggling yesterday, crying on the phone. I think after more than a month the novelty has worn off and now she's just looking at the next five months. But she rallied by the end of the day after talking with her best friend on the phone, so now she's more settled down and determined to just soldier on.

Philip filled out an online form about our concerns and I called them, and they were very responsive, sending two counselors to talk with her, with the post officer present, one of the ones she likes. They've arranged for her to meet weekly with one of their counseling interns, which will be a good thing, I think. I'm sure the young counselors are very motivated and all caught up with the latest data, theories, and techniques, and Andrea is very articulate and knows how therapy works, so I'm sure it will be a good thing for both her and for the counselor trainee. She really benefits from being able to talk things through with someone who knows how to listen.

She called back again last evening, after we had registered our concerns, and she sounded much better.

I miss NYC so much. There's no place like it. The last time I was there was in January 2020. I took the bus into Port Authority, walked all the way down to Abingdon Square Park in Greenwich Village and met a wonderful old theater friend for brunch. We sat and talked for a couple of hours, then went out and sat in the park and talked for a couple hours more. We joked that you had to be a gay couple with a Frenchie in order to come into Abingdon Square Park, because we were the only two people there who didn't fit that description. The weather was beautiful, a cool and crisp January Sunday morning.

I walked back up to Port Authority, feeling fine, and got on my bus back out to Jersey. Forty-five minutes later when I disembarked, I tried to thank the driver, but had inexplicably lost my voice. The next morning I was too fatigued to get out of bed, and I couldn't talk anyway, so I stayed home from school for the next three days. All I had was laryngitis, fatigue, and a dry cough. I finally went back in to school on the Thursday and joined the half dozen of my colleagues who had also experienced something "weird" that winter. Flu-like, but not the flu. Everyone had had their flu shots, but those hadn't worked, and neither did the doctor-prescribed Tamiflu.

Two months later we shut down the world.

I think that January 2020 week may have been my first experience of SARS-CoV-2, the next one coming in September of 2021.

So many stories to be written and told...

If you want to get more impatient with the contraband restrictions at TCCC, here's another one for you. I had Amazon send Andrea a copy of a book called "My Year of Rest and Relaxation." It's a novel about a woman who is depressed, so she tries to sleep for a year (and the "merry mishaps" that occur). I thought she might appreciate it under her circumstances.

It was sent back because the front cover depicted "partial nudity." A no-no. If you looked really, really closely, and I mean super-close, you could just barely make out the shadowy outline of a nipple through the diaphanous bodice. Horrors!

This means that every Jane Austen book cover (which this one parodies) and every great work of art in the Metropolitan Museum constitutes contraband at Travis County Correctional Complex.

Absurd.

Day 40: November 10, 2022, 22.72%

DD! You are certainly free to write to whatever authority figure you please. I know you're a writer of letters to authority! I don't think they would retaliate against Andrea. We have another friend in Maryland who is as up-in-arms as you are about the contraband. He's trying to send her script pages for a TV show he thinks she would be interested in ("Severance"), and these keep bouncing back to him, for some unknown reason.

She also says she's allowed to have earphones for her tablet, but no dental floss. So you're allowed to hang yourself with your earphone cord, but not with your dental floss.

What I object to most is that they're not given anything to do. I thought at least there would be some structure, kitchen patrol, laundry, cleaning, something. But, no. They just sit in their cells all day long. It's cruel. She'd be better off on a chain gang, outside in the sun, picking up trash from the side of the road. At least she would get some fresh air, vitamin D, exercise, structure, even "purpose" of a sort.

It's just so wrong. Especially with hardened, career criminals being released on the street every day to reoffend.

Because they live in close quarters, and she's in a cell with three other women, Andrea has bonded with many of the other inmates, most of whom are in jail for minor drug-related or financial crimes of one kind or another. She says, "When you get out of jail, your probation officer will caution you that you're not allowed to associate with others who have a criminal history. But often, the only people you know, and the only people who are willing to socialize with you are others who have a criminal history. The only places you're allowed to live are places where other people with criminal backgrounds are allowed to live."

We really have to do some serious work on our criminal justice system.

Day 44: November 15, 2022, 25%

To: Bart

Andrea has struggled over the past almost-five years with whether or not to tell people about her situation, when to tell people about her situation. She has ten years of probation and 300 hours of community service to work off, so if she wants people to be close, she has to let them in on her life. She worries that if she tells people too soon, they won't be invested in her enough to continue the relationship, but if she waits too long, they might feel as though she was withholding the information from them, waiting until they had become attached to her, like playing a dirty trick on them, sucking them in.

How and when do you tell someone about the worst day of your life, the worst thing you've ever done?

Day 45: November 15, 2022, 25.56%

Dear Alan,

She's been struggling lately. I just found out yesterday that they haven't prescribed her antidepressants for her, so she's been off them for 45 days, cold turkey, which is not recommended, to say the least. She's on a "mood stabilizer," whatever that is. So she's been having bouts of crying for the past week or so, especially since the reality of being only a quarter of the way through her sentence is sinking in.

She also hasn't gotten any of the mail that I've sent, nor any of the four books I've sent. I sent the first couple of books so long ago, I thought she would have had them and read them by now. But she hasn't had any. So she just sits there with nothing. What is the point, really? Punishment? I guess, if spending the rest of your life knowing you were responsible for the death of another human being is not punishment enough.

I'll bet you can't treat prisoners at Guantanamo this way. The Geneva Convention would never allow it.

Day 46: November 16, 2022, 26.14%
Dear Alan,

Pink form: "Literature on drug use, names of drugs not allowed." Earlier I had tried to have sent to Andrea a copy of a book with a cover picture deemed too sensational, provocative, and pornographic. Yes, if you looked hard at it really, really closely, you might find the merest suggestion of a nipple. You had to want to find a problem with this cover. And someone did. So then I tried to type the book into letter form to "sneak" it in. But there are drug names cited in the story such as Librium, Ativan, and Ambien, because the main character is taking those drugs. Apparently, jail inmates are not allowed to read the names of drugs. Or at least some drugs. I'm not sure if they're allowed to read words like acetaminophen, ibuprofen, or acetylsalicylic acid. Sigh.

Day 57: November 27, 2022, 32.39%
To: Bart

I'm always so pleased to see your email address pop up in my Inbox.

Thank you for staying in touch with Andrea, and I'm glad she's still staying in touch with you. Six months is a bit of a haul, and I worry that, with people getting busy during the holidays, the novelty of having a friend in jail will wear off and her friends will stop writing to her. It may be cool, initially, to say, "Hey, I'm writing to my friend who's doing six months in jail in Texas for manslaughter" (sounds so bad-ass for them, doesn't it?), but then will that be sustained over the next four months and beyond? We've stopped writing for the most part, because we're able to speak with her on the phone every evening, which is a blessing.

I'm actually a bit relieved to hear you say that you get angry about your case. Anger is something that I'm afraid we often feel too guilty to allow ourselves to feel, but I think it's understandable and even healthy. We're human, after all. And while I do get all the "honor our victims" narrative, I don't think it's wrong to acknowledge that something happened to us as well.

For example, I think that what is happening to Andrea right now is pointless and cruel. Yes, if roles had been reversed, and if Mr. Boyd had been the drunk driver and she the victim, six months in jail would seem a pitiful price to pay for taking a life. I would want him to be in jail forever. Or dead. I get it, believe me, I do.

But even beloved television icon Mary Tyler Moore wrote in her autobiography "After All," "In case there's any doubt about the acute state of my alcoholism, I can recall with sickening clarity that on more than one occasion I played Russian roulette with my car." America's Sweetheart was a drunk driver. One of the lucky ones.

My daughter is a good person, who did a bad thing. What is the point, really, of sticking her in a hole for six months? It's been hard to get any reading material to her. She's not allowed to have a journal. This is what we do to kindergartners who have misbehaved. "Now you just sit there in that corner and think about what you did."

And since it was four years and eight months between the incident and reporting for jail, this is similar to the admonition dog trainers give you that you can't punish a dog when you get home for peeing on the carpet, because the dog can't make the connection between something he did five hours ago and the way you're treating him now.

When she comes home after this "punishment" Mr. Boyd will still be dead. But I don't know what kind of damage she will have sustained in the interim, and to what end? What is the point, really? To never do it again? Well, since she had never gotten so much as a parking ticket before or after the incident, it's not as though she's a career criminal and scofflaw. As her mother, I suppose it makes sense that she feels guilty, while I mostly just feel sad and angry. I'm surprised to note that it took me several years to realize that the emotion I was feeling all this time was simply grief. Yes, there was fear and sadness and worry and anger and hope and terror. But the overriding feeling has been one of grief. I've been mourning the life

I had -- we had -- and the life I dreamed of for her. That life is gone; the people we were don't exist anymore.

We have this little parable that we tell to parents who have children with developmental disabilities. We all have dreams about and for our children, that their lives will be special, better than ours, that we'll do everything we can to ensure that. But it's like planning a vacation in Hawaii and then finding yourself getting off the plane in Norway. At first you're bound to be very disappointed. You were expecting Hawaii. You packed shorts and bathing suits and loud shirts. But after a while you realize that Norway can be a nice vacation, too. Not what you were expecting, different challenges and rewards, but you can make it work if you set your mind to it.

So I'm working my way out of the grief phase and into acceptance. Acceptance of Norway.

She likes her three "bunkies," as she calls them, but they're all meth heads, so speak very rapidly and non-stop. And loud. Whenever she calls us, every day, there is a constant din of talking and shouting and screaming and shrieking in the background, so there is never a quiet moment to just sit inside her head and meditate, be at peace.

And even though her crime was a one-off, it was very serious, of course: manslaughter. So she is classified "maximum security" and thus does not qualify to participate in any of the jail "programs" that might be interesting, diverting, and get her out of her head -- health and wellness; education; re-entry; workforce development; pet therapy; women, families, and children. So all she can do is sit in her cell all day and night, ruminating.

Lately she's been worrying about us, about the dogs. What will happen if something happens to one of us, both of us? She worries when we travel together or separately, worries about something happening to the pugs and her not being able to get to them because she's in jail. She's been crying on the phone with me lately, and we've submitted online mental health reports on her, so they've sent counselors to her cell to make sure she's okay, which is good. They're very responsive, even though they're so understaffed.

The food is awful, so that also contributes to depression, because it's all carbs and processed sugar. Bread, doughnuts. And she has a history of eating disorders, whipsawing back and forth from being too thin and over-exercising, to gaining about 30 pounds the first two months of college. She may end up gaining a lot of weight in there, so that will be another contributor to depression, even after she comes out. Everything is over-sugared and over-salted. They've been getting bagged food for a few days, because I'm sure they're even more short-staffed during the holidays, but she says the bagged food is better than the trays anyway. I'm sure she whips back and forth between sugar highs and sugar crashes all day every day, so the depression is not surprising.

She was also taken off her anti-depressants cold turkey when she entered jail on October 2, because they don't prescribe her anti-depressant in there. So all those warnings on television about how you shouldn't come off these things suddenly because of suicidal ideation, depression, and anxiety. Yeah. There's that.

So I guess this is modern criminal justice and rehabilitation theory. Mr. Boyd will be no less dead, but at least we'll do everything we can to destroy my daughter. Yeah, that makes sense.

A woman came into the unit recently who had been arrested for killing a friend and then stealing her baby, attempting to pass the infant off as her own. Andrea said she's really nice and funny and kinda sweet, a good person to be around and to talk to. As long as you're not her best friend with a tiny baby. (This turns out to be a fairly common crime, at least in Texas. If you google "Texas woman kills friend, steals baby," several stories pop up, all about different women. The fairer sex, indeed.)

She and I have pledged to work on reform of some aspects of this system. I hope we don't get lazy and forget once she's out and we don't have to deal with it anymore. There will still be others rotting away in there, and to what end? No wonder recidivism is so high. We don't do anything to give people hope, meaning, purpose.

After this, she will have gone through and survived something unimaginable to most people, so I hope she'll be a force to be reckoned with. She won't sweat the small stuff.

Day 60: November 30, 2022, 34.09%
Dear Kevin and Daniel,

I hope you had a lovely Thanksgiving and that you received our holiday and gift cards.

We spoke with Andrea yesterday -- we speak with her every day -- and she sounds very bad. She hasn't been able to see a counselor or counseling intern regularly because they're so severely understaffed. The staff do what they can, but there is only so much.

We heard on the news this morning that the percentage of inmates in Travis County with "unmet mental health needs" has risen from 21% to 45%, post-SARS-CoV-2, and she is certainly among that rise. And we are, of course, concerned about the possibility of a spike this winter in institutional SARS-CoV-2 and other respiratory infections. She had an abnormal pap smear a couple of weeks ago, but has been assured that it's nothing to be concerned about. But doesn't the phrase "abnormal pap smear" automatically conjure up a frisson of worry? After all, if abnormal ones are okay, why do we check them in the first place?

Day 61: December 1, 2022, 34.66%
Nadia! I remember that I took turning 50 a bit hard because I realized that so many things changed for me between being 10 and 20, of course, and then between 20 and 30, then 30 and 40, and even 40 and 50 (because Andrea was born when I was 42). But between 50 and 60, not that much had changed for me, except that my child was growing up and away from me. But I felt that I had hit cruising altitude and that this would be it for the rest of my life.

Of course, that turned out not to be the case, in spectacular fashion, but this is about you, not me. %-)

It sounds as though you have an excellent plan, and that's the most important first step. Too often, at our age, people tend to just let things happen, rather than being proactive. Please give my love to your sisters and mom as you make your way forward. I found a new quotation today that I'm sending to Andrea: "You never know how strong you are until being strong is your only choice." Thank you, Bob Marley!

She tells us that some of the ladies become what's called "Gay for the Stay" (see, you learn something new every day %-), so they have girlfriends, and problems tend to develop with territory and possessiveness. Andrea says that the gossip a couple of days ago was that one inmate was angry at another for making a play for her girlfriend, so she went to the offender's cell but only found her bunkmate there, so she beat her up instead. Not sure if I quite get the logic at play, but if these ladies could work at IBM, with some notable exceptions, they wouldn't be in county jail.

Women will masturbate right in front of you, and not in a "fun" way. And Andrea says the farts are real. One of her bunk mates told her that the etiquette in jail is: when you feel that you are about to fart, you're supposed to sit on the toilet and then flush as you're farting, in order to flush it away. And "crop dusting" in the Day Room is a severely punishable offense.

So it's not a nice place. "I hate it here," she says every day. I guess that's the point. Andrea says she's most looking forward to sleeping on a real mattress again, so we'll have to make sure that she spends at least her first week out in bed most of the time, catching up. I'm also going to arrange for hair, nails, massage, and waxing. Instead of tying a yellow ribbon 'round the old oak tree, we'll give her a spa weekend.

There's an idea. Wouldn't it be great if a big spa chain offered ladies in jail some pro bono services as a corporate charitable contribution, help these women to feel good about themselves, at least for an afternoon?

"A misogynist is a man who hates women as much as women hate one another."

H. L. Mencken

Day 63: December 3, 2022, 35.8%

Dear Mom,

I'm sorry, I was going to tell you what's been going on in my head, but then I thought, "maybe they listen to the Global TelLink recordings and heard her ask if we go through her mail and read it before sending it, so now they have me on a list to go through my mail," so this is actually just going to be a blank letter. NICE TRY, TRAVIS COUNTY.

Kidding – but that thought did legitimately enter my mind. No, what's actually going on is that all three of my cellmates are making hooch in the room (tell no one – if I get a reputation in here for being a snitch, I'll get the shit kicked out of me, so there's nothing Kevin or anyone else can do to help me with this, and I don't want it coming up on the phone either – I'm being so serious) and I'm worried it'll get found during a shakedown, and I'll be associated with it even though I have nothing to do with it at all.

I think I'm just flipping out because I don't believe deep down that I deserve to have a good life, so when I hear you and Dad talking about me getting out of here and getting to live with my dogs again, my brain can't accept that that's actually going to happen, so it starts doing all kinds of gymnastics thinking of everything that could go wrong.

One of my cellmates just got moved out of the room because she was in a jail relationship with my other cellmate and this blew up in everyone's faces. If this story sounds familiar, it's because one of my cellmates, Nilah, is a wonderful person, but has bipolar disorder and schizoaffective disorder, which means she acts out in hypersexual ways – in layman's terms, she won't stop fucking literally everyone who comes into this bunk. She's tried to fuck me, too. The situation got out of hand because Soljah, Nilah's girlfriend, found out that C.W. and Nilah hooked up weeks ago when C.W. was in a different bunk, but now we're all rooming together, so then when Nilah gave C.W. her last mustard packet (this is not a euphemism; the mustard packet symbolized a lot more to Soljah), Soljah had a meltdown and started screaming at her and the officers got involved and now we're waiting to see who our next roommate is going to be. Thank God I'm straight.

So, yeah, I'm in Hell, but it's okay. It's all going to be fine. I'm just really fucking tired of living with other women who are always coming at each other over sugars and mustards and other stupid ass motherfucking nonsense talking about how it's about "respect" shut the fuck up no one cares just shut your stupid methhead ass mouth up and sit quietly in your bunk and mind your own goddam business = how Andrea actually feels, but doesn't say out loud, BECAUSE I WASN'T RAISED BY FUCKING ANIMALS JESUS. DIDN'T ANYBODY EVER TEACH YOU BITCHES HOW TO BE FUCKING QUIET?

This has been a diary entry. Nothing in this letter may come up over the phone, lest I get in trouble with the powers that be. Thank you for providing this invaluable service; your sacrifice will not be forgotten.

Love you and miss you much. Kiss The Boys for me and tell them I love them, too.

Love, Andrea

Day 64: December 4, 2022, 36.36%
Dear Mom,
Let's get into the real minutiae of the things that are bothering me here because the last letter was too watered down, honestly, to accurately represent how frustrated I am with my current living situation. I WANT TO FLOSS MY TEETH. I also don't know off the top of my head how to spell the word minutiae and I can't check because one of my bunkies has a tablet that has a broken charging port and has to tell one of the guards every night that the tablet needs to be charged on an extra port instead of 104-D's port, because evidently it's too hard for them to just write that down somewhere to save

everyone the headache of having the same fucking conversation over and over again, but guess what else? My bunkie is one of your school kids all grown up, so she can't communicate with the guards to tell them this, which means that I have to either a) tell the guards for her every night, or 2) let her use my tablet when hers is dead in the morning because neither of us told them, so that's why I can't check how minutiae is spelled right now. No tablet for me; C.W. has it. I suppose I could just let this be her problem, but no, I can't, because that's not the way I was designed, so I'm just going to be annoyed with everyone (but mostly myself), thank you very much.

Then the ridiculous sex stuff. I genuinely do not know how, when, or why these women are fucking each other in this room, but evidently it's happening. And I would really appreciate it if they would stop it, because it is not in keeping with the generally accepted guidelines for harmonious living, and it keeps turning disagreements about mustard packets into "I have people outside of here who actually care about me and you can't get anyone to answer the phone when you call," which is just uncalled for and about 12,000 steps above mustard, and then before I know it, someone's moving out of the room and I have a new stranger I have to get used to urinating in front of. I want to believe that you don't like causing/starting drama, I really do... but when you insist upon taking everyone who crosses the threshold of 104 to Pound Town and then crying foul (fowl? help!) the second someone says you're "ran through" for behaving this way... I don't know how to help you on this one.

I can't wash my hair here because the water is too hot, and the only shampoo they have is full of sulfates (sulphates? help!), so if I wash it more than once a month it'll dry up and fall out, literally. So I have to just try to avoid letting the water touch my hair, or my face, because I'm also trying to protect my skin's moisture barrier as much as I can so I don't get crazy acne. So far it's working okay, except around my chin once a month, but there's not much I can do about that because it's hormonal. This place actually has me looking forward to my period because it means I'm closer to being out of here. I only have four more phantom periods until I'm free! Joy.

Since sending the previous letter yesterday, I've been paranoid that they're going to open it and read through it because of all the "contraband" mail you've sent me, since it's addressed to you. I'm worried they're going to do the same thing with this one. But I think it's still a federal offense for them to open your mail without your consent, so I sincerely hope they won't, but I just have a lot of paranoia in here about everything. I have no privacy in here at all. When I get out, boundaries and privacy are going to be really important to me – more so than before. Jail has been and will continue to be an extremely violating experience, so entering a bathroom I'm in without knocking will reduce me to tears, fair warning.

I miss my clothes. I miss being able to wear something I actually feel comfortable in instead of these weird canvas-bag material uniforms or the bizarre fucking off-white men's thermal underwear we sleep in. I also really miss shaving my legs. I got the weird magic shave stuff from the commissary a few weeks ago, the stuff that's like Nair, but I don't like to use it because you have to do it in the sink in your cell and it makes a big mess, plus you're not supposed to be naked in your cell because you never know when a male officer is going to come into the tank and announce "male on post," and if you're undressed in front of a male officer you can get in trouble. So it's really just not worth it to me to try to "shave" my legs or armpits in here, honestly. But I want to rid myself of all of my body hair within five hours of my release, please. That's like Item #1 on my agenda. I'm gonna need a bikini trimmer, which I think I already have in my apartment in a little purple case in my bathroom, but I might need a new one, and I'm gonna need the clippers (with a shower cap to protect my long hair) that are under the sink in my bathroom (they should be with their charger) to get my undercut under control, and I'm also gonna need the mega exfoliating mitt that should still be hanging up on my shower door (but Anastasia might have moved it elsewhere in my bathroom). And I'm gonna need some Dial liquid antibacterial soap (I think this exists), and the rest of my usual in-shower products that I left in my bathroom.

Sorry this is so detailed; I haven't felt clean since I left my apartment. Jail is a really dirty place. There's black mold growing on the showers we use every day that no one's doing anything about and I don't think anyone cleans the stalls at all, ever. I know no one cleans the toilet, because we aren't offered a brush to scrub it with. This entire place is just teeming with bacteria.

That's all for now. I love and miss you lots.

xoxo gossip me

Day 66: December 6, 2022, 37.5%

Dear Andrea,

Even though we speak every day, I wanted to try to write a letter. It's hard to know what to say, not really knowing what you're going through. And every little thing reminds me of you, as though I'm not already thinking about you all the time.

When I leave the elementary school on Wednesday and Thursday afternoons, there is a line of parents' cars come to pick up their kids, and I think about meeting you in the courtyard at school, waiting for you outside Stillman, picking you up in the middle school car line, dropping you off at THS in the mornings, with all the terrible drivers cutting one another off. Yun Ji and I used to marvel that parents could be so nasty to each other, knowing that we were all there for the same reason; we weren't exactly anonymous drivers you could engage with in some random road rage encounter. We were parents at the same school. It was weird. Some of the parents in Tenafly were so Type A.

I just took one of my students back to class in the school elevator. It's only two floors, but he has a congenital orthopedic disability and just had another leg surgery over Thanksgiving break, so I wanted to spare him the stairs. He walks with a rocking gate, side to side, and his bones are brittle. So then I thought about that time we were leaving Courtney's apartment down in Edgewater, and you begged me to let you ride the elevator down the one floor by yourself. Like an idiot, I said yes, because you really wanted to.

Of course, as soon as the doors slid closed, you screamed at the top of your lungs. I guess the reality of being alone in the elevator suddenly struck you. So, in a panic, I ran down the stairs, and you were crying in the lobby. No one was there, or they would have thought I was a terrible parent. (LOL! Maybe I was. %-)

That made me think of two other times I made you burst into tears. One was when you were supposed to have your very first sleepover, at Makayla's, the night of the school Benefit. I was hosting, along with Bryce Levin and somebody else I don't remember. But Jack O'Malley was in the process of losing his mind over the divorce, and he was supposed to supervise the sleepover, so he decided to go all passive-aggressive with Brandi and her friends, and say that he wasn't sure whether he would be home with the kids after all, because he might just go do something else while Brandi was planning to be at the Benefit, and make her figure out some other childcare arrangement. Or maybe he would also attend the Benefit, and just take you kids with him.

You came into the kitchen while I was talking with him on the phone, heard my side of the conversation, figured out what was going down, and burst into tears.

The other time I remember was when you asked me if there was really a Santa Claus. I forget how old you were, but you were young. Because you were so smart, I always made the same mistake of thinking that you were more mature than you were, ready for things you weren't ready for. People make that mistake with kids who are tall for their age, too.

I remember I asked you, "Do you really want to know?" And, of course, you said yes. So like a moron I said, "No," and you burst into tears. I should have realized that you still wanted desperately to be lied to. I think I've made you cry even more than men have. Horrible thought. %-)

I work with broken kids, as you know, and some of them can be real pains in the ass. I have a couple of them, I think, whose disability definition in the DSM is actually "pain in the ass." Needless to say, they're always here, never absent. One of them, Bruce, came in one day a few weeks ago and was clearly sick as a dog. He was coughing and sneezing all over the place, his nose was runny and red. We work in close quarters in my tiny room.

I told him that he should have stayed home. We're just coming off a two-year viral respiratory pandemic, so he could do us all a solid. We learned only two things from this pandemic, what with all the lies about masks and vaccines: wash your hands a lot and stay home when you're sick.

But he said, "I can't. I drive my mom crazy enough as it is, so she needs the time when I'm at school. She won't let me stay home."

So this woman is willing to put the rest of us at risk for some sort of virus – SARS-CoV-2, the flu, the common cold – just so she can get rid of her annoying kid for a few hours. Thanks, chum.

I never had that problem with you. I looked for any excuse to keep you home. I don't know, I just liked hanging out with you. I should have homeschooled you. I found out years later that all my friends in Maryland had a bet that I would.

I think it may have been the first time I took you down to Lexington Park, you were just barely walking, so you may have been anywhere from 10 months to a year old. You took your first steps at 10 months, down in my mother's apartment in the house in North Bergen.

Anyway, Dad was with us. And I remember Joanne's little kids were all fascinated with you, and kept following you around. But whenever you headed toward the stairs, instead of trying to stop you, they all just tagged along, I think, to see if you would fall down the stairs. So there I was, frantically tossing her kids out of my way so that I could get to you before you plunged head first down onto the concrete floor of the basement den.

I asked Joanne what she did about the stairs when her kids were little. She said that she initially put up gates, but that eventually there were more people in the house who were inconvenienced than protected by them, so she took them down, "And we just let the littlest kids fall down the stairs until they stopped doing it."

Dad and I were so obsessed with you. Still are, I guess. (Although Dad does sometimes tease me with that Tom Papa joke about going out for dinner, leaving the kids with the babysitter, they getting in the car, his wife putting her face in her hands and sobbing, "I miss them already," and Tom Papa confesses to the audience, "I don't even know who she's talking about.")

Every time I start a sentence with the word "She," knowing full well that he knows full well who I'm talking about, your Dad will feign innocence and say, "Who?"

I remember sitting on Joanne's porch with everyone, and you needed a diaper change, so I picked you up and started to leave the room, and Dad was following right behind me. As we were going I heard Dawn say to Alan, "How long do you need two people to change a diaper?" and Alan replied, "Until you have a second kid." LOL! I guess that's true.

I just always got such a kick out of you. I never wanted to have kids, and then I read "Calvin and Hobbes" and thought, "Well, if I could have a kid like that...". And I did! You've always been so smart and funny; that's why we called you "The Portable Friend" and took you everywhere. I never understood people who wanted to leave their kids at home. After you were born, Dad and I might go out for a meal together, and we would just talk about you anyway, so you might as well have been there. I honestly don't remember what we talked about before you were born.

Of course, now we talk about The Boys. They're so funny. Giacomo is like an old bachelor who just wants to be left alone (as your father says, "He is his own pug"), and Bonsai is always trying to get him to play, lunging at him playfully and nipping at his neck skin. And Giaco puppy secretly enjoys it. He usually comes around. Sometimes he even initiates the play, which throws everyone off.

When Ben and Althea were leaving on Saturday afternoon, Giacomo was barking and jumping at them at the door, and Bonsai tried to do the same, but then Giaco did that thing he does where he rounds on Bonsai and yells at him, because barking at stuff is his thing, and he wants Bonsai to back off and let him take charge. Althea thought this was hilarious. "They're yelling at each other!" she said.

Hang in there, kiddo. You're the strongest person I know. When I go to bed at night, it kills me to think that I'm settling into a nice, soft, comfortable, warm bed, while you're lying on that thin mattress over a metal slab. We'll make sure that you come home to a nice comfy bed, and you can stay there until you're ready to come out.

I will close with one of my favorite quotations, from Theodore Roosevelt:

"Far better it is to dare mighty things, to win glorious triumphs, even though checkered by failure, than to take rank with those poor spirits who neither enjoy much nor suffer much, because they live in the gray twilight that knows neither victory nor defeat."

As I type this, you're on Day 66, 37.5% of the way through, 110 days to go. I will kiss The Boys for you, as I do every day.

xoxo Gossip Mom

Day 69: December 9, 2022, 39.2%
INMATE: GRIEVANCE
To: Sgt. On Duty   From: Andrea Scott
We need to get out of our cells more than this; the frequency with which these 23-hour-in-cell days are happening is really outrageous. This unit is virtually indistinguishable from lockdown – the only difference is the number of women there are in a room. That's why fights keep breaking out. Please do something to fix this. We deserve to be treated like human beings.

Staff Action/Response:
Please be patient as we continue to work with Travis County and jail standards to come up with solutions to our shared problems.

Dear Mom,

"Our shared problems" my butthole. We do not "share" this problem. Also, tell me why I got back both copies of this carbon sheet thing. Something tells me Jail Standards never saw this grievance. I don't trust these hoes. I'm telling y'all, this jail's shit stinks to high heaven. But whatever. Almost halfway there.

Much love, xoxo, Andrea

P.S. I think the state should have to prove that a person poses an ongoing threat to society greater than that of the average citizen in order to justify locking them up for any length of time. No more silly arrests over nonsense things.

P.P.S. My bunkie pronounces "pancakes" like "panda cakes" and "pandemic" like "pin debit." I thought you might find that amusing, since your colleague pronounces "Kleenex" like "clinics." She also pronounces one of the guard's names, Jimenez, as "Himmendez," which would be right, were it not for the extra "d." She's funny, I like her. She's here because she was on probation and kept having dirty urinalyses because she smokes weed. Bullshit reason to put someone in jail. She's maximum security because she's a hothead with no respect for the guards.

Day 71: December 11, 2022, 40.34%

Dear Mom,

12-11-2022: Me again, writing to you from this place where time stands still. Finally broke 40% today, and yet completion still feels aeons away, despite aeons only being 15 total weeks. I think I may call Kevin at some point this week to see if I can get answers out of him faster that way.

What I do know is that the Tom Boyd who's been described to me would not have wanted me to be spending 22-24 hours a day locked in a cell that only sometimes has a working toilet, with a rotating cast of mentally unstable women who could at any moment decide to rip one another's heads off over a missing sugar packet because that's what happens when you force four grown adults to share space like they're a sleepaway camp without giving them any privacy or any of their own space. He wouldn't have wanted me to be forced off my antidepressants, or ripped away from my therapist, or separated from the support system that's kept me stable for the last several years.

12-12-2022: On the subject of stability, this jail evidently doesn't have the resources or capability to make appropriate housing determinations based on level of need for psychiatric care. How do I know this? I've now been placed in a room with more than one person who needed to be in special psychiatric housing, but wasn't. This has the potential to put my other bunkies and me literally in mortal danger. The rules in the special psychiatric building are much more strictly enforced to make sure everyone is safe; in this building, it's a free-for-all where inmates are swiping things from officers' desks like "free world pens" that could be used as weapons.

Last night, our schizophrenic bunkie ended up in crisis (likely because of how infrequently we get let out of this godforsaken cell), and the first thing I did was tell Nilah to hide her pen, because Uneek is in here for assault related to one of her crises getting out of hand when police were called instead of EMS. We have no EMS here; we only have police, and we needed to get her out of our room because as compassionate as we are, we can't just pretend she's not pacing in a circle around our room, talking about the devil, saying, "Don't look at me," and going so fast she could fall at any second. Eventually, she did fall. She also tapped Nilah and me in the face a couple of times before the post officer got clearance from the sergeant to intervene.

After all this happened and Uneek was removed from the room, they did a shakedown, meaning they made us go outside in the cold for 30 minutes while they turned our room completely upside down. And when I say completely, I mean completely – papers out of manila folders, dirty laundry mixed up with clean, wet wash cloth left under the mattress, papers taken off the walls – everything taken apart and left a mess. I don't know if they were looking for evidence that we were the ones who had driven her to madness to minimize their exposure, or what the fuck was going on, but they were thorough, and *the whole experience was extremely violating, especially after already having been afraid for our physical safety just minutes before.*

No part of me believes my victim would have wanted this. I'm glad I've seen what I've seen because it makes me angry enough that I'm never going to shut up about it once I get out of here, but I've seen enough, you know? I've seen fucking enough.

Thanks for not giving up on me. I love you and I can't wait to get out of here and come home.

Love, Andrea

Day 72: December 12, 2022, 40.9%
Dear Kevin,

There was an incident last night in Andrea's cell, which she shares with three other women.

Apparently, the psych unit is overcrowded, so inmates are being moved from that unit into cells with the general jail population. One of the women in the cell had a psychotic break last night: screaming, rocking, seeing the devil, touching the other inmates. Post officers responded, removed the woman, and then tossed the cell looking for contraband. Andrea was rattled, but she's okay. She spoke with Philip on the phone for about an hour today.

Philip tried calling over there today, but was hung up on once as soon as he heard the phone answered, and then the phone just rang unanswered when he tried to call back. He submitted a Mental Health form, just because we're concerned about Andrea's general health at this point. We certainly wouldn't want to see her come to harm because the facility is so inadequately staffed.

Day 72: December 12, 2022, 40.9%
Dear Mom,
Since the tone of the other letter was very negative, I wanted to counteract

that somewhat with this one. I'm so unbelievably incredibly lucky. I could've gone to prison for literally years, decades, and most of the women I'm in here with aren't fortunate enough to get the kind of deal I got for the charge I got. I was unlucky that one night of my life, but I was lucky every night before it, and I've been lucky every night since.

I don't have schizophrenia. I don't know what Uneek was seeing in this room last night, I'm so glad I don't know what she sees, and I'm so sorry she sees what she does. I'm grateful for the mental health I do have.

I'm lucky people have rooted for me to succeed instead of rooting for me to fail. I'm lucky to have been blessed with the opportunities I've been extended these past few years. I'm lucky to have the best dogs in the world. I'm lucky to have the best therapist in the world. I'm lucky to have Sam.

Most of all, though, I'm lucky to have parents who love and support me through absolutely anything and everything. I don't know what I would do without you. That's why I get so needy about having a third number in case y'all don't pick up one day; I would instantly spiral into complete panic. You're the best parents in the world and I miss you desperately. (Doesn't all this sincerity make you miss when I was free and took you for granted like a normal adult offspring? Kidding.)

But in all seriousness, if it weren't for you and Dad I don't know where I would be right now, so I hope you're taking really good care of yourselves – correction, you'd better be taking really good care of yourselves – because I know taking care of me and The Boys and everything else during this time and making it seem like it's no sweat can't be a cake walk, and I need you both too desperately to have there be any fallen soldiers in this battle. Put as many band aids on your nipples as you need to, but we must all finish this marathon together. Okay now this letter is getting away from me a little. Apologies.

I love you both so much, we will all get through this – the only way out is through, and we're almost halfway there now. Progress.

xoxo gossip me

Day 73: December 13, 2022, 41.47%

Dear Dawn,

One of Andrea's cellmates left the other day when her charges were dropped, and Andrea was quite sad. She cried. She and this other woman had apparently bonded. Humans make connections, no matter what the circumstances. Perhaps because of the circumstances.

We hit 40% of the way through on Sunday, and I told Andrea that was good, but she was unconvinced. Forty percent doesn't sound like much compared to sixty percent. But I pointed out to her that, if she went to the airport and they told her that her flight had a 40% chance of crashing into the sea, she wouldn't board the plane, because 40% is actually a lot when it comes to air travel and jail sentences, at least. She laughed and allowed that, well, yeah, if you look at it that way... ;-)

Oh, I had a funny conversation with one of my 3rd graders yesterday. I asked what she had done over the weekend, and she said she went to a party. I asked what kind. "A birthday party." Who was it for? Her brow furrowed. "I don't remember." You don't remember whose birthday party you celebrated? Was it a friend? A relative, someone in your family? She still looked perplexed.

"I don't remember. But he died."

He died? You went to a birthday party for someone who died? So was it, like, a memorial celebration? A celebration of someone's life? Something like that?

She nodded, but still seemed unsure.

Then, when I walked her back to class, she suddenly turned to me and said, "Oh! I remember whose party I went to! It was Jesus!" Okay, so I can see where there are celebrations of the birth of Jesus in December; that's the whole point. But I have other friends who were born in December -- my high school friends Hannah and Dawn, for example. But I think that if I went to a birthday party celebration over the weekend I would remember whether it was for Hannah or Dawn... or JESUS! %-)

Kids are so strange. ;-)

Day 74: December 14, 2022, 42.04%

Dear Bart,

I know today is a rough day for you, an unhappy anniversary, so I wanted you to know that I'm thinking about you and will have you in my head and heart all day long, as I see the kids, as I speak with colleagues, as I feed the cats, as I walk the dogs, as I make myself a pitiful salad for dinner (still trying to take off those pesky 20 pounds), as I watch TV, and as I say my prayers tonight.

You are such a good person, it pains me to think of you being in pain. But we feel what we feel, so I just want you to know that you are not alone; you are never alone.

I don't know if you're familiar with Viktor Frankl and his "Man's Search for Meaning," but it's a great book. Frankl survived the Holocaust, and most of his philosophy stems from that experience.

These are just some of the things he wrote that I find helpful and inspiring when I'm in my darkest places:

"If there is meaning in life at all, then there must be meaning in suffering."

"No man should judge unless he asks himself in absolute honesty whether in a similar situation he might not have done the same."

"When we are no longer able to change a situation, we are challenged to change ourselves."

"But there was no need to be ashamed of tears, for tears bore witness that a man had the greatest of courage: the courage to suffer."

Anyway, I hope you're moving toward a greater and deeper understanding of your value, what you mean to your friends and family, the good you do as a member of the Hyacinth Fellowship. I truly believe that we were all brought together for a reason, and that we can accomplish a lot together.

You are much more than the worst day of your life. You have turned out to be one of the most important people in my life, one of my favorite people on the planet.

Proof that every day holds new possibilities. ;-)

Day: 75 December 15, 2022, 42.61%

Dear Bart,

I know what you mean. I know I've thought about Mr. Boyd every single day since the incident, and I've often thought to myself, "I wonder if his brother and his best friend think about him every single day the way I do, or have they absorbed this tragedy into their lives by now and moved on?" In my heart of hearts, I honestly don't believe that his brother and his best friend think about Mr. Boyd as much as I do, as much as Andrea does.

I believe this simply because: people die.

I have a very funny old friend named Ezra Weinberg, who is a lot like Woody Allen in that he is a borderline hypochondriac and is obsessed with his own mortality. One day I tried to comfort him about the inevitable by shaking my head sadly and saying, "But Ezra, everybody dies," to which he immediately replied, "So far!"

I think he's still holding out hope. Playing the percentages.

Weighing his options. %-)

Your victim was young, so she wasn't supposed to go when she did, so there is that element of the unexpected. Mr. Boyd was only 46, so probably had many good years ahead of him. But people do gradually accept death as a part of life. My parents have been gone for a while now, 26 and 24 years. I think about them a lot, but probably not every single day at this point. Death is absorbed into life. Somehow we move on.

But what you're going through, and what Andrea is enduring, and everyone else at the Hyacinth Fellowship is not common. It's more common than people think, but not "common." The guilt, the shame, the moral injury, the anxiety, the second-guessing, the loss of confidence and trust in the rightness of things, the terrifying awareness of the fragility of life. This is a different kind of suffering than the suffering we experience when we lose a loved one. It's not more or less suffering, not better or worse suffering, but it's a different brand of suffering.

And, as Viktor Frankl observed, it takes courage to endure suffering. If you weren't the person you are, you wouldn't be experiencing this suffering. What happened to you doesn't mean you are bad, and the way you have been processing it only confirms your innate goodness.

So hang onto that. Give yourself a break. Think of how you would treat a friend going through what you go through every day. Think of how you would want to lift that burden from them. Think of the compassion you would show them. Think how much they would deserve that compassion. Think how much you deserve it.

You deserve it.

Day 78: December 18, 2022, 44.32%
Dear Mom,
My findings indicate that, for adult females, believing that pads, panty liners, and tampons are flushable items and feeling the need to announce when someone ELSE has farted are major predictors of eventual incarceration. Sorry, sorry. I'm being snide, I know. But I guess jail doesn't exactly bring out the best in me for some reason; I can't imagine why. December is dragging a bit. Again, I can't imagine why.

Here I go being NEGATIVE again – I don't like it when it feels like all I bring to the table is negativity, and right now I'm forced into that headspace until the end of March. I am sad that I will miss Christmas, but to be fair, Christmas has never really felt like Christmas in Texas because it's never been snowy, and in the grand scheme of things, missing this one is really no big deal.

I'm going to call you guys really early on the 25th – like freakishly early, probably, otherwise we probably won't be able to talk that day. Everyone's going to be calling their families all day, so if I don't take an earlier slot I might not get another one. I have my period-ish, meaning I have a bunch of symptoms of my period, but no actual bleeding – thank God for the IUD; I would be so miserable without it – so only three more phantom periods until I come home!!! Progress.

I'm scared that when Sam goes to Australia in January I won't be able to talk to him pretty much that entire month. I'm also scared that Australia will try to kill him, because there are about 8,000 bizarre ass species running around that place waiting to terrorize human beings, like buff kangaroos that'll come up to you and punch you in the face or weird little cute-looking octopuses (I think that's the plural, but who knows/cares) that are actually extremely venomous. And it's in like an opposite time zone, too, so how will I know when is an appropriate time to call him?? (Also, will I even be able to call him at all? I DON'T KNOW!!)

It's okay, I want him to go and have his adventure, he's just my favorite person and he's playing a crucial role in keeping me sane while I'm in here, so I'm scared to let him go somewhere so far away for so long. It's like a three-week trip. But it's okay. I'm handling it.

Oh, and I think Carl might've blocked the jail's number, so there's that. Finally got under a guy's skin enough for him to block me – milestone moment, tbh.

Miss and love you muchly, more letters to come soon.

xoxo gossip me

Day 80: December 20, 2022, 45.45 %

Dear Mom,

It's me again, and I'm back with more Roommate Qualms, TMI. Today when our newest bunkie, with whom I get along fine (and we all at least act like we get along fine), left the room briefly, my other two bunkies took it as an opportunity to start talking about her, because why not be catty and small, and go after the topic of choice? "I feel like if someone has the ability to communicate that they can't take care of themselves, then they can take care of themselves."

So what you're saying then is that you think our bunkie is "faking" her matted hair, orange teeth, smelly armpits, and bruised knees from the times she fell on them because she was being tormented by the voices in her head? For fuck's sake, Ellen. She's schizophrenic. What would possess you to say something so fucked up about somebody. WHAT IS WRONG WITH WOMEN? WHY IS THIS THE WAY WE INTERACT WITH ONE ANOTHER?

I had been reading my book, minding my business, not a part of the conversation, but then I got dragged in with a "What do you think, Andi?" and it felt like I was being made to choose sides and I felt like a SIM when an interaction starts going south with one of their friends and you see a little people-y squiggle over their heads as the relationship bar starts to dip into the red. I can't remember losing affection for someone that quickly in a long time but like, wow, man. That's just a helluva thing to say about a perfectly nice girl who's finally taking her medicine as directed to the point where she was stable enough to be moved to our building and functioning well enough that she could take a shower yesterday and start conditioning her hair to get some of the tangles out. She says she wants to just shave her head because it would be easier than combing it all out, and her mom usually helps her comb it, but this time she's in jail so her mom's not here. Like, have a little compassion.

Sorry, that just pissed me the fuck off, so I had to angrily write about it for a few minutes. She's like, "Well, I have schizoaffective disorder..." Bitch, that's not the same thing. Just the other day you were telling your friend on the phone that you have bipolar disorder and borderline personality disorder, and that they're "basically the same thing." WHOA, hold up, nope, stop, not even close. Not even in the same family. One is a personality disorder, one is a mood disorder; you don't know what you're talking about, shut the hell up.

I think jail might be Hell designed specifically and personally for me.

Love, and miss you loads.

xoxo gossip me

Day 82: December 22, 2022, 46.59%

So far, we have had mail returned to us undeliverable to Andrea because it was "not from a bookstore, could not locate," "printed out book not allowed," "map," "books must come from a U.S. publisher, no individuals," "literature on drug use, names of drugs not allowed," "attempt to print out book from internet," "multiple attempts to send individual book page – not allowed," and "threatening language."

Andrea also sent us something called a "TCSO (Medline) Sick Call Request" form that contained the following question: "What is Your "Medical" Problem? (Be Specific)." She found it hilarious that "Medical" was in scare quotes, as though the question was really "What is Your Problem?" and you're just trying to make it "Medical."

My Problem? Have you ever seen "One Flew Over the Cuckoo's Nest?"

Day 105: January 14, 2023, 59.66%
Dear Anna Louise,

Thank you so much for thinking of us, and for keeping Andrea in your prayers. As I've said before, it really makes a difference.

They were lined up at the cart for their meds the other day when the male nurse dishing it out surveyed the line and said, "Gosh, this cart is full of meds, and y'all are still crazy as hell." A little gallows humor. LOL!

She gets along well with her rotating cast of three rotating "bunkies." She's been there longer than the others, who are mostly in briefly for some sort of drug possession, so she's had a couple dozen cell mates by now.

Her unit is currently "hot" because there have been a couple of SARS-CoV-2 cases, so no programs or visitors for a while, but she is able to call us every day. Yesterday she got a form, late, that listed all the programs she was supposed to have participated in last week, but which have been suspended due to SARS-CoV-2: support animals, one-to-one counseling, clergy. She said, "It was like a cruel little note telling me how great my week could have been."

Day 111: January 20, 2023, 63.07%
Dawn and Alan and Maddie!

Andrea sings to herself all the time, always has, and has been singing to herself in jail, which is a positive indicator of her mood. Her "bunkies" have heard her, of course, so when everyone was in the Day Room the other day, they encouraged her to sing something. She sang Rhianna's "Love on the Brain," and said that everyone stopped talking and stopped what they were doing and people started coming out of their rooms and offices, inmates and guards, and when she finished, everybody applauded. She said it was like a scene in a movie.

Now she's taking requests, and sang Adele's "Hello" the other day, and "Earth Sway" by Loony. Next thing you know she'll be assembling a musical theater troupe called the Jailbirds to perform "Prisoners of Love" from the movie "The Producers." One of the other inmates gave Andrea her mother's phone number, so she could call and sing "Happy Birthday" to her on a tablet call, which she did.

We spoke last night and she told us that she was awakened from a nap and told that they would be moving her to another cell. It seems that there was a personality conflict in one of the other rooms, so they were moving one of the participants into Andrea's bunk and moving her in with the other group, because everyone knows that Andrea gets along with everybody.

But her three current "bunkies" staged a "mutiny" of sorts, an insurrection, if you will; they protested and refused to let her go. So the staff backed down and moved someone else around. LOL! Winning a popularity contest in jail? That's a new one. %-) "Inmate of the Month."

Her unit is still "hot" with SARS-CoV-2, so no programs, but we're hoping that will be lifted soon. Philip will be visiting next week, and I'll be down the week after.

Day 134: February 12, 2023, 76.14%

Dear Sam,

Can I just take a minute to complain about my newest bunkie okay great thanks love you [heart emoji]

So this bitch and I had an arrangement where she was borrowing my spare headphones (which I had in case mine ever stopped working, because they're cheap and terrible quality and I didn't want them to break and then have to wait up to a week for new ones) until she got her own headphones from the commissary, and in exchange for renting them for a few days, she got me a Snickers. A Snickers is like $1.65. The headphones are about $11.00. At no point did I tell her she could commandeer my fucking headphones. At NO POINT did we enter into any contract stating that a single Snickers bar would (or even could) be considered an appropriate substitute for my $11.00 motherfucking headphones, AND YET she shows NO SIGN of returning them to me or addressing the fact that they are not now and never were hers to enjoy, FOREVER.

But that's just my personal beef with the hoe. Last night, she decided that she wanted to tell us stories about her life, and I sincerely wish she hadn't because now I must ask God's forgiveness for yet another series of intrusive thoughts. She said that "every time she gets in a car with a random man he tries to fuck her or pull out his dick," and I was like Well Then Maybe You Should Consider Another Mode Of Transportation Because WHAT THE FUCK ARE YOU THINKING, GETTING INTO CARS WITH RANDOM MEN seemed like it might be too direct for her. I don't know if my message made it in anywhere, who's to say if she even heard me or if she had my FUCKING HEADPHONES TURNED UP TOO LOUD (yes I am still on the headphones thing).

But wait, there's more! This morning, shortly after breakfast trays were served and while my other two bunkies and I were half asleep, we heard a noise that sounded like a little "ploop, ploop, ploop" in the toilet, followed by NO flushing or hand-washing, and then the sound of her getting back in bed.

I convinced myself I was having an auditory hallucination and started to drift back off to sleep, only to be rudely awakened shortly thereafter by the sound (and smell) of her full-on vomiting into the toilet, and then peeing on top of her vomit, because why not, I guess. When we looked, we saw that she threw up all over the floor on the way to the toilet and we are convinced that the "ploop, ploop" sound was her vomiting (or at least pre-vomiting) in the toilet before vomiting on the floor, WHICH SHOULD HAVE BEEN ENOUGH WARNING THAT YOU WERE GONNA BLOW, TO STOP YOU FROM THROWING UP ON THE FUCKING FLOOR IN THE FIRST PLACE. YOU ARE AN ADULT AND YOU ARE SOBER. GROW THE FUCK UP.

Seriously, who the fuck does ANYTHING that makes a "ploop" sound in the toilet and then doesn't flush it when you share the fucking toilet with three other people. The series of events was like this, in case it was confusing before:

Everyone is asleep.

Trays are served.

Everyone goes back to sleep(ish).

Ploop, ploop, no flush, no hand washing.

Calm before the storm.

Vomit everywhere. Sad times.

Why, MY GOD WHY, would a sober adult human being not be able to make it to the toilet in time to vomit into it? She's on the bottom fucking bunk. It's not hard. I just – I can't with these people, Sam, I can't anymore. But the state of Texas says I have to, so I guess I'm fucking gonna.

So, my favorite of my bunkies – and the only one who's a mom in the free world – ended up cleaning it up because she was going to vomit herself if she didn't address the stench, and because Alon (Gabrielle is her government name, but she literally gave herself the jail nickname "Alon" - pronounced "alone" - because no one likes her. I wish I were making this up, but I'm not.)

used a vomit-soaked wad of toilet paper to "clean" vomit off the toilet and then fucking got back in bed as though the job was fucking done, so obviously someone had to step up.

I was too busy to be useful as I was trying to process the fact that a grown adult human being had failed to make it to the toilet in time, despite drugs/alcohol playing absolutely no role whatsoever. Plus I'm highly vomit-averse, so I'm incredibly grateful to Anna for taking one for the team this morning. Alon, meanwhile, did not thank Anna, that I can recall, and is now eating DRY RAMEN like it's a bag of fucking corn chips. I'm done.

Maybe she keeps getting in cars with strange men because she figures there's no way they're more terrifying than she is, so what's there to fear? Lord forgive me.

Thank you ever so much for indulging this vent session. Your sacrifice will be rewarded handsomely upon my release. [Smiley face emoji] Miss and love you.

xoxo me

Day 157: March 7, 2023, 89.2%
Hi family,
Just me being anxious again, but it occurred to me that Kevin may need my Texas state ID for the occupational license, which I think I was supposed to get within 30 days of my sentencing, but I never did. My Jail Fear Demon is whispering in my ear that they'll use this as an excuse to keep me in here longer, so I didn't want to talk about it over the recorded line until Kevin confirmed that it wasn't a concern, so I chose instead to send it in a letter. So here's that letter.

Hi. I really don't have the temperament for this. He probably doesn't need it if he hasn't already asked for it. I need to calm down. I just don't want them to pull the "just kidding" bullshit on me on the 26th that they like to pull on people. Lots of people get told they'll be getting out on a certain date, and then some bullshit happens (they catch a new charge, their lawyer doesn't show up for court, their court date gets pushed back, they get indicted again on their 89th day of a 90-day term, etc.), so I've seen shit go wrong so many times, it's hard not to be nervous.

Separately, could you do me a kindness and order me d-mannose and bromelain supplements from Amazon? The d-mannose will clear my urinary tract (if the antibiotic hasn't, which I never really trust it to, to be honest), and the bromelain will help regulate my digestion, so those'll be good to get back on ASAP when I get out. Also, I don't want too much time to go by before I'm able to make an appointment with my psychiatrist, because I don't think these folks are going to give me a five-day supply of meds to tide me over or anything like that when they release me; I'm pretty sure they just send me back out on the street to fend for myself. Oh, and that reminds me, please bring the Aplenzin and Zyprexa I was prescribed six months ago when you come pick me up. I'll probably only take the Zyprexa to avoid shocking my system, but I want to have them both just in case.

Thank you so much for everything you've done throughout these past several months and are continuing to do for me, and sorry for being such a worrier – you've handled my worries very well. I can't wait to get out and see you and The Boys and do my taxes on time. %-)

xoxo me

"For it will not do to betray the conspiracy and tamper with the courage of the living; there is nothing better than to be alive, everyone has agreed on that; it is past argument, and who attempts to deny it is justly outlawed."

Katherine Anne Porter, "Pale Horse, Pale Rider"

In the end, there was no hiccup, no last minute revocation of her discharge, no surprises. On the morning of March 26, 2023, she simply filled up a paper bag with all of the books and correspondence she had accumulated over six months and walked out into the cool Del Valle dawn and into the rest of her life.

Upon her release from her jail sentence, Andrea began the next nine years of her probation, her 300 hours of community service, and started looking for a job. When friends and loved ones asked me how she was doing, I told them that she was in the process of putting the "P" in "PTSD." After all, it's not called "Traumatic Stress Disorder." Much of what had happened and what was yet to come would just be settling in for the long haul, for a lifetime of adjustment, a lifetime of "disenfranchised grief" or even "demonized grief." For is one permitted to grieve for a lost life of one's own when one has taken the life of another, even unintentionally? I suppose we'll find out.

But Andrea at least has a chance to rebuild something. The same cannot be said for so many of the people – many, but by no means all of them, black and brown – we have encountered thus far on our journey through this system.

As I write this, there is much sturm and drang in the news about the Supreme Court striking down institutional racism in college admissions. But just the very fact that there are populations requiring "affirmative action" once they encounter the Ivy-covered gates of Harvard, Princeton, and Yale means that we have already let those populations down, or they wouldn't be in need of "affirmative action" at this stage of their lives in the first place.

Andrea came from a white, middle-class family with some modest means. She was educated and well cared for throughout her life. We made some mistakes. She made some mistakes. But she had the support of family and friends, and has it still. The same cannot be said for most of the women with whom she shared a cell block for six months. Most of them never had a chance "from the git."

The total Travis County jail population as of 6:00 a.m. on Monday, July 10, 2023 was 2,205. The terms "jail" and "prison" are often used interchangeably, but there is a big difference. Most inmates in jail are there temporarily, awaiting trial or disposition of their cases, or are there, as was Andrea, serving relatively brief sentences.

The population on this day was 87% male, 13% female, 65.76% white, 33.24% black, 59% non-Hispanic, 41% Hispanic. The Asian population was less than 1%, because there are clearly some fields in which Asians do not excel. These statistics indicate neither racism nor favoritism, but culture. The majority of current inmates, over 50%, are between the ages of 25 and 40, the prime working, producing, contributing, and earning years.

These sad statistics are repeated across the country, and they represent a failure of imagination on the part of a society that simply does not know what to do with people when they are in distress, traumatized, mentally ill, alone, abused, drug-addicted, or lacking in any kind of social support.

Most of Andrea's bunkies gave her advice based on their previous experiences in jail, because jail has a revolving door. Why?

The men in Del Valle reportedly worked in their units, doing k.p. duty, cleaning, laundry, what have you. They also exercised outside, presumably on the baseball field provided for that purpose. The women, on the other hand, had no jobs and got no exercise. They simply sat there: sleeping, eating, watching "Suits" on their tablets, peeing, farting, shitting, masturbating. They would be released on their release dates, and would be back relatively soon.

Upon release, most inmates return to the terrible lives that landed them in jail in the first place. Background checks bar them from renting apartments, getting jobs, applying for insurance. They're not supposed to hang around with a "bad element," but bad elements are the only elements in their orbit.

Instead of worrying about whether or not a black student with an SAT score of 926 can get into Harvard over an Asian kid with a 1229, we should be paying more attention to the K-12 education that got them there in the first place, and to the family dynamics at play. Race-based admissions in college simply reflect the fact that we are letting our children down for the first 18 years of their lives and then attempting to make ourselves feel better on the back end by pushing black and brown students up into colleges for which they may be mismatched. In 2023, 67% of white students had finished the four-year degrees they started, while 46% of black students finished on time, compared to 72% completion rates for Asian students.

As I write this, Andrea's bunkies are still rotting in jail, or they have been replaced by other young and early middle-aged women who will rot in jail, to be replaced yet again by Andrea's bunkies back for another round. I think about those women every day. About the waste, the suffering, the dysfunction that becomes multi-generational. We have no plan for these women, no purpose for them to aspire to, no resources to pull them out of this cycle. We aren't taking this time to educate them, train them, counsel them. Many – most – jail staffers are good, well-intentioned people who do what they can, but they face insurmountable obstacles. Putting people's lives back together after incarceration is simply not a priority for us as a society. It should be.

I'm currently writing to women who are incarcerated in Michigan, Alabama, Florida, and South Carolina, and they write back to me. These women are bright, thoughtful, remorseful. They want to be better, they want to do better. But we don't know how to build jails and prisons that can be incubators for better lives rather than simply temporary warehouses of lost lives. We need to redefine the mission of jails and prisons.

Instead of wringing our hands because now Omar won't be able to get into Cornell because of the mean old Supreme Court justices, but will have to settle for Ithaca College instead, why can't we put some of our energy and some of our resources toward the most needy and helpless and marginalized among us? Affirmative action in college admissions is like affirmative action in criminal justice: too little, too late on the back end of the problem.

We're always saying we want to have a "National Conversation About Race," but do we really? Because some truths are hard to hear, or forbidden to be spoken aloud.

Perhaps we should focus on what I believe are the two biggest factors in tackling equal opportunity on the front end: K through 12 education and fathers. The best thing that ever happened to the American automobile industry was the Japanese automobile industry. Competition. Let's have competition in K-12 education: charter schools, vouchers. Give people a choice and we all grow stronger. Every school will have to raise its game to stay competitive.

And let's get fathers back in the home. Men in general have taken it on the chops in recent years, but we need men, strong men, men with purpose. Children need women and men, in any combination you like, but let's get two parents back in the home. Raising children is tough enough when you have two people or a village, but trying to do it alone is the least desirable option. Be honest: which do you think is better? One arm or two? One leg or two? One eye or two? One ear or two? Let's give our children everything we possibly can.

We can do better. We should do better. We must do better. We're letting people down. Let us lift them up. And let's start early, while the light is good.

~Twelve~

"Children begin by loving their parents; as they grow older they judge them; sometimes they forgive them."

Oscar Wilde, "The Picture of Dorian Gray"

An Open Letter to My Daughter

Dear Andrea,

I wasn't a particularly good daughter to my parents. I never gave them very much cause for worry, at least nothing that they knew about. I simply left home for my sophomore year of college at 19, and never really looked back (except when I needed money).

I loved them, and I still do. They were the best parents I could possibly imagine: taking care of me when I needed care, encouraging my independence when I needed that encouragement. But at a certain point they had served their purpose in my life, raising me to young adulthood, so I was happy to be out of the nest and on my own (except when I needed money ;-).

Like many or perhaps most adult children, I became somewhat dismissive of my parents. They were old and old-fashioned, I thought. I was cool and hip; they were quaint and benign. I thought I knew more than they did, but I didn't then and I still don't even now, as it turns out. In return, they humored me, never challenging my elevated vision of myself, never countering with their own experience and wisdom, never taking me down a peg. They were wise enough to know that my mistakes were mine to make, and wisdom was mine to work for, and there was no point in their trying to intervene to make things easier for me.

As I write this, I am almost two years older than my mother was when she died, and about six months younger than my father was when he died. I wish we could spend some time with our parents as contemporaries. I would love to hang out with them now, to compare aches and pains, to "swap lies" as my father used to characterize his barroom conversations with compatriots. As is true with everyone we think we know well, we have no idea what they're like when they're alone, or with others when we're not around.

And I would like to apologize. I would like to apologize to my parents. For everything. For the slights large and small, for seeing them as merely supporting characters in my life, rather than the stars of their own. For appreciating them, but not nearly as much as I should have.

The truth is that if you had horrible parents, you can never really get past that, even with all the therapy in the world. But it's also true that if you had wonderful parents – and I had wonderful parents – you can never get past that either. At least the people with horrible parents don't have to spend the rest of their lives feeling guilty because they never appreciated their parents enough.

I think I was what Donald Winnicott termed "the good enough parent." I'm sure I've been disappointing, disillusioning, perhaps even horrifying at times, but I think that's the way things are supposed to be. It would be worse if you spent your whole life thinking that I knew everything, the way you did when you were, say, five years old.

There was a movie back in 1994 called "Quiz Show" about scandals in the 1950s that apparently rocked the nation's psyche when it was discovered that game shows were sometimes rigged in favor of one contestant over another. The premise of the movie seemed to be that this discovery was a terrible thing, that this loss of faith and confidence in the integrity of game shows specifically and television more generally was a dreadful cultural blow.

But I disagree. If people were believing everything they saw and heard on television, isn't it a good thing that they were disabused of the wild notion that television presented only objective truth, and that this valuable lesson was learned early in the life of the medium and through the relatively benign conduit of the quiz show format? Isn't it best that we were encouraged to be skeptical early on? Imagine the damage and chaos that would ensue if we believed everything we saw on television today? It hardly bears thinking about.

In much the same vein, it may be horrifying to realize later in life that those two people in the front seat of the car while you were sleeping peacefully and blissfully ignorant in the back had absolutely no idea where they were going or what they were doing. But this epiphany turns out to be the gateway to your own independence as a "good enough" adult. If those two clowns could do it, so can you.

We will never be contemporaries, you and I. I will never know what it is like for you to be 27 years old, but I'm pretty sure it's harder for you than it was for me. You will never know what it's like for me to be 69 years old, but I hope it will be easier for you than it has been for me.

I don't want you to ever feel guilty when you think of me, never for even a second. Like Walter White (my spirit animal), everything I've ever done for you and for your father has ultimately been for me in the end, because I couldn't live with myself if I didn't do everything I could to make things as good as I possibly could for you, your father, and myself.

And I never felt more purposeful, felt more meaning in my life, than I have when I've been doing whatever I could for you, from the moment I first gazed into those little almond-shaped eyes right up through this very moment, and beyond. In a strange, perverse way I feel a little let down that the "worst" of our travails over the past six years are essentially over, all but the shouting. Like Jesse Pinkman's "Mr. White," I may have felt most alive when circumstances were at their worst.

I've had a great life. I had the best parents in the world. I've been blessed with a lifetime of dogs and cats and a teddy bear hamster, all of whom I adored and who provided me with untold joy in exchange for only food, water, shelter, and something to chew on. I've been engaged in two fascinating careers, both of which have had their share of challenges and rewards. I was born and have lived most of my life in the greatest country in the world. And I've basked in creature comforts my ancestors, even as recently as a single generation ago, could never have imagined. (Four beds and three baths! Two thousand nine hundred thirty square feet! And this for a woman who is only two generations removed from steerage!)

I drive a car that is more sophisticated than the first lunar module. But for the wonky left knee and the cataracts, I'm in blessedly amazing health. I have friends I've had for 50 years, and while they sometimes drive me crazy with their insane politics, I'm more slender than all but one of them, so that simple circumstance provides me with the requisite amount of schadenfreude to be able to see past their foibles.

And I have a daughter I would not trade for another. She's funny (but not fun, as she frequently reminds me), she's smart, talented, with a soft heart and a hard head. She surprises me constantly with the novel twists in the labyrinth of her mind. She told me once that, "No one ever gets bored with me. People get tired of me, but never bored."

And she's the bravest person I've ever known. She has endured hardships her peers, I hope, will never encounter, and this has armed her with an understanding of the tenuousness of our hold on life and on our conceptions of ourselves that is the foundation of wisdom.

My daughter is demanding of herself and others, but she doesn't judge (unless judgment is richly deserved). I don't know her, I will never know her, and I suspect that I never really knew her even back when I thought I did, back when she was three years old and we went everywhere with her hand in mine. We can never truly know another, any more than we can ever truly know ourselves, I suspect. Coming to know others and knowing ourselves is the unfinished work of a lifetime.

"Love" is a gift. "Fear" is an obstacle. "Despair" and "Hope" are two sides of the same coin, both reaching out toward a future neither can control. "Manslaughter" is a word, while "Remorse" is a sentence.

I would only say this to you, my darling. You have always been the best thing that ever happened to me, and being your mother has been the greatest joy of my life.

I won't be here for most of your life, alas, so in the immortal words of Lee Ann Womack: "when you get the chance to sit it out or dance, I hope you dance."

Love,
xoxo gossip mom

~Thirteen~

"*A merchant in Baghdad sends his servant to the marketplace for provisions. Soon afterwards, the servant comes home white and trembling and tells him that in the marketplace, he was jostled by a woman, whom he recognized as Death, who made a threatening gesture. Borrowing the merchant's horse, he flees at great speed to Samarra, a distance of about 75 miles (125 km), where he believes Death will not find him. The merchant then goes to the marketplace and finds Death, and asks why she made the threatening gesture to his servant. She replies, 'That was not a threatening gesture, it was only a start of surprise. I was astonished to see him in Baghdad, for I have an appointment with him tonight in Samarra.'*"

W. Somerset Maugham

Tom woke up before the alarm rang, but then he always did. He only set the alarms throughout the day because he liked to keep to a routine, and while he almost never deviated from his self-imposed schedule, he liked the serenity of knowing that he had the alarms set, just in case.

He was in the habit of getting up a couple of hours before leaving the house, because he enjoyed the quiet of the night. He could sense everyone else asleep and at peace, all around him. The apartment building, the neighborhood, the city, and on out across the land, like quiet ripples made by a stone thrown into a lake. The universe exhaling, letting out a sigh. He would often lie still for a few minutes with his right ear on the pillow. It was so quiet he could hear the blood coursing rhythmically through his veins and arteries, his heartbeat, the rise and fall of his breath.

He watched his digital clock click over to 1:04 a.m. so that he could count his resting heartbeat.

...1...2...3...4...5...6...7...8...9...10...11...12...13...
14...15...16...17...18...19...20...21...22...23...24...
25...26...27...28...29...30...31...32...33...34...35...
36...37...38...39...40...41...42...43...44...45...46...
47...48...49...50...51...52...53...54...,

then the clock clicked over to 1:05 a.m. Even allowing for a slight uptick in his heart rate when the alarm went off, which he was trying to train himself to resist, 54 was a pretty good resting heartbeat.   His doctor told him that he usually only observed that slow a heart rate in athletes. Tom wasn't an athlete, not by any means, but he felt flattered to be compared to one.

He had gone to bed shortly after sundown, as was his customary practice, so with sundown the night before at 6:14 p.m. and allowing for an hour or so to read before sleeping, he had probably gotten close to five hours of sleep, which was pretty good. He would take a nap later on in the day. He found that two shorter periods of sleep worked better for him than trying to sleep for one longer stretch, like grazing throughout the day rather than sitting down for two or three larger meals.

He would have gotten closer to six hours of sleep, but he had woken up around 10:45 and had a little trouble getting back to sleep. Whenever he woke up in the night, his mind immediately ran to trivial but excruciating memories. Why did he do this to himself? Minor slights, minor mistakes, minor embarrassments, some from decades before would creep into his thoughts, embed themselves, and refuse to leave. Did this happen to other people?

Last night it was that time when he was having a dorm room debate with Sarah and Peter, and Tom had used the word "tantamount" when he meant to say "paramount." He could still wince and flush with embarrassment. It had been too late to pull it back, to correct himself, so he could only hope that Peter and Sarah didn't notice.

But of course they did. They must have. What did they think in that moment? Did they think that he didn't know the difference between "tantamount" and "paramount?" That was even more painfully unthinkable than the possibility that he had simply misspoken, which was the truth. He should have corrected himself immediately, that's what he should have done, to remove all doubt, make a joke out of it.

It must have been at least 25 years ago now, but the memory still burned. If he thought about it when he woke up in the night, it would take him ages to fall back to sleep. If he thought about it when he was awake, he had to distract himself with reading or television, to push the memory back into the box. Sometimes when uncomfortable thoughts intruded he would find himself shaking his head rapidly and emitting a tiny sort of yelp, as though he had just been startled or flicked on the ear.

Where were memories like that kept? He had dozens of them, humiliating memories he couldn't suppress. He had once said, "with retrospect to" instead of "with respect to." What was wrong with him? Were these memories all stored in the same part of the brain? He would like to dig in and scoop that part of his brain out with a sharp spoon.

He was reading Pierce Brown's "Iron Gold," the fourth installment of the Red Rising Series. So far he was liking the changes in Darrow, and all the new characters. After the first trilogy, it was time to shake things up a bit. Darrow was now 33 in this book, the age Jesus was on the cross, and Tom wondered if there was any symbolic significance to this. His favorite was still "Morning Star," but he was willing to give this one a chance.

He sat up, threw off the covers, and swung his legs over the side of the bed, drawing his feet into his slippers. He never walked barefoot, not even in the middle of the night when he got up to go to the bathroom. It was a habit he had cultivated since childhood. His father had never gone barefoot, having what his mother called "a thing" about his feet. In fact, Tom had never seen his father's naked feet, not once in his life. To have done so would have been shocking and embarrassing, more intimately intrusive than walking in on someone having sex.

He flipped open his laptop on the dresser and keyed in his password, then fired up Youtube and searched for "New World Man" by Rush, a musical jump start to his day. *"He's a rebel and a runner, he's a signal turning green..."*

He had thought about writing some science/fantasy fiction of his own, maybe starting out with some fan fiction online to see if he could get any followers. He already had some character names picked out: Ohev, Panagiota, Jiwon, Calen, Darius, Yixuan, Arjun, Kavya, Yasin, Daniyal, Jooha, Aws, Zinu, Mars, and Or.

He shuffled into the kitchen and turned on the coffee maker, set up from the evening before, then pulled half-and-half and two eggs out of the refrigerator. The coffee machine began to make its bubbling, wheezing hum. Why did coffee never taste quite as good as it smelled? And why was there no coffee cologne or perfume or air freshener? Lavender was so cloying, yet there was plenty of that. But didn't everyone love the smell of coffee? And vanilla. That would also make a great perfume. But maybe there already was a vanilla perfume.

"He's got a problem with his poisons, but you know he'll find a cure..."

It was early days, nothing yet committed to paper, but he thought the story might be about a family from Earth that had colonized a small planet in another solar system when climate change rendered life on Earth untenable. They had lived peacefully on this new planet for generations, slowly rebuilding civilization, when they found themselves suddenly occupied by a refugee family from another planet, fleeing persecution by warlords. The two families then started out living peacefully side by side, sharing their wealth and technological expertise, but rival factions started to stir up tribal animosity, while romances began to develop between younger members of the two families. He pictured it as an interstellar "Romeo and Juliet" or "West Side Story." He wanted crossover appeal between men and women, targeting male readers for the warrior conflicts and female readers for the romantic storylines.

Should he shave? He walked around the corner into the bathroom, looked in the mirror, and thoughtfully rubbed his jaw. Not really necessary, but maybe he should go ahead. Rosa Santiago was usually working the only open register at three a.m. at H.E.B., and he liked her, as much as he was able to like someone with whom he had only exchanged a few socially scripted words. "Hi. How are you?" "Fine, thanks." "Do you have shopping bags with you?" "Yes, thanks." "Here's your receipt. Have a nice night." "Yes, you too." Once she had said, "Here's your receipt," and he had responded, automatically, "Yes, you do the same." That one made him wince, too. What an idiot.

Or perhaps the story should take place at the depths of the ocean, truly the final frontier. Deep sea, he reasoned, was actually less understood and less explored than deep space. And the special effects possibilities from a potential movie sale were staggering.

He was accustomed to Rosa now, almost comfortable, although "comfortable" was never a word he associated with himself. She was short and a little plump, with apple cheeks and her black hair pulled back in a French braid. She looked like a kindergarten teacher. She was brisk and efficient scanning his meager groceries, never overly friendly, but she always gave him a small shy smile that allowed him to practice smiling back.

"He's noble enough to win the world, but weak enough to lose it..."

He already had titles for all three volumes of his projected trilogy, titles derived from "Romeo and Juliet." They were: "Violent Delights," "Fire and Powder," and "Violent Ends." It could be "The Violent Trilogy" by Thomas Boyd. Had a solid ring to it.

Two weeks before, when he went to H.E.B. on a Friday morning, Rosa had been out and another cashier – Roberto – had been covering. Tom wasn't happy, of course, and he felt his palms turn to sweat when he walked into the store and assessed the situation. He briefly thought of turning right around and going home.

Wait. Would he have to meet with people if there was a movie deal in the works? Maybe the writers didn't do that. Maybe that was why they had agents. But would he have to meet with an agent in the first place, or could he just send in his manuscript and have a long distance relationship?

He heard the gurgle and final wheeze from the kitchen, indicating that the coffee was ready, but he was already lathering up to shave. When he finished scraping his face and neck, he rinsed off the razor, then splashed and dried his face before checking the weather on his phone. Dry and 54 degrees. Perfect biking weather. He had his list of seven grocery items on his phone. He always bought only seven items, partly because that was usually about all he could fit in the basket on his bike, and partly because he liked the number seven. There was something mystical about it. To Tom it represented totality, completion, the sum of all things. After all, what was eight, really, but an unnecessary step onward? Who had a special relationship with the number eight? No one. Except maybe those people who turned it on its side to invoke infinity. But infinity was a frightening concept. If he needed more than seven items at the store, he would prioritize them and leave any excess for his next errand.

"He's got to walk a fine line, and keep his self-control..."

His seven items this morning were: a quart of milk, a box of corn flakes, a dozen eggs, a loaf of bread, a package of sliced lunch meat, a package of sliced cheese, and a jar of mustard. He had wanted to put light bulbs on the list, because he had used the last 75-watt on Wednesday and he didn't like to be caught short when a bulb burned out. But he was willing to take his chances. If he lost an important bulb before Rosa's next shift on Tuesday morning, he would steal a bulb from a less frequently used light source, like the second lamp in his bedroom, and just make do.

Thomas poured just the right amount of half-and-half into his mug before adding the coffee. He did it this way because he enjoyed seeing the warm, creamy tannish brown rising up to meet him as he added the coffee, somewhere between a chartreuse and a chateaubriand, he thought. Look at you, Tom; so fancy!

For some reason, this method was so much more beautiful and satisfying than pouring in the cream later and stirring the coffee. And he didn't need to stir when he put the half-and-half in first, so he didn't have to use a spoon. And a spoon he didn't have to use was a spoon he didn't have to wash and dry.

He carried his mug back into the bedroom and set it down on the coaster on top of his dresser. With that, he began to strip the bed. First the pillows, then the comforter, then the top sheet, and he placed these on the seat of his bedroom chair. He walked around the bed, smoothing and brushing the bottom sheet with his hand as he went. He reached under the mattress on both sides and the bottom, pulling taut on the edge of the fitted sheet and firmly tucking it under the mattress so as to tighten the sheet across the top.

He made his bed like this every morning, even if he was planning to take a nap later, and he made his bed after every nap as well. He liked the cool feeling of sliding into a smoothly made bed. He also showered before bed, even if he had not gone out all day, because he didn't want to go to bed feeling dirty, waking up feeling dirty. That was no way to start the day.

He flapped the top sheet over the bed and watched it billow to the ceiling, tugging gently on it as it wafted down. Then he evened up the edge on the bottom and around the sides. He never tucked his top sheet in at the bottom because he didn't like the tight feeling of the sheet pressing down on his toes when he was in bed. His feet had to be able to move freely, as did he, so he didn't tuck the top sheet in anywhere. He always went to sleep on his left side, but for some reason always woke up on his back.

"He's not concerned with yesterday; he knows constant change is here to-day..."

Why did anyone, anywhere, go grocery shopping other than at three o'clock in the morning? Even if one didn't have difficulty managing people and crowds and lights, grocery shopping was a nightmare. If there was a Hell, he would spend it for eternity making his way miserably up and down grocery store aisles, weaving within the mob. Enochlophobia. Maybe that's what he had. Must have been named after some poor bastard named Enoch who, for sure, never went to Times Square on New Year's Eve.

In the grocery store, he was acutely aware of the existence of other people, but he felt himself alone in this sensitivity. People in grocery stores, he felt, behaved as though they were the only people in the world, much less in this store, in this aisle. They parked their carts diagonally in the center and then wandered up and down and around, blocking all manner of egress. Rather than say, "excuse me," Tom would turn around at any roadblock and go back up the aisle in the opposite direction.

He hated the fact that, if he ran into someone annoying in one aisle, he would invariably meet them again in the next aisle, doing their same annoying thing, as people often shopped at the same pace. Sometimes, in an aisle in which he had no more shopping to do, he would trot up the aisle so as to increase the time and distance between himself and another shopper. And sometimes there were aisles where he didn't need to buy anything, like baby items, so he could skip that one entirely and gain a whole aisle's advantage over the approaching offenders.

And when he was after a specific item, such as a can of tuna fish or a jar of peanut butter, at any time other than three a.m. there was invariably someone – usually a conscientious mom – standing, parked, right in front of his array of items, intently reading every ingredient listed on every single label as though searching for the antidote to a poison she had just swallowed.

He flapped the comforter over the bed and watched it float down, then straightened the bottom edge and sides. Then he folded over the top edge of the comforter and folded the top edge of the sheet down over that. He smoothed the hem of the sheet, and patted the bed. Lastly, he fluffed the pillows and set them up at the headboard, tugging on the edge of each pillow case to straighten and tighten them.

"He's a new world man, he's a new world man..."

Tom sipped his coffee as he returned to the kitchenette. He pulled his small frying pan out of the lower cabinet and placed it on the front left burner, turning the dial to settle between two and three, which was where he did most of his cooking: eggs, burgers, pancakes.

He had to keep working on that song he was writing for Maureen. She was coming in to town from Boulder next weekend, and he wanted to surprise her. He'd worked out the tune on his guitar and now had to iron out the lyrics. Which did singer-songwriters do first, the music or the lyrics? Wade had recently gifted him with a brand new Taylor 114ce Grand Auditorium acoustic guitar Tom now had hanging on the bedroom wall, and he had started to pluck out a tune he thought Maureen would like. A little ballad-y with the refrain, sentimental, but with a sense of humor.

Tom slid an oven mitt under his plate, picked up his fork, went into the living room, and sat down on the sofa, then picked up the TV remote and pointed it toward the television.

He liked to start the day with at least part of an episode of a cooking show, like "Top Chef." He wasn't a cook, didn't even like to cook, but he had found himself loving cooking shows. He had recorded last night's episode, which was shot in The Stanley Hotel in Colorado, the inspiration for and setting of Stephen King's "The Shining." He wanted Bruce to win this season, but also had a soft spot for Mustache Joe. Tom admired people who were this good at and this passionate about a single thing. He had always had trouble focusing on one form of expression for his talents and energies, spreading himself so thin that he was okay at a lot of things, but not particularly accomplished at anything.

How long had he and Maureen known each other now? It must be 30 years. They had met in high school, dated briefly (and not particularly successfully), and then stayed friends forever. He remembered thinking, back when they were 16 and had just started seeing each other as boyfriend and girlfriend, a trial balloon, "Don't screw this up, because one way or another you don't want to lose this girl."

After about two months of bike rides and shared confidences, some fumbling around on the sofa in her parents' living room after her folks had gone to bed, she looked at him after one particularly unsatisfying session of French kissing and said, "Can we just talk for a while?"

And they had been talking – and listening – ever since. He told her about his failed relationships and failed jobs, she told him about her failed relationships and successful jobs. Maureen had a grown son now and sold insurance in Colorado, her boy's father long since out of the picture. She still came to Austin a few times a year, and they would share a bed and some hugs, some comfortable snuggling, but nothing else. He didn't want to lose her.

Tom took his plate and fork back into the kitchen, rinsed them in the sink, and put them in the dishwasher. He opened the refrigerator and poured himself a glass of orange juice, drinking it down in one long gulp, rinsing out the glass, and putting it in the top rack. He washed out the frying pan in the sink, because you weren't supposed to put it in the dishwasher. Then he went to the bedroom and unhooked his Taylor from the wall.

He went into the living room, sat down on the edge of a cushioned straight-backed chair, and began to strum. The song lyrics and a pencil were on the coffee table in front of him, the paper covered with scribbles and arrows pointing up to the top of the page, down to the bottom. He could have erased, but he didn't like to, because sometimes he went back to those old cross-outs.

This was what he had so far. He wanted to title it "For Maureen," but thought maybe the refrain would be catchier: "If It Were That Easy." But he would call it "For Maureen" when he sang it to her, for sure.

> When I was just a kid, my older brother taught me to shoot
> hoops.
> He was six feet tall, and I was two feet smaller.
> He won every game we ever played, but I told him that my
> plan
> Was that if he was tall, then I would just get taller.
> My brother smiled sadly at me, shook his head and said,
> "Hell, if it were that easy, everyone would do it."
>
> If it were that easy, everyone would do it.
> If it were that easy, everyone would do it.
> If it were that easy, everyone would do it.
> Hell, if it were that easy, everyone would do it.

Should he say "smiled sadly" or "smiled ruefully?" When he thought about Wade's smiles when they were kids, and even now, they always seemed more rueful than sad. But is "rueful" a country song word? Anyway...

When I was in high school, I fell in love for the very first time.
She was a ten, I was a five, but I had hope.
I was smart, I was funny, and had a heart that wouldn't falter.
Her football captain boyfriend was just a handsome dope.
My best friend smiled sadly at me, shook her head and said,
"Hell, if it were that easy, everyone would do it."

If it were that easy, everyone would do it.
If it were that easy, everyone would do it.
If it were that easy, everyone would do it.
Hell, if it were that easy, everyone would do it.

So he had the smile "sadly" again. Should he leave them both "sadly," or change one of them to "ruefully?" How in the world does Kenny Chesney do it?

When I was 31, my girlfriend left me for another man.
I think I stayed in bed for almost 13 days.
Then I watched a movie where a guy tried to commit suicide
By eating pizza and doughnuts in a drunken haze.
My trusty therapist sadly shook his head and said,
"Hell, if it were that easy, everyone would do it."

If it were that easy, everyone would do it.
If it were that easy, everyone would do it.
If it were that easy, everyone would do it.
Hell, if it were that easy, everyone would do it.

Okay, he was going to have to leave it "sadly," since he had it in every stanza. And how many times can you smile differently at someone, in two syllables? Sadly? Shyly? Grimly? Weirdly? Oddly? Barely? Badly?

> Then I remembered you, Maureen, my best friend since we
> were both kids.
> I called you up, asked why don't we get together.
> I wondered at the strength of our bond, why other folks don't
> have it.
> A lifetime of our sunny days and stormy weather.
> You just smiled sweetly at me, shook your head and said,
> "Hell, if it were that easy, everyone would do it."

> If it were that easy, everyone would do it.
> If it were that easy, everyone would do it.
> If it were that easy, everyone would do it.
> Hell, if it were that easy, everyone would do it.

Hey, "sweetly!" So he should keep "sadly" through the first three stanzas, and then change it to "sweetly" at the end, because Maureen is different from anyone else; she sure is.

He checked his watch, time to go. Hang up the guitar for later. Rosa must be in the middle of her night shift by now.

He picked up his wallet and scooter keys off the counter and headed out the door, pulled it closed and put the key in the lock, turned it. He tried the knob for safety, and it shook tight in his hand.

He stopped. Had he turned off the stove after the eggs? He had, hadn't he? He was trying to break the compulsive habit of unlocking the door and going back in to check again, one last time, trying to be more conscious and in the moment when he turned off the burner, remembering to think to himself, "Okay, you're turning it off now, remember, no need to check it again later." He was getting better at this, one day at a time.

No, he definitely remembered: he had turned it off. What a relief to have that monkey off his back. Things were looking up, after all. The night was clear, crisp, cool, and quiet. He turned from the door and took a deep breath of the bracing Austin February night air. Nothing to worry about. He pivoted to jiggle the doorknob one last time – some habits take longer to break – then turned toward the parking lot and stepped off into the rest of his life.

"The most beautiful people we have known are those who have known defeat, known suffering, known struggle, known loss, and have found their way out of the depths. These persons have an appreciation, a sensitivity, and an understanding of life that fills them with compassion, gentleness, and a deep loving concern. Beautiful people do not just happen."

Elisabeth Kübler-Ross

Gratitude and Acknowledgements

Cover art by JuliAnn Gessler,
artbyjuliann, Saratoga Springs, NY, ArtbyJuliAnn.Etsy.com.

Lyrics to "New World Man" by Rush;
written by Neil Pearl, Geddy Lee, and Alex Lifeson, 1982.

First thoughts are always with my husband Stephen and my daughter Olivia. God only knows what I'd be without you. Sure, I'd be able to quit my job, sleep in, read all day, walk at my own pace, quit the gym, binge-watch Netflix, adopt more cats, eat whatever I want, go to bed early, and never have another worry in my head. But what would be the fun in that?

My heart is with the members of The Hyacinth Fellowship. A merciful providence led me to you all, and I could never express in words what it has meant to me to meet you, to hear your stories, and to share your pain.

Thank you to the ladies I write to in prison: Wendy B., Jennifer B., Olivia H., Jamie K. Your strength inspires me, as well as your refusal to be defined by the worst decision you ever made on the worst day of your life. 1-Peter 3:8 – "Finally, all of you, be like-minded, be sympathetic, love one another, be compassionate and humble."

Without pets, how do we even know what it means to be human? Thanks to Basil, the Cat of My Heart; to Bonsai the Baby; to Giacomo the Wonder Pug; and to cats Wilma (nobody has ever looked at me the way you did, and no one ever will), and to Betty, who got me through those first two miserable years. Thanks to Jasmine, the only rodent I have ever truly loved. And thanks to Gertrude and Alice, who don't seem to mind being feline also-rans, as long as they have a screened-in porch, and now Runcible, "World's Cutest Dog" and our Easter Bunny. I couldn't have done it without you, all of you.

Thank you to the friends of my daughter who stuck by us in those early days: Taryn Buttram, Julie and Adam Carr, Minh Chau, Chris Costas, Stuart Day, Jay Dayaram, Casey Hayasaki, Sam Hayes, Will Honig (Guest of the Year), Bradley Lombardo, Sydney McQuade (who hit the therapy jackpot!), Saul Ortega, Taylor Rohrer, Sabina Tamang, Alena Zhukova; and to those loyal folks in the neighborhood: Cody Davis, Dean the Mailman, Sara Herlick, Susan Young and Stephen Wolff.

Thank you to my church families: Pastor Rich and everyone at First Presbyterian Church of Englewood, New Jersey, and Pastor Robert Balduc and everyone at St. Peter Lutheran. Ephesians 4:32 - "Be kind and compassionate to one another, forgiving each other, just as God in Christ has forgiven you."

Thank you to the various and sundry members of our legal support team: Michael Clay Arendes, Jr. (sorry about the fence; thanks for the attorney referrals), Ronald L. Clark, William Coltharp, Milan the Custodian, Karen Sage, Jon Tapia, and especially Kyle Lowe, Esq. and David B. Frank, Esq., the Abbott and Costello of criminal defense.

And to all those friends, family, and loved ones who have been with us all the way: Adriana Bate and Bert Pigg, Therese Bruck and Patrick Boll, Taeok Chong, Dorothy Cox and her Louie, Jodie Craft, Dr. Mitchell Essig and Dr. Peter Sarosi, Barbara Friedman, Amy and Robert Hand, Caitlin Kelly and John Camera, John Kennedy, Jill Knowles and Paul Sullivan,

Brian Norcia, Christine Norcia, Kathleen Norcia, Cyd Quilling, Julie and Doug Samuels, and the late great Dr. Frank C. Vanore (who first warned me that life would be "tough for her, Mary").

Finally, this work is humbly dedicated to Timothy Wayne Boykin (October 15, 1971 – February 9, 2018), and also to my parents, Morva A. Hamalainen (1929 – 1998) and William M. Hamalainen (1925 – 1996), whose hearts would be broken, but also uplifted.

I also dedicate this book to Maryann Gray, founder of The Hyacinth Fellowship, because her gift for understanding and compassion enabled her to take her own pain and use it to help relieve the anguish of so many others, those of us suffering from disenfranchised grief, demonized grief, but legitimate grief: our grief. Thank you, Maryann; we miss you.

About the Author

Mary Kay Hamalainen is and has been a daughter, wife, mother, and friend. She graduated from Hofstra University in 1977 and began her working life as an editorial researcher, then theater administrator, before becoming a speech-language pathologist working with developmentally disabled children, adolescents, and young adults. Mary Kay has lived in Washington, D.C., the Philippines, Hawaii, Maryland, New York, and New Jersey. She currently lives in north Texas with her husband, two cats, and one dog, just three hours north of her daughter and two grandpugs.

www.ingramcontent.com/pod-product-compliance
Lightning Source LLC
Chambersburg PA
CBHW060851120626
46553CB00001B/49